Co-operative

This book gives recognition to the importance of co-operative learning, in contrast to the traditional classroom, as an effective approach to teaching. Its coverage of the subject ranges across the educational spectrum, from pre-school years to university, and offers a fresh perspective on a topic that has gained increasing interest worldwide.

With contributors from an international panel of leading experts in the field, this engaging text succeeds in providing key insights, linking the theories that underpin the study of group dynamics to their practical application in the classroom. It presents a comprehensive overview of this alternative educative approach; illustrating how co-operative learning experiences can promote socialization and friendships, and facilitate learning.

The editors assemble a range of well-researched essays, covering such aspects as:

- the importance of teacher and student interactions;
- small group, virtual and non-virtual teaching environments;
- assessment practices for measuring the outcomes of individual and group progress;
- the effect of co-operative learning on relationships among students with diverse cultural, social and learning needs.

Illustrated with practical examples throughout, this book will be a crucial read for teacher educators, educational psychologists, student teachers, academics and researchers who wish to attain a fuller understanding of the subject and unleash the significant potential of co-operative learning in any educational setting.

Robyn M. Gillies is Associate Professor in the School of Education, University of Queensland. **Adrian F. Ashman** is Professor of Education at the University of Queensland.

Co-operative Learning

The social and intellectual outcomes
of learning in groups

Edited by
Robyn M. Gillies and
Adrian F. Ashman

RoutledgeFalmer
Taylor & Francis Group

LONDON AND NEW YORK

First published 2003
by RoutledgeFalmer
11 New Fetter Lane, London EC4P 4EE

Simultaneously published in the USA and Canada
by RoutledgeFalmer
29 West 35th Street, New York, NY 10001

RoutledgeFalmer is an imprint of the Taylor & Francis Group

© 2003 Robyn M. Gillies and Adrian F. Ashman

Typeset in Times by Wearset Ltd, Boldon, Tyne and Wear
Printed and bound in Great Britain by MPG Books Ltd,
Bodmin, Cornwall

British Library Cataloguing in Publication Data
A catalogue record for this book is available from the British
Library

Library of Congress Cataloging in Publication Data
Cooperative learning : the social and intellectual outcomes of
learning in groups / edited by Robyn M. Gillies and Adrian F.
Ashman.
    p. cm.
  Includes bibliographical references and index.
  1. Group work in education. I. Gillies, Robyn M., 1949–
II. Ashman, A.F. (Adrian F.)
LB1032.C5935 2003
71.39'5–dc13

2003046519

ISBN 0–415–30340–0 (hbk)
ISBN 0–415–30341–9 (pbk)

Contents

Contributors

Philip C. Abrami is Professor of Education and Director of the Centre for the Study of Learning and Performance at Concordia University in Montreal, Canada. His areas of interest include social psychology of education, instructional effectiveness, quantitative synthesis and educational technology. He has authored a book on co-operative learning published in both English and French and is currently conducting research on technology integration in schools and the uses of technology to promote early literacy.

Adrian F. Ashman is Professor of Education in the School of Education at The University of Queensland, Brisbane, Australia. He has a twenty-five-year history of publication in the education, psychology and disability fields, and is known internationally for his work in the application of cognitive psychology to regular and special education contexts. He has published twenty books and major monographs, and more than 150 research articles and book chapters including many on co-operative learning.

Victor Battistich is an applied developmental psychologist and Deputy Director of Research at the Developmental Studies Center, Oakland, California. He has conducted research on schooling and school reform/intervention programmes, including co-operative/collaborative learning, for twenty years, and has written several articles and book chapters on co-operative/collaborative learning.

Hugh Foot is Professor of Psychology at the University of Strathclyde in Scotland. His research interests are in children's social skills, particularly in relation to collaborative learning and peer tutoring. He also has a long-term interest in child pedestrian behaviour.

Robyn M. Gillies is an Associate Professor in the School of Education at The University of Queensland. Her research interests include small group processes in learning, career development and disability studies. She is a trained teacher, counsellor and psychologist.

David W. Johnson is Professor of Educational Psychology at the University of Minnesota where he holds the Emma M. Birkmaier Professorship in Educational Leadership. He is Co-Director of the Cooperative Learning Center. He is a past editor of the *American Educational Research Journal*. He has published over 350 research articles and book chapters. He is the author of over forty books (most co-authored with R. Johnson). He has received numerous national awards in the USA for his teaching and research. For the past thirty-five years David Johnson has served as an organizational consultant to schools and businesses in such areas as management training, team building, ethnic relations, conflict resolution, interpersonal and group skills training, drug abuse prevention, and the evaluating of attitudinal/affective outcomes of educational and training programmes. He is a recognized authority on experiential learning and currently provides training for clients in North America, Central America, Europe, Asia, the Middle East and the Pacific Region. He is a practising psychotherapist.

Roger T. Johnson is Professor in the Department of Curriculum and Instruction with an emphasis in Science Education at the University of Minnesota. He is an authority on inquiry teaching and has worked at the national level in science education in the USA and the UK. He is the author of numerous articles and book chapters, and co-author with David Johnson of *Learning Together and Alone* (4th edn, 1991); *Circles of Learning: Association of Supervision and Curriculum Development* (1984); *Cooperation and Competition: Theory and Research* (1989). Roger Johnson has been the recipient of several national awards in the USA including the Research Award in Social Studies Education presented by the National Council for the Social Studies, the Helen Plants Award from the American Society for Engineering Education, the Gordon Allport Intergroup Relations Award from the Society for the Psychological Study of Social Issues (Division 9 of the American Psychological Association), the Alumni of the Year Award from Teachers College, Ball State University, and the Outstanding Contribution to Research and Practice in Cooperative Learning Award from the American Educational Research Association Special Interest Group on Cooperative Learning. He is Co-director of the Cooperative Learning Center, which conducts research and training within the USA and internationally on changing the structure of classrooms and schools to a more co-operative environment.

Katherine McWhaw is a graduate in educational technology from Concordia University in Montreal, Canada, and has been a member of the Centre for the Study of Learning and Performance since 1992. She is currently co-researching how to improve the problem-solving skills of preservice teachers through computer-supported collaborative learning.

She has also developed and led workshops with undergraduate and graduate students on collaborative learning. Her current research interests focus on self-regulated learning and computer-supported collaborative learning.

Sheila Morrison was employed at the University of Strathclyde, Glasgow as a Research Fellow on the child pedestrian skills programme. Following this she worked at Glasgow Caledonian University on a project concerned with men's health. Her research interests include 'theory of mind' and children's humour.

Carol Rolheiser is an Associate Dean of the Ontario Institute for Studies in Education at the University of Toronto. The scholarship path she has taken is multi-dimensional but continues to be based strongly in co-operative learning; an area of research, development and teaching expertise. Her work as an international staff development consultant has focused on instructional and assessment innovation, teacher education reform, school improvement and managing educational change.

John A. Ross is Professor of Curriculum, Teaching, and Learning at the Ontario Institute for Studies in Education at the University of Toronto. He has worked with teachers in one of OISE/UT's field centres for thirty years, designing, implementing and evaluating curriculum, as well as teaching in the graduate studies programme. His research focuses on student assessment, especially in co-operative learning contexts, school improvement and programme evaluation.

Pepi Sarvary is a Research Fellow at the University of Strathclyde, Glasgow responsible for the design and development of the interactive software simulation used in the pedestrian training programme.

Heidi L. Schnackenberg is an Associate Professor of Educational Technology at Plattsburgh State University in Plattsburgh, New York. Her areas of research interest include preservice and inservice teacher integration of technology into pedagogy and higher education faculty professional development. In 1999 she was awarded a Special Commendation as a Young Researcher from the Association for Educational Communication and Technology (AECT) and in 1997, the AECT Dean and Sybil McKlusky Research Award.

Jennifer Sclater is an MA candidate in educational technology at Concordia University, Montreal, and a member of the Centre for the Study of Learning and Performance. For the past two years she has taught an undergraduate course on integrating technology into the K-12 classroom, both at a distance and on site, at Concordia University. Her area of interest is in collaborative learning within online and face-to-face learning environments.

Hanna Shachar is Professor of Educational Psychology at Tel-Aviv University, Israel. Together with Professor Shlomo Sharan, she has written numerous articles and book chapters on the group investigation approach to using co-operative learning strategies in schools. She is a co-author of *The Innovative School: Organization and Instruction*, which deals with co-operation in the classroom.

Shlomo Sharan is Emeritus Professor of Educational Psychology, School of Education, Tel-Aviv University, Israel. He is the leading proponent of the group investigation approach to co-operative learning that places an emphasis on the cognitive benefits students derive from working together on problem-solving tasks. He edited *Cooperative Learning: Theory and Research* (1990), which was very positively received internationally, and has recently written (with colleagues) *The Innovative School: Organization and Instruction* (1999) in which he suggests ways in which co-operative learning strategies can be implemented in schools at a systems level.

Jan Terwel is Head of the Department of Educational Psychology at Vrije University, Amsterdam, The Netherlands. He has been actively involved in six major studies on educational reform in The Netherlands and has published widely on the application of co-operative, small-group learning to the school reform agenda, particularly in secondary schools.

James Thomson is Professor of Psychology at the University of Strathclyde in Scotland. His theoretical interests in the visual control of locomotion have formed the basis of a long series of experimental studies of child pedestrian behaviour. These in turn have been used to construct programmes of practical training aimed at young children, one of which (Kerbcraft) is currently undergoing national evaluation across the UK.

Andrew Tolmie is Senior Lecturer in Psychology at the University of Strathclyde in Glasgow. For the past fifteen years he has researched on the development of children's skills and their understanding of their physical and social environment, effective means of educational support for this development, and the application of this research to the development of pedestrian skills.

Marilyn Watson was the Director of Programs at the Developmental Studies Centre and, prior to that, the head of Early Childhood Development at Mills College. She has written many curriculum materials in the area of co-operative/collaborative learning.

Kirstie Whelan is Senior Research Associate at the Sir James Spence Institute for Child Health, University of Newcastle, involved in the evaluation of the National Network Pilot for child pedestrian training. She was formerly a Research Fellow at the University of Strathclyde in Glasgow working on the child pedestrian skills programme.

Chapter 1

An historical review of the use of groups to promote socialization and learning

Robyn M. Gillies and Adrian F. Ashman

Introduction

One of the most influential educators of the early twentieth century was the philosopher, John Dewey. He believed that education was a process of living and that schools had a responsibility to capture children's interests, to expand and develop their horizons, and assist them in responding appropriately to new ideas and influences. Moreover, learning should be an active and dynamic process based on children's expanding curiosity in their world. It should be child-centred and responsive to the child's own developing social interests and activities. In this regard, he believed that schools had a responsibility to build on students' natural interest in their social environment by fostering interpersonal communication and group involvement. By interacting with others, children receive feedback on their activities, they learn socially appropriate behaviours, and they understand what is involved in co-operating and working together (Dewey 1940, 1966). Dewey's ideas were quite revolutionary at the time and had a profound influence on education, particularly as the effects of developments in the field of group dynamics began to be realized.

Group dynamics

Research into the behaviours of people in groups grew markedly in the second half of the twentieth century. This can be attributed largely to two movements in the social sciences. The first involved the recognition that groups affect individuals in different ways and these effects need to be measured. The second involved the development of a number of innovative behavioural science methodologies that enabled group behaviours to be recorded and measured.

During the two decades before World War 2, a number of studies on individuals' behaviours in groups demonstrated that their behaviours changed when they were exposed to the influence of others. For example, Allport (1924) found that there was a distinct increase in the quantity and quality of individuals' work when they were able to see and hear others working; Watson (1928) noted that groups think more efficiently than the best member of the group working alone; and Shaw (1932) observed that individuals were more productive when they worked in groups than when they worked alone. In fact, Mead (1937) observed that people worked co-operatively when they sought to obtain mutual outcomes, and May and Doob (1937) noted that individuals co-operate when they are in close contact and expected to work together to achieve a shared goal. In contrast, individuals compete when they have limited contact and are not expected to achieve a shared goal. In effect, the expectations placed on groups affect how members behave towards each other.

The power of the group to influence members' behaviours was demonstrated clearly in two experiments on group leadership styles reported by Lewin and colleagues (1939). In the first experiment, two groups of 10-year-old boys were exposed to either autocratic or democratic leadership as they participated in boys' club activities. The researchers noted that the children in the authoritarian group became more dominating and aggressive towards each other with each successive meeting while their attitude to the group leader was either one of submission or of persistent demands for his attention. In contrast in the democratic group, the members were more open and friendly towards each other while their relationship with their leader was egalitarian and free.

When the groups were compared for overt hostility, language and behaviour, boys in the authoritarian group were forty times more aggressive, they used more egocentric language, and they were less work-focused than the democratic group. In fact, the authoritarian group became so aggressive that on two occasions during the course of the meetings, the focus of the aggression shifted from mutual aggression to one another to one of concentrated aggression towards one member by the other four. This scapegoating became so unpleasant that two of the boys who were targeted left the group.

In the second experiment, four groups of 10-year-old boys were exposed to successive experiences of autocratic, democratic and *laissez-faire* leadership while participating in similar club activities. While only one of the four autocracies showed the same level of aggression as occurred in the first experiment, the researchers argued that it was suppressed by the presence of the autocratic leader. This became apparent when the autocrat left the room and there was a sharp rise in aggression among group members. The lack of smiling and joking, and the fact that nineteen out of twenty boys preferred their democratic leader to the autocratic one, were further indications of the repression the boys believed they experienced. In effect, these two studies demonstrated the dramatic effects that different leadership styles can have on group behaviours and that psychological and social phenomena can be observed and measured.

Concurrently with Lewin's research on group behaviours, Moreno (1934) began researching the psychological properties of populations and the communal problems that these properties produce. Moreno developed his interests in groups when, as a young doctor, he observed the effects of relocating thousand of peasants who were wine growers or mountaineers from rural areas near the Austrian alps to a suburban industrial district near Vienna to avoid the advancing Italian army during World War 1. While the primary concern was for the safety of the people, it soon became apparent that despite the outward manifestations of community life, there was great unhappiness and friction among the people. When Moreno and his colleagues investigated they found that most of the relocated peasants had been brought together randomly in a strange urban environment where they were unprepared for their changed circumstances. It was this experience that helped Moreno realize how important it was to plan for the psychological needs of a whole community and the science of socionomy emerged.

Socionomy is concerned with the way different groups in the community interact and how this affects the psychological well-being of the whole community. However, to be able to measure organization within social groups, Moreno developed a number of sociometric techniques that enabled him to depict graphically the evolution and organization of groups and the affiliation of individuals within them. Interestingly, he found that these preferences were dynamic and changed depending upon group membership and the problems facing the group.

The development of different sociometric techniques such as group observations and interview techniques enabled data to be collected on the structural properties of groups, on the relationship between groups and subgroups, and on the relationship between a group and its individual members. Lewin (1948) saw the potential these methods had for solving research questions of significant social value and he encouraged researchers to use them to develop theories that could be applied to important social issues such as how group actions and behaviours affect group life and cultural values.

Co-operative groups

Although different social theorists (Allport 1924; Shaw 1932; Watson 1928) had commented on co-operative and competitive behaviour by individuals as they worked either in groups or individually on problem-solving activities, it was May and Doob (1937) who developed the first comprehensive theory on the distinction between these two behaviours. They observed that individuals co-operate when they strive to achieve the same or complementary goals, are required to achieve the goal in equitable amounts, and when they are in close contact with one another. In contrast, individuals compete when they are striving to achieve the same goal which is scarce, are not required to achieve the goal in equitable amounts, and when they have few close contacts with one another.

While many researchers had observed that individuals in groups are either co-operative or competitive in the ways in which they interact with each other to obtain their goals, Morton Deutsch (1949a) was the first to investigate interactions between individuals and group processes that emerged as a consequence of the co-operative or competitive social situation. In a now famous study conducted with first-year university students, Deutsch set about to determine how individuals perceive they are either co-operatively or competitively linked. He hypothesized that if individuals are working co-operatively together to attain a group goal they will perceive themselves to be more psychologically interdependent than individuals who are in a competitive social situation. When this happens, group members will actively co-ordinate their efforts, ensure that others have opportunities to contribute, provide help and assistance when it is needed, and encourage others' efforts. As a consequence of the co-operative group experience, Deutsch hypothesized that group members would be friendlier, more cohesive and motivated than their peers in the competitive situation. Furthermore, groups would be more productive as members demonstrate a willingness to listen to each other and work together to produce a group product that is qualitatively better than those who work competitively.

Using fifty volunteers allocated to ten groups, Deutsch (1949b) ranked and paired groups with each other on the basis of the productivity of their discussions. The rationale for matching groups and not individuals was that groups were seen as functioning entities and not merely the sum of their parts. Deutsch, like Lewin, believed that the behaviour of groups is quite different to the sum of the behaviours of individual members.

One group from each pair was then assigned to the co-operative condition while the other was exposed to a competitive one. During the following five weeks, the groups met weekly and discussed problems designed to test their ability to engage in clear, logical thinking and social problem-solving. Each group was observed and rated on the basis of their discussion, orientation, self-centredness, involvement, communication difficulties, attentiveness, and acceptance or rejection of the ideas of others. In addition, the participants completed a weekly questionnaire which included items that paralleled those on the observers' rating scales as well as items that were designed to elicit their perceptions on group feeling, amount of group co-operation, group productivity, individual productivity, interest in the activities, and the reactions of others to their contributions.

The results showed that students in the co-operative condition were rated by the observers as having a stronger sense of group-centredness or group feeling than their peers in the competitive groups. In contrast, students in the competitive groups were observed to be more self-centred and, interestingly, this observation was confirmed when the students in this condition rated themselves as being more self-oriented. Students in the co-operative groups worked together more frequently, were more highly co-ordinated, and ensured that tasks were divided up so that there was no duplication of labour. They were also more attentive to what others had to say, communicated more effectively, were more motivated to achieve, and were more productive in their achievements than were their peers in the competitive groups. Furthermore, these observations were confirmed by the students' responses on the weekly follow-up questionnaire. In essence, Deutsch's (1949b) study provided evidence that when groups co-operate, they are more productive and motivated to achieve, communicate better, and have better intra-group relations than groups that compete. The implications of this study were to challenge the traditionally accepted notion that students who compete to receive awards work better than students who co-operate and facilitate each other's efforts.

Research on the dynamics of group behaviours continued over the next decade with Deutsch (1959, 1960) examining achievement motivation among group members and the nature of trust in co-operative groups while others, such as Bales (1950), focused on investigating the nature of group interactions. However, Johnson and Johnson (2000) argued that much of the momentum of group dynamics dissipated during the 1950s because of a focus on the individual rather than on the group. Asch's (1952) thesis on how individuals are influenced by others, Festinger's theories of social comparison (1954) and cognitive dissonance (1957), and Kelly's (1955) theory of personal constructs focused on individual attitudes, values and thoughts to explain social rather than group behaviour. This focus may be attributed, in part, to methodological difficulties of collecting, analysing and interpreting multiple data from groups in field settings (Johnson and Johnson 2000). Furthermore, the technology that later allowed audio- and videotaping of group behaviours and interactions was cumbersome and not readily available.

Groups to enhance learning

Interest in groups re-emerged in the 1970s, stimulated, in part, by the empirical research on peer tutoring that reported the academic and social outcomes of children assisting others to learn (e.g. Brown *et al.* 1971; Cloward 1967; Epstein 1978; Gartner *et al.* 1971; Lane *et al.* 1972). These studies showed that peers could be trained to facilitate academic accomplishments, reduce incidents of deviant and disruptive behaviour, increase work and study skills, and teach social interactional skills (Damon 1984; Greenwood and Hops 1981). The benefits derived were quite exciting and this, coupled with other research which showed that benefits also accrue to tutors (e.g. Allen 1976; Cohen *et al.* 1982; Dineen *et al.* 1977), helped to stimulate renewed interest in groups and how they could be used to facilitate learning and socialization. Johnson and Johnson (2000) suggested that these findings contributed to growing interest in a number of group issues such as co-operative learning versus competitive and individual learning, conflict resolution, group interaction, distributive justice and cross-cultural interaction (e.g. Deutsch 1969, 1979, 1983; Johnson and Johnson 1974, 1979, 1981; Sharan 1980). However, the overriding focus in the research that followed was on the benefits of co-operative learning in comparison to competitive or individual learning.

In 1981, Johnson and colleagues published the results of a meta-analysis they conducted on 122 studies that examined the effects of co-operative, competitive and individualistic learning on achievement. The results showed that co-operation promotes higher achievement and productivity (i.e. encouragement to learn) than interpersonal competition or working individually, and that these results were consistent across all subject areas (language arts, reading, mathematics, science, social studies, psychology, physical education), for all age groups (elementary, secondary, college, adult), and for a variety of cognitively challenging tasks. Furthermore, when intergroup competition was introduced into the co-operative, competitive and individual conditions, the superiority of co-operation increased the more the group members were required to produce a group product.

In a follow-up meta-analysis of ninety-eight studies that examined the impact of co-operative, competitive and individualistic learning experiences on interpersonal attraction among homogeneous and heterogeneous individuals, Johnson *et al.* (1983) found that co-operative learning experiences promoted greater interpersonal attraction among homogeneous students, students from different ethnic groups, and handicapped and non-handicapped students. The effects of Johnson *et al.*'s (1981, 1983) studies were to focus attention on identifying the variables that mediate and moderate the relationship between co-operative learning and achievement with the intention of understanding under what conditions these variables affect learning.

Understanding how co-operative learning methods affect academic achievement has been addressed by several researchers. In a review of twenty-six studies conducted from 1972 to 1984, for example, Johnson and Johnson (1985) identified eleven variables that potentially mediate or moderate the relationship between co-operation, productivity and interpersonal attraction. These variables were grouped into three clusters and include cognitive process variables (i.e. quality of learning), social variables (i.e. mutual support among group members), and instructional variables (i.e. type of task). While the effect of many of the variables still needs to be determined, the authors did suggest that the processes which may promote higher achievement and liking among students include the promotion of high-quality cognitive strategies, the constructive management of controversy and debate, time on task, elaborate sharing and processing of information, peer encouragement of efforts, active peer group involvement in learning, interaction between students of different achievement levels, perceptions of psychological support, positive attitudes towards subject areas, and perceptions of fairness in grading.

The implications of these findings were that co-operative learning could be used with any type of academic task. Disagreement and debate among group members are readily managed constructively and students can be encouraged to support each other's efforts to achieve. Co-operative groups should contain high-, medium- and low-ability students, and the fairness of joint outcomes should be discussed with group members (Johnson and Johnson 1985). Because of the emphasis on working together and helping each other, this approach to co-operative learning has become known as learning together.

In a review of sixty studies of co-operative learning conducted in elementary and secondary schools between 1972 and 1987, Slavin (1989) found that while co-operative learning may be an effective means of increasing student achievement, opportunities for learning can be maximized only if group goals and individual accountability are embedded in the co-operative method used. The critical difference between studies that incorporated these criteria and others is the importance attached to group members working together as a team to attain group rewards. In the student team learning approach advocated by Slavin, all group members are required to learn the information assigned to their achievement level (i.e. high-, medium- or low-achievement) and are able to earn rewards for their group on the basis of being able to do so. Motivation to achieve is enhanced because children are competing against others from the same achievement level and not against those from different achievement levels. In effect, group rewards and individual accountability may be used to enhance academic achievement by creating peer norms and sanctions that encourage children to learn.

Sharan (1980) reviewed five methods for conducting co-operative small-group learning in classrooms and examined their effects on achievement, attitudes and ethnic relations. The five methods included in this review were jigsaw (Aronson *et al.* 1978), teams-games-tournaments (DeVries and Edwards 1973), student team learning (Slavin 1977), learning together (Johnson and Johnson 1975), and group investigation (Sharan and Sharan 1976). Interestingly, Sharan classified the first three methods as peer tutoring because the tasks were limited and well defined, communication was primarily unilateral or bilateral, and rewards for achievement of set tasks were extrinsic. In contrast, the remaining two approaches were classified as group investigation because tasks were diverse and encouraged students to gather and evaluate information from different sources, communication was bilateral and multilateral, and rewards were primarily intrinsic. In fact, Sharan argued that peer tutoring techniques are similar to traditional whole class instruction in the emphasis on basic skills acquisition, individual accountability through assessment, and limited discussion of ideas and, because the dyads work independently of others, there is no common learning goal they are trying to achieve. In contrast, the techniques used in group investigation are complex and involve high-level thinking processes, group members are accountable to the group for the contributions they make, and discussion is encouraged as members collaborate on solving the group task and achieving the group goal.

Sharan found that children perform more effectively in small groups (e.g. peer tutoring and group investigation) than they do when they work in traditional whole class settings. However, the group investigation method promoted higher levels of cognitive functioning than peer tutoring. He attributed this to the interpersonal exchanges among group members which helped to clarify misunderstandings, and developed their problem-solving skills. The interpersonal exchanges among students who worked in the different types of small groups increased helping behaviour, perceptions of being helpful to others, and a sense of being able to manage the classroom demands. Students felt more liked, accepted and included than their peers in traditional classroom settings, and these feelings extended to the development of positive cross-ethnic relationships.

The studies and reviews by Johnson et al. (1983), Johnson and Johnson (1985), Slavin (1989) and Sharan (1980) confirm co-operative learning as an effective teaching strategy that can be used to enhance achievement and socialization among students and contribute to improved attitudes towards learning and working with others, including developing a better understanding of children from diverse cultural backgrounds. However, while co-operative learning gained acceptance as a strategy for promoting positive academic, social and attitudinal outcomes, researchers at the time were still debating how the different methods influenced academic achievement. Although a number of researchers (e.g. Johnson and Johnson 1985; Slavin 1983) had suggested potential mediating variables, Knight and Bohlmeyer (1990) argued that the research had only demonstrated that the co-operative learning experience causes variance in many of these proposed mediating variables and it was not established that these variables were the mechanisms through which co-operative learning influenced achievement. Clarification within this debate was important because it would enable researchers to predict how co-operative learning influenced academic achievement and under what circumstances.

Knight and Bohlmeyer (1990) suggested that two research strategies may be used to identify possible causal mechanisms. The first involves field-based, experimental studies in which specific variables can be manipulated under controlled conditions to identify potential causal mechanisms. The second involves research using specific data analysis techniques (e.g. path analysis, causal modelling) designed to identify causal relations predicted from theory or research. Certainly, both research strategies have been pursued in recent years as researchers have sought to test hypotheses about potential mediating variables, particularly as they apply to academic achievement.

Interaction as a variable mediating academic achievement

Numerous studies on co-operative learning have documented the benefits that accrue to students who interact with others, yet few have examined how different interactions affect the learning that occurs. In a series of studies which examined the role of interaction on achievement, Webb (1985) demonstrated that it was the explanations which children received in response to requests for help that were related positively to achievement, whereas giving non-elaborated help did not facilitate higher than expected outcomes. However, in a more recent study of the relationship between receiving explanations and problem-solving behaviour, Webb *et al.* (1995) found that children only benefited from the explanations they received when they were timely, relevant to the student's need for help, correct, and of sufficient detail to enable the student to construct a clearer understanding of the problem. When these conditions were met, children were more likely to continue to engage in problem-solving behaviour and it was this ongoing engagement that was likely to contribute to high achievement outcomes for all students, irrespective of prior achievement or ability level.

In contrast to Webb's studies on the effects of different types of interaction on student achievement, Cohen (1994) argued that it is the frequency of task-related interactions that is related to conceptual and achievement gains in mathematics, science and writing activities. These findings are consistent whether the focus is on the individual learner or on the percentage of students who are observed talking together as they work on a shared task.

The results of these two bodies of research (i.e. Cohen 1994; Webb 1985) are markedly different. Cohen argued that the differences may be explained by the types of task the groups undertook and by the nature of the work assigned to the groups. With the former, all members of the group were interdependent because no one could complete the group task without at least some input from the others. With the latter, the types of interaction that occurred among group members were dependent on the structure required to solve the work the children had been given. For example, work assignments that are well structured, such as mathematical and computational tasks, often have a set procedure to follow to obtain a correct answer, so there is little need to discuss ideas or pool information. In this case, the most effective type of help is providing explanations. In contrast, work assignments that lack structure, such as open-ended or dis-covery-based ones, often have no set procedures to follow or correct answers to obtain, so exchanging ideas and information is crucial if the problem is to be resolved or underlying concepts and themes identified. In effect, when groups work on an ill-structured work assignment, productiv-ity depends on task-related interaction; for example, in a study of student interaction of 782 children in Grades 3–8, Hertz-Lazarowitz (1989) found that when the task involved high-level co-operation (i.e. students are required to talk and share ideas to produce a group product), 78 per cent of the interaction involved higher level thinking such as analysing, synthe-sizing and evaluating information, whereas only 44 per cent of the inter-action in low-level co-operative tasks involved higher level thinking. These findings suggest that tasks which require high levels of co-operation promote higher reasoning and thinking interactions. Teachers need to be aware of the differences in interactions that can occur when children work on high- or low-level co-operative tasks and the effect these different types of interaction are likely to have on students' learning and thinking.

Cognitive language strategies

One of the first studies to document the cognitive strategies children use as they interact together in co-operative groups was conducted by Sharan and Shachar (1988). This study involved 351 Grade 8 students from nine classrooms in a junior high school in Israel, and sought to determine if children who study in classrooms that used the group investigation approach to teaching achieved more academically than did their peers in classrooms that used the whole class teaching approach. Furthermore, the study sought to determine if students in the group investigation classes engage in more extensive verbal interactions with each other than do their peers in whole class situations. The results showed that not only did the children in the group investigation classes achieve more academically than their peers in whole class settings but also they were more interactive in their groups, were more focused on the problem they were trying to solve, and used more sophisticated language strategies. Sharan and Shachar proposed that this occurred because the children who worked in the co-operative groups had opportunities to practise using different verbal and cognitive strategies they had heard their teachers use as part of the teach-ing and learning process in their classrooms. In contrast, the children in the whole class groups may have heard the same verbal and cognitive strategies but, because they did not have the opportunities to practise them, these strategies may not have had the same impact. In essence, chil-dren need opportunities to interact with each other if they are to develop an understanding of their world and find new ways of expressing their thoughts and feelings.

There is some evidence that children can be taught specific interactional strategies to enhance thinking and learning. In a study of forty-six Grade 5 children who worked in pairs in three conditions to solve computer-assisted problems, King (1991) found that the children who had been taught to use strategic questions to guide their cognitive processing and develop their metacognitive awareness asked more strategic questions and gave more elaborated explanations than children who had been told simply to ask and answer questions and a control group who received no training or instructions in questioning. Furthermore, the strategic questioners outperformed both the unguided questioners and the control students on a follow-up written problem-solving test and a novel problem-solving activity. King suggested that training children to use strategic questioning prompts them to offer more detailed explanations, and that this, in turn, promotes problem-solving success.

In a more recent study of Grade 7 students who were assigned randomly to one of three peer tutoring conditions, King et al. (1998) found that students who had been trained to sequence questions and provide explanations during peer tutoring outperformed students who were taught to give explanations only, ask questions, and provide explanations on their ability to engage in higher level discourse and construct knowledge both during tutorial interactions and on a follow-up retention test. King et al. maintained that the study demonstrated the importance of teaching students to use strategic questioning techniques coupled with providing detailed explanations to help tutoring partners to ask thought-provoking questions that promote the development of high-level discourse and complex knowledge construction.

Theoretical perspectives on learning in groups

The social context for learning is a key feature of peer-mediated discussion approaches. One of the more prominent theoretical perspectives on how students learn from interacting with others is based on the social constructivist view of Vygotsky (1978). According to this perspective, children's mental functioning develops first at the interpersonal level where they learn to internalize and transform the content of interpersonal interactions with others, to the intra-personal level where it becomes part of their repertoire of new understanding and skills. In essence, children learn by interacting with adults or more capable peers who scaffold or mediate learning so that they are able to complete tasks they could not do alone.

When children work together on group tasks, they often provide information, prompts, reminders and encouragement to others' requests for help or perceived need for help (Gillies and Ashman 1998). In fact,

Webb and Farivar (1994) observed that children are often more aware of what other children do not understand, so, by helping them to focus on the relevant features of the problem, they can often explain it to them in a way that can be readily understood. Moreover, as children interact together, they have opportunities to model their thinking, reasoning and problem-solving skills on each other, receive feedback, and as a result socially construct new understandings, knowledge and skills (King 1999). When they have to justify or explain their position or ideas to others, they are forced to reorganize their understandings so that their explanations can be easily understood. In so doing, they often develop better comprehension of the problem than before and this, in turn, has a positive effect on their own learning and performance (Wittrock 1990).

Another perspective on small group learning is based on Piaget's (1932) theory of sociocognitive conflict, which occurs when children are forced to re-examine their understandings and perspectives in the light of contradictions that occur from interacting with others. When this happens, children reflect on their own understandings, seek additional information to clarify the contradictions, and attempt to reconcile their perspectives and understandings to resolve any inconsistencies. Cognitive conflict is a catalyst for change as it motivates children to reassess their understandings of the world and to construct new ones that fit better with the feedback they are receiving.

Interacting with peers is a primary impetus for change because children are very forthright when stating their ideas. They speak directly to each other in ways that can be understood easily, and children are strongly motivated to reconcile differences between themselves and others (Damon 1984). Furthermore, children are often more receptive to their peers' ideas than to those of their teachers because peers' ideas are seen as more personal and less threatening.

In summary, the Vygotskian and Piagetian approaches represent two perspectives on how children learn from each other. On one hand, the social constructivist's perspective proposes that more capable peers and adults scaffold or mediate learning by providing the language and strategies for problem-solving. On the other hand, the personal constructivist's perspective proposes that when children interact with others, they are challenged to reconsider their own understandings, seek additional information on how to resolve conflicts, and reconcile differences between themselves and others. However, the main work of constructing new understandings and knowledge is undertaken by the individual in solitary reflection rather than by co-constructing new understandings, knowledge and skills with others. While there are clear differences between the social and personal constructivists' perspectives, advocates of each acknowledge the importance of social interaction and discourse in prompting and challenging individual perspectives and cognitions, and promoting learning and thinking.

Current developments in co-operative learning

Co-operative learning is well recognized as a pedagogical practice that promotes learning, higher level thinking, prosocial behaviour, and a greater understanding of children with diverse learning, social and adjustment needs (Cohen 1994). In fact, Johnson *et al.* (2000) have suggested that there is no other pedagogical practice that simultaneously achieves such diverse outcomes. Interest in co-operative learning has burgeoned over the past three decades as more research has been published that clearly demonstrates the benefits which accrue to students who work co-operatively as opposed to those who work in traditional classrooms (Johnson *et al.* 2000; Slavin 1995). The purpose of this book is to outline current developments in co-operative learning and how this approach to learning has been used to promote socialization and learning among diverse groups of students.

The preceding material has provided a broad introduction to the collection of chapters in this book. It reviewed the emergence of the field of group dynamics, tracing the contributions of Dewey, Moreno and Lewin. It elaborated on differences between co-operation, competition and individual goal-directed behaviour, highlighting the work of Deutsch and the development of three key schools of co-operative learning proposed by Johnson and Johnson (learning together), Sharan (group investigation) and Slavin (student team learning). We also highlighted the key role that interaction plays in facilitating learning and the development of higher level thinking and reasoning skills.

Chapter 2, by Battistich and Watson, focuses on the use of co-operative and collaborative learning techniques with preschool and early elementary children. It emphasizes the role of learning groups in the socialization process and in promoting inclusion, respect for diversity and social understanding. Practical issues around group-based learning with young children are suggested based on theory, research and classroom experience about the types of activities that are most likely to be effective with young children.

Chapters 3 and 4 discuss key issues relating to the implementation of collaborative approaches in primary and secondary school classrooms. In Chapter 3 these include the component parts of structured co-operative learning, the importance of training in establishing structured, co-operative learning experiences, the advantages of different ability and gender compositions for small group learning, and the role of structuring interactions in groups to promote giving more detailed explanations to assist problem-solving, develop metacognitive awareness and promote learning.

Terwel effectively extends the ideas presented in Chapter 3 but with specific reference to the educational factors that lead to successful learning in secondary school. He discusses the importance of instructing students in the social and cognitive strategies needed to work effectively in co-operative groups on problem-solving tasks and the benefits accruing to low-achieving students following strategy instruction in problem-solving activities. The cognitive apprenticeship model of Collins, Brown and Newman is presented and its appropriateness for low-achieving students discussed.

In Chapter 5, McWhaw, Schnackenberg, Sclater and Abrami focus on how educators can help college and university students to develop the skills they need to learn collaboratively either face-to-face or virtually without imposing a teacher-directed structure of positive interdependence and individual accountability. They argue that the scope, depth and type of projects students are being asked to develop and the recognition that students learn valuable skills that can be put to good use upon graduation has led to an increased emphasis on collaborative learning in tertiary institutions.

In Chapter 6, Ashman addresses the breadth of educational situations that include students with diverse learning needs. While the focus of attention in many co-operative learning projects has been students with intellectual disabilities and learning difficulties, there are many others who have diverse learning needs and who can be assisted to achieve both academic and social learning goals through collaboration. This chapter not only provides an overview of research and practice already undertaken using students with special education needs, but also addresses the diversity of learning and social needs of students at various levels of education.

In Chapter 7, Hanna Shachar presents an overview of data from seven studies that investigated the different effects of co-operative learning on students representing different achievement levels. The results demonstrate how low-achieving students are hampered by traditional whole class teaching and benefit from co-operative learning.

In Chapter 8, Ross and Rolheiser examine current assessment practices in co-operative learning with particular attention to the use of self-evaluation in everyday classroom activities and the effects of collaborative assessment in mandated assessments. They demonstrate that the use of specific assessment strategies in co-operative learning contributes to higher student achievement and positive student dispositions.

Motivation plays an important role in the development of social skills and the facilitation of interactions between peers. David and Roger Johnson (Chapter 9) draw upon the extensive experience they have had in conducting research on co-operative learning to highlight the important role motivation plays in academic success and ways in which schools can foster motivation in their students.

Chapter 10 by Foot, Tolmie, Thomson, Whelan, Morrison and Sarvary deals with a specific application of collaborative learning as children interact under adult guidance around a computer-based training package. Evidence is presented that training on computer simulations of road traffic situations not only promotes children's performance on simulated road-crossing tasks and on their understanding of features and concepts relevant to safe crossing strategies, but also has an impact on practical roadside performance.

Chapters 11 and 12 deal with ways of connecting individuals to peer or system networks. A significant number of children and young people experience alienation and disengagement from learning. In Chapter 11 we consider how these networks promote learning, socialization and friendships among students. In Chapter 12, Shlomo Sharan highlights the benefits of applying a systems approach to classroom organization and instruction as a way of connecting people to maximize the flow of information and facilitate the resolution of complex problems confronting teachers and students. He argues that by adopting a systems perspective, schools can deal effectively with communication between people, the integration of domains of teaching and studying, flexible scheduling of classes, and co-operative team work among teachers and students. With this type of flexibility, the distressing phenomenon of large classes can become a non-issue because of the alternative methods of organization and instruction employed.

In the final chapter, the editors draw together the major themes to emerge from the previous chapters and present a model of co-operation and collaboration which includes those factors that enhance learning in the intellectual, social and personal domains. The authors consider person, context and curriculum domains to demonstrate how teachers, parents and education professionals can contribute to the development of students of all ages through the application of the principles of co-operation.

References

Allen, V. (1976) 'Children helping children: psychological processes in tutoring', in J. Levin and V. Allen (eds) *Cognitive Learning in Children: Theories and Strategies*, 241–90, New York: Academic Press.

Allport, F.H. (1924) *Social Psychology*, Boston, MA: Houghton Mifflin.

Aronson, E., Stephan, C., Sikes, J., Blaney, N. and Snapp, M. (1978) *The Jigsaw Classroom*, Beverly Hills, CA: Sage.

Asch, S. (1952) *Social Psychology*, New York: Prentice Hall.

Bales, R.F. (1950) *Interaction Process Analysis: A Method for the Study of Small Groups*, Cambridge, MA: Addison-Wesley.

Brown, L., Fenwick, N. and Klemme, H. (1971) 'Trainable pupils learn to teach each other', *Teaching Exceptional Children*, 4: 36–49.

Cloward, R. (1967) 'Studies in tutoring', *Journal of Experimental Education*, 36: 14–25.

Cohen, E. (1994) 'Restructuring the classroom: conditions for productive groups', *Review of Educational Research*, 64: 1–35.

Cohen, P., Kulik, J. and Kulik, C. (1982) 'Educational outcomes of tutoring: a meta-analysis of findings', *American Educational Research Journal*, 19: 237–48.

Damon, W. (1984) 'Peer education: the untapped potential', *Journal of Applied Developmental Psychology*, 5: 331–43.

Deutsch, M. (1949a) 'A theory of cooperation and competition', *Human Relations*, 2: 129–52.

—— (1949b) 'An experimental study on the effects of cooperation and competition upon group process', *Human Relations*, 2: 199–231.

—— (1959) 'Some factors affecting membership motivation and achievement motivation in a group', *Human Relations*, 12: 81–95.

—— (1960) 'The effects of motivational orientation upon trust and suspicion', *Human Relations*, 13: 123–39.

—— (1969) 'Socially relevant science: reflections on some studies in interpersonal conflict', *American Psychologist*, 24: 1076–92.

—— (1979) 'Education and distributive justice: some reflections on grading systems', *American Psychologist*, 34: 391–401.

—— (1983) 'Current social psychological perspectives on justice', *European Journal of Social Psychology*, 13: 305–19.

DeVries, D. and Edwards, K. (1973) 'Learning games and student teams: their effects on classroom process', *American Educational Research Journal*, 10: 307–18.

Dewey, J. (1940) *Education Today*, New York: Greenwood Press.

—— (1966) *Democracy and Education*, New York: The Free Press.

Dineen, J., Clark, H. and Risley, T. (1977) 'Peer tutoring among elementary students: educational benefits to the tutor', *Journal of Applied Behaviour Analysis*, 10: 231–8.

Epstein, L. (1978) 'The effects of interclass peer tutoring on the vocabulary development of learning disabled children', *Journal of Learning Disabilities*, 11: 63–6.

Festinger, L. (1954) 'A theory of social comparison processes', *Human Relations*, 7: 117–40.

—— (1957) *A Theory of Cognitive Dissonance*, Stanford, CA: Stanford University Press.

Gartner, A., Kohler, M. and Riesman, F. (1971) *Children Teach Children: Learning by Teaching*, New York: Harper & Row.

Gillies, R. and Ashman, A. (1998) 'Behavior and interactions of children in cooperative groups in lower and middle elementary grades', *Journal of Educational Psychology*, 90: 746–57.

Greenwood, C. and Hops, H. (1981) 'Group-oriented contingencies and peer behaviour change', in P. Strain (ed.) *The Utilization of Classroom Peers as Behaviour Change Agents*, 189–259, New York: Plenum Press.

Greenwood, C., Carta, J. and Hall, V. (1988) 'The use of peer tutoring strategies in classroom management and educational instruction', *School Psychology Review*, 17: 258–75.

Hertz-Lazarowitz, R. (1989) 'Cooperation and helping in the classroom: a contextual approach', *Journal of Educational Research*, 13: 113–19.

Johnson, D.W. and Johnson, F.P. (2000) *Joining Together: Group Theory and Group Skills* (7th edn), Boston, MA: Allyn & Bacon.

Johnson, D.W. and Johnson, R. (1974) 'Instructional goal structure: cooperative, competitive, or individualistic', *Review of Educational Research*, 44: 213–40.

—— (1975) *Learning Together and Alone*, Englewood Cliffs, NJ: Prentice Hall.

—— (1979) 'Conflict in the classroom: controversy and learning', *Review of Educational Research*, 49: 51–70.

—— (1981) 'Effects of cooperative and individualistic learning experiences on interethnic interaction', *Journal of Educational Psychology*, 73: 454–59.

—— (1985) 'The internal dynamics of cooperative learning groups', in R. Slavin, S. Sharan, S. Kagan, R. Hertz-Lazarowitz, C. Webb and R. Schmuck (eds) *Learning to Cooperate, Cooperating to Learn*, 103–24, New York: Plenum Press.

Johnson, D.W., Johnson, R. and Maruyama, G. (1983) 'Interdependence and interpersonal attraction among heterogeneous and homogeneous individuals: a theoretical formulation and a meta-analysis of the research', *Review of Educational Research*, 53: 5–54.

Johnson, D.W., Johnson, R. and Stanne, M. (2000) *Cooperative Learning Methods: A Meta-analysis*. Online. Available at: <http:/www.clcrc.com/pages/cl-methods.html> (accessed 29 January 2001).

Johnson, D.W., Maruyama, G., Johnson, R., Nelson, D. and Skon, L. (1981) 'Effects of cooperative, competitive, and individualistic goal structures on achievement: a meta-analysis', *Psychological Bulletin*, 89: 47–62.

Kelly, G. (1955) *The Psychology of Personal Constructs*, New York: W.W. Norton.

King, A. (1991) 'Effects of training in strategic questioning on children's problem-solving performance', *Journal of Educational Psychology*, 83: 307–17.

—— (1999) 'Discourse patterns for mediating peer learning', in A. O'Donnell and A. King (eds) *Cognitive Perspectives on Peer Learning*, 87–115, Mahwah, NJ: Lawrence Erlbaum.

King, A., Staffieri, A. and Adelgais, A. (1998) 'Mutual peer tutoring: effects of structuring tutorial interaction to scaffold peer learning', *Journal of Educational Psychology*, 90: 134–52.

Knight, G. and Bohlmeyer, E. (1990) 'Cooperative learning and achievement: methods for assessing causal mechanism', in S. Sharan (ed.) *Cooperative Learning: Theory and Research*, 1–22, New York: Praeger.

Lane, C., Pollock, C. and Sher, N. (1972) 'Remotivation of disruptive adolescents', *Journal of Reading*, 15: 351–4.

Lewin, K. (1948) *Resolving Social Conflicts: Selected Papers on Group Dynamics*, New York: Harper & Brothers.

Lewin, K., Lippitt, R. and White, R. (1939) 'Patterns of aggressive behaviour in experimentally created social climates', *The Journal of Social Psychology*, 10: 271–99.

May, M. and Doob, L. (1937) *Cooperation and Competition*, New York: Social Sciences Research Council.

Mead, M. (1937) *Cooperation and Competition Among Primitive Peoples*, New York: McGraw-Hill.

Moreno, J.L. (1934) *Who Shall Survive? A New Approach to the Problem of Human Interrelations*, Washington, DC: Nervous and Mental Disease Publishing.

Piaget, J. (1932) *The Language and Thought of the Child* (2nd edn), London: Routledge & Kegan Paul.

Sharan, S. (1980) 'Cooperative learning in small groups: recent methods and effects on achievement, attitudes, and ethnic relations', *Review of Educational Research*, 50: 241–71.

Sharan, S. and Sharan, Y. (1976) *Small-Group Teaching*, Englewood Cliffs, NJ: Educational Technology Publications.

Sharan, S. and Shachar, H. (1988) *Language and Learning in the Cooperative Classroom*, New York: Springer-Verlag.

Shaw, M. (1932) 'A comparison of individuals and small groups in the rational solution of complex problems', *American Journal of Psychology*, 17: 491–504.

Slavin, R. (1977) 'Classroom reward structure: an analytical and practical review', *Review of Educational Research*, 47: 633–50.

—— (1983) 'When does cooperative learning increase student motivation?', *Psychological Bulletin*, 94: 429–45.

—— (1989) 'Cooperative learning and student achievement', in R.E. Slavin (ed.) *School and Classroom Organization*, Englewood Cliffs, NJ: Lawrence Erlbaum.

—— (1995) *Cooperative Learning: Theory, Research, and Practice* (2nd edn), Boston, MA: Allyn & Bacon.

Vygotsky, L.S. (1978). *Mind in Society: The Development of Higher Psychological Processes*, ed. and trans. M. Cole, V. John-Steiner, S. Scribner and E. Souberman, Cambridge, MA: Harvard University Press.

Watson, G. (1928). 'Do groups think more efficiently than individuals', *Journal of Abnormal Psychology*, 17: 328–36.

Webb, N. (1985). 'Student interaction and learning in small groups: a research summary', in R. Slavin, S. Sharan, S. Kagan, R. Hertz-Lazarowitz, C. Webb and R. Schmuck (eds) *Learning to Cooperate, Cooperating to Learn*, 5–15, New York: Plenum Press.

Webb, N. and Farivar, S. (1994) 'Promoting helping behaviour in cooperative small groups in middle school mathematics', *American Educational Research Journal*, 31: 369–95.

Webb, N., Troper, J. and Fall, R. (1995) 'Constructive ability and learning in collaborative small groups', *Journal of Educational Psychology*, 87: 406–23.

Wittrock, M. (1990) 'Generative processes of comprehension', *Educational Psychologist*, 24: 345–76.

Chapter 2

Fostering social development in preschool and the early elementary grades through co-operative classroom activities

Victor Battistich and Marilyn Watson

The crucial importance of peer group experience for the development of children's co-operative skills, as well as for their social, moral and intellectual development in general, has long been emphasized by prominent developmental theorists (Dewey 1900; Piaget 1932/1965; Sullivan 1953; Vygotsky 1978; Youniss 1980). The development of social skills, interpersonal understanding and concern for others continues into adulthood, but the foundation of these critical competencies occurs in early childhood (Watson *et al.* 1988). For many children the early childhood classroom provides their first group learning experiences outside of the home and, through such interactions, they come to understand themselves as learners (Buzzelli 1996), and as social beings.

In this chapter, we discuss the importance of co-operative learning for promoting young children's social and emotional development, review research on co-operative learning in early childhood education, and discuss implications for educational practice.

Why co-operative learning is important in early childhood education

When young children first come to a structured educational setting, their fledgling social and emotional skills and understandings are challenged in new and more complex ways. They will need to interact and negotiate with a large number of unfamiliar peers with different levels of social and emotional competencies, interests, cognitive abilities and interaction styles. Many will need their teacher's help to successfully manage these new challenges. If children do not learn successful strategies for interacting with their peers, the classroom environment will be peppered with disruptions and academic learning is likely to be seriously undermined (Howes and Ritchie 2002). Equally important, the ability to interact competently and positively with others is as important for success in life as the acquisition of academic skills and knowledge (Goleman 1995).

Co-operative learning activities provide an ideal vehicle for teachers to structure the environment for successful peer interactions and to provide students with the coaching and support they need to develop their social and emotional skills and understanding. Co-operative learning in early childhood can develop positive attitudes towards school and learning, and towards peers, and can provide abundant opportunities for learning how other people think, for developing language skills, and for learning how to solve interpersonal problems. Children who learn to interact successfully with their peers during the preschool and early elementary years tend to be well accepted by their peers throughout their school career, while children who fail to learn these skills in the early grades tend to be rejected by their classmates throughout their school career (Coie 1990). Teaching the skills needed for effective peer interaction early in children's school life can provide the foundation for success at school, and for success in life.

There is no question that children need to interact with other children. This desire to play derives from the basic human need to belong to a group (Baumeister and Leary 1995), which results in an intrinsic motivation to co-operate with others towards some common goal. For young children in particular, interest in co-operative play with others comes primarily from the need for social interaction, rather than from the specific content of the activity (DeVries and Zan 1994). Such co-operative interactions are essential for developing children's emerging understanding of fundamental social values of justice, caring and fairness, as well as their social skills and understanding.

Particularly in preschool, adults tend to underestimate children's ability to engage in co-operative interactions. Early childhood teachers used to be taught that infants and young children could not share or engage in reciprocal interactions (Howes and Tonyan 1999). Observation of the play and interactions of infants and toddlers made possible by the increased numbers of very young children in daycare settings has revealed that they are capable of interactive play and of building friendships (Howes and Tonyan 1999). Co-operative learning activities can provide young children with opportunities to develop not only their social and emotional skills, but also responsibility for their social environment, and to feel a personal commitment to the rules that are necessary for positive social relationships. However, as most teachers are keenly aware, children's activities are not always co-operative and not always beneficial to the children involved. For children to engage successfully in co-operative activities they need to experience a trusting, co-operative relationship with their teachers (Howes and Ritchie 2002; Watson in press). Children who experience their teacher's co-operation are likely to reciprocate by co-operating willingly with the teacher and their peers (DeVries and Zan 1994; Howes and Ritchie 2002).

Consistent with the educational theories of both Piaget and Vygotsky, young children benefit socially and morally from their interactions with peers (Piaget 1932/1965; Vygotsky 1978). We have found that both the social constructivist theory of Vygotsky and the attachment theory of John Bowlby (1969) and Mary Ainsworth (Ainsworth *et al.* 1978) that stress the child's apprenticeship role with nurturing adults to be equally important (Rogoff 1990). In the school setting, young children need both the autonomy to manage their own behaviour and their teacher's supportive presence and assistance. Many children need their teacher to organize their activities for success and to provide ongoing support, guidance, modelling and coaching (Howes and Ritchie 2002; Watson in press). Encountering conflict and the necessity of solving problems is important for social and moral growth, as is the coaching and modelling by adults of effective, fair and considerate ways to resolve conflict (Bloom *et al.* 1991).

When co-operative groups function well, children learn from one another, and come to like and respect one another, yet at the same time they learn to think for themselves and to explain the reasons for their opinions. Shy children can become contributors to the group, assertive children can learn to solicit the opinions of others, and all group members deepen their understanding of what it means to collaborate, negotiate and compromise to achieve fairness for everyone (Watson *et al.* 1988).

Research on co-operative learning in early childhood education

Although there is an extensive body of research on co-operative learning (e.g. Johnson *et al.* 1981; Slavin 1990), very little of this research has involved children of preschool or early elementary age. In their comprehensive meta-analysis of over 500 studies of co-operative learning, Johnson and Johnson (1989) found only four studies of co-operative learning (less than 1 per cent of the research) involving preschool children. Perhaps this reflects the widespread, although erroneous belief noted above that young children are developmentally incapable of 'true' co-operation. Nevertheless, the small body of research on co-operation and co-operative learning in early childhood education suggests that young children, like older children, benefit from co-operative learning.

For example, Vaughan (1996) introduced co-operative learning into a classroom environment characterized by disrespect, unfairness and intolerance between 5- to 7-year-old boys and girls. She found that co-operative learning resulted in more collaboration, less competitive behaviour, improved communication skills, better tolerance and respect for others, improved self-esteem, and a more positive and productive classroom in general. However, such positive outcomes are not a certainty. Howes and Ritchie (2002) found that for successful co-operative learning, the classroom needed to be a safe place for all students, the children needed to possess the social skills required by the activity, and the children needed to have a collaborative and trusting relationship with the teacher. Similar conclusions were reached by Rheta DeVries and her colleagues from their extensive research on children in constructivist preschools (see DeVries and Zan 1994). That is, young children are capable of effective co-operation if the teacher establishes a supportive classroom environment, models co-operative skills, and has a positive and personal relationship with students.

General implications for educational practice

It seems likely that, at least for young children, a caring and collaborative teacher–child relationship and a safe and caring classroom environment are both conditions for – and outcomes of – successful co-operative learning activities. However, many children, especially those who live in difficult circumstances, enter the classroom predisposed to mistrust their teacher as well as their classmates (Howes and Ritchie 2002; Watson in press). To be successful with co-operative learning activities, teachers will need to concentrate both on establishing a trusting, co-operative relationship with each of their students and on helping their students to develop co-operative relationships with one another. It will be impossible for a teacher to establish such relationships with students if the teacher cannot make the classroom a safe environment – an environment that meets students' needs for belonging, competence and autonomy (Baumeister and Leary 1995; Deci and Ryan 1985; Watson in press). The successful implementation of a co-operative learning programme will involve building co-operative relationships will each student and working towards creating a caring and supportive classroom community.

That said, let us now focus more specifically on the aspects of instruction that are likely to make co-operative learning activities succeed in fostering students' social and emotional development and supporting their academic motivation and learning.

As noted, although there has been considerable theoretical, empirical and practical work on co-operative learning during the past twenty-five years, extant approaches have been focused almost exclusively on upper elementary through university students (Johnson and Johnson 1984, 1991; Sharan 1990; Sharan and Shachar 1988; Slavin 1983, 1990). This work has not explicitly paid much attention to developmental considerations in co-operative activities for younger children (Watson et al. 1988). Consequently, recommendations derived from the existing research regarding group size, amount of teacher support, social skills instruction and lesson format are often too developmentally advanced for the skills and motivational levels of preschool and early primary children. Co-operative activities with young children must be appropriate to their skills, abilities and interests if they are to be effective at promoting their social development.

Group size

Good co-operative lessons challenge children to work together to achieve common goals. Most co-operative activities described in the literature involve groups of four or more. Groups of this size are generally too large for preschool and primary children. Groups of even four or five young children can work co-operatively if the activity is open-ended and loosely structured, such as block play, dramatic play or mural painting. In such activities, several children can be involved at the same time because there are many different functions to be filled, many ways to engage in them, and the actions of one child provide little constraint on the actions of the other group members (Watson *et al.* 1988). For activities that are more structured (e.g. playing a game with rules), involve a defined end-point (e.g. matching blocks to a pattern), or require high levels of academic skills (e.g. composing a role-play), it is best if young children work in pairs, so that each child has to co-ordinate activities with only one other person (Watson *et al.* 1988).

Amount of teacher support

With any co-operative activity, and with students of any age, teachers need to inform children of the goals and likely challenges of the task as clearly as possible, and to provide or elicit from the children concrete examples of the behaviours that will help them achieve these goals and successfully meet the challenges. Because young children are likely to have fewer of the basic social and emotional competencies needed for successful co-operation, and assumed to be in place in much of the literature on co-operative learning, teachers of young children will need to structure activities carefully and provide considerable support to their students as they struggle to work respectfully and productively with their classmates. For example, young children frequently have difficulty listening to one another. If the teacher constructs a partner interview activity in which each child's task is to draw or write about what their partner tells them, listening to a partner will be easier because it is necessary to doing the task. As the children work on the task they will receive constant positive and negative feedback on their listening skills, and with repeated interview activities the children's listening skills will increase.

However, even with carefully structured activities, some young children will fail to even engage with their partner, let alone co-operate. Teachers who used co-operative learning as part of their involvement with the Child Development Project (CDP) (see Dalton and Watson 1997; Solomon *et al.* 1990; Watson *et al.* 1988) frequently found that they needed to provide direct instruction to their students on basic competencies. For example, when Laura Ecken first introduced partner work to her early primary students, she found that several had trouble accepting and working smoothly with their assigned partners. Some of them did not even know how to say 'Hello'. Laura found that she needed to engage in some direct instruction to get co-operative learning activities off the ground.

> I think it makes a big difference to provide some direct teaching in what you do when you get with a partner. It helps to teach them very basic things. I might role-play with a student how to look at your partner and smile.
>
> With Louise, for example, I think it was very important that we talked about how to let people know you want them for a partner. She didn't have a clue. She would get with a partner and then grab the pencil out of their hand or kick them under the table. After we had some conversations about how to greet our partners, she started having positive partner experiences simply because she smiled at people and they smiled back. And those smiles were a wonderful thing for that kid.
>
> The other day she and Tyrone drew each other, and it was precious because she was happy to have him and she showed it. For his part, Tyrone's been having a lot of problems in his partnerships because people see him as not serious, and he does play around some. So when he got a partner who smiled and was happy to work with him, it was just great for both of them.
>
> (Watson in press)

While CDP teachers generally engage in whole class direct instruction of one or two of the social, emotional or moral competencies that are needed to engage successfully in a particular co-operative learning activity, they also provide individualized instruction or support as they notice problems arising in individual partnerships. In another example from Laura Ecken's classroom, there were many things that Laura's students did not under-stand about working collaboratively – some did not know how to say what they wanted without being bossy, some did not seem to care about their partner's needs, and some withdrew at the slightest disagreement or con-flict. Repeatedly, Laura provided brief lessons to partnerships on how to work fairly and considerately, how to express one's needs without giving up or withdrawing, how to give reasons for opinions, and how to look for compromise solutions:

> Ella was working with Gabrielle on a role-play. I happened to be nearby and I heard Ella say in a bossy way, 'You're Sarah Ida. I'm the dad.'
>
> So I asked, 'Did you all talk about who you want to be?'
> Ella said, 'No.'

So I said, 'Well, Gabrielle, how do you feel about Ella telling you that you're Sarah Ida, and she's the dad?'

She looked up and in a real quiet voice she said, 'I'm embarrassed.'

I said, 'Okay, you're embarrassed by that? Ella, what can you do?'

Ella snapped, 'I don't know!'

So I asked Gabrielle, and she said, 'We could talk about it.'

I said, 'El, what do you think about that?'

And she said, 'Nothing,' and just sat there.

So I said, 'I've got a suggestion for you, Ella. If you really want to be the dad, a way you could say that to Gabrielle is, "Maybe you could be Sarah Ida, and I could be the dad. What do you think about that?" Or, you could say "I'd like to be the dad, would you mind being Sarah Ida?" Ella, do you think that could work?'

It was interesting, because she immediately agreed, 'Yeah, okay, I can try that.'

(Watson in press)

A great strength of co-operative learning is that it provides teachers with many opportunities to instruct children in the social, emotional or moral domains at a time when such instruction is immediately relevant. Howes and Ritchie (2002) compare such embedded instruction or support to coaching and present convincing evidence of its effectiveness in the early childhood classroom. Embedding instruction in the context of ongoing classroom learning is similar to the ways that nurturing parents instruct children in the social and moral domains, and is likely to be more effective than decontextualized lessons in good character or social skills (Noddings 2002; Watson in press).

If young children are to benefit as much as possible from co-operative learning, it is imperative that the teacher observe their group interactions. Even with older children co-operative activities do not always go well, and when the quality of interaction is poor, children do not benefit – either socially or academically (Battistich *et al.* 1993).

At the same time, one of the goals of using co-operative learning is to facilitate children's development by giving them opportunities to solve problems on their own. Too much adult surveillance and guidance works against this goal, and must be balanced with the goals of making co-operative activities intellectually productive, positive and growth enhancing experiences for all. For example, struggling to solve an interpersonal problem in a co-operative learning activity can provide young children with the opportunity to learn why rules are necessary and later, with teacher guidance, help them to decide for themselves what they need to do to get along better with one another (DeVries and Zan 1994). Through observation and trial and error, teachers can develop their understanding of when and how to provide support to a group and when to let the group struggle on their own. One helpful step that teachers can take is to establish with the class the ground rule that children try first to solve their problem before coming to the teacher for help. Such a ground rule not only keeps children from bringing every trivial problem to the teacher; it also frees the teacher to observe the whole class and to provide focused help when needed to a particular group or partnership.

When the inevitable problems and conflicts occur during co-operative learning activities, the teacher's goal should be to facilitate the children's social development, rather than circumventing it by immediately intervening to solve the problem for the group.

Sometimes, just the teacher's supportive presence is sufficient to help children to muster the self-control needed to keep their behaviour organized and do what they need to do for successful interaction (Howes and Ritchie 2002). At other times more direct support may be needed. For example, the teacher may ask questions that will help children to understand what the problem is and how they might resolve it, or join the group and model the desired behaviour, or offer a suggestion or two to the children about how a problem might be resolved. It is important that groups of young (and older) children struggle and even fail on occasion, so that they learn the value of working hard to accomplish difficult tasks and experience the pleasure of solving difficult problems. If co-operative learning activities in a classroom almost never fail, it is likely that either the activities are too structured or too easy, or that the teacher is intervening too much in the groups' interactions. Conversely, if groups frequently have serious difficulties, the activities may be too hard for the children's abilities, or the teacher may not be providing enough instruction or support to enable the children to maintain positive interpersonal relationships (Watson *et al.* 1988).

Finally, it is important that the teacher 'debrief' co-operative activities with children after they are completed, and help them reflect on the activity and the ways in which their interactions could be improved. With preschool and early primary children such debriefing might be as simple as gathering the children into a circle and asking such open-ended questions as 'Can anyone tell us about a way their partner helped them?' 'Did any partnership have a problem? How did you solve it?' and 'Does anyone have something they're proud of about the way they worked with their partner?' Reflecting on the problems and successes encountered in co-operative activities maximizes children's ability to learn from their experiences, and thus helps to establish their inclination to be lifelong learners and to be personally committed to values of caring, justice and personal responsibility (Watson *et al.* 1988).

Social skills instruction

Approaches to co-operative learning designed for upper elementary, middle and secondary school students often focus on teaching roles such as 'leader' (Cohen 1987) and 'facilitator' (Johnson and Johnson 1991), or specific behaviours facilitative of group work such as paying compliments (Johnson and Johnson 1991). While young children do compliment their classmates on occasion and sometimes act as leaders in group play, asking them to consciously perform such roles and behaviours is more likely to disrupt than facilitate their co-operation. Many preschool and early primary children are still working on such social and emotional competencies as not crying when they are upset, listening to their partners, greeting a partner in a welcoming way, keeping their behaviour organized when they are excited, using their words to tell their partners what they are feeling, or even knowing what they are feeling. (For detailed discussions of the social and emotional competencies that young children need to develop during the preschool and early primary years see Howes and Ritchie (2002) and Watson (in press).) Early childhood teachers need to bring to co-operative learning the approach they have used for years in monitoring and facilitating children's group play: (1) structure the environment for both challenge and success, and (2) be ready, when needed, to facilitate children's interactions or teach social skills and understandings. By raising children's consciousness that they will be working on particular social competencies and debriefing their experiences at the end of an activity, as should be customary in co-operative learning with young children, teachers will simply be making their teaching more explicit for their students.

Lesson formats

Watson *et al.* (1988) identified four basic types of co-operative tasks, according to the source of co-ordination (internal vs. external) and the degree of interdependence required, that provide a very practical framework for thinking about how to design co-operative learning activities for young children.

The simplest type of co-operative task is one that is externally regulated (i.e. by the teacher) and involves a simple, structured division of labour, such as building a class caterpillar or dragon from the individually decorated paper plates of all the children in the class, or creating a class mural or bulletin board on which each child in the class places his or her own contribution. In activities such as these, each child works independently to produce something that is combined into a single group product. Each child's contribution is essentially prescribed and self-contained, and the teacher has the responsibility for co-ordinating the individual pieces into the group product. This type of co-operation thus involves little or no interaction among children. The teacher's primary role is to help children to recognize the relationship between their individual efforts and the group's common goal and product. The primary purpose of this type of activity in an overall co-operative learning programme is to help students see themselves as contributing group members and to underscore for children the value of people co-operating to produce a single product.

Slightly more demanding are tasks that involve an informal and incomplete division of labour, such as building with blocks, exploring the properties of water at the water table, or cutting out of magazines different pictures of objects that begin with a particular letter of the alphabet. These open-ended and self-directing tasks have many semi-independent parts, allowing children with varying levels of social skills to engage successfully in joint activity. Children with only rudimentary co-operative skills can work successfully in a group because they can keep their collaboration to a minimum. At the same time, children with more advanced skills can engage in more collaboration on the same tasks. Co-operative activities of this type are particularly useful with groups of children who have varying levels of skill.

The next most difficult level of collaboration involves clearly defined interdependent roles that help group members co-ordinate their behaviour. For example, when children work together to act out a well-known story, they are guided by their shared understanding of the story. Most games also fall into this category, and many are clearly within the abilities of young children. Activities such as these can be handled by young children working in groups of two or three, depending upon the complexity of the task. Like the structured division of labour tasks described above, these activities provide external supports in the form of shared scripts or agreed-upon 'rules'.

An important caveat when using games with young children is the extra strain competition can place on children's ability to co-operate successfully. While Hildebrandt and Zan (2001) found no difference in egoistic or aggressive behaviour when first grade children in constructivist classrooms played competitive or co-operative board games, in many settings children can become so upset at losing that they disintegrate into tears or aggression, or become so focused on winning that they ignore or belittle their partner/opponent (Howes and Ritchie 2002; Watson in press).

Clearly, young children need to be taught how to win or lose with grace, but such teaching might best wait until the children have had more opportunities to learn how to play co-operatively with success or until the classroom has developed a general spirit of co-operation. Hildebrandt and Zan (2001) also found that the first grade children in their study engaged in higher levels of negotiation and shared experiences when playing co-operative games rather than competitive games. Co-operative games are likely to be particularly useful at the beginning of the school year, when the co-operative atmosphere is being built, and for young children who have difficulty controlling the strong emotions that often accompany winning and losing. (Kamii and DeVries (1980) is a good source for competitive games suitable for young children, while Orlick (1982) is a good source for co-operative games for all ages, and Family Pastimes (www.familypastimes.org) produces many wonderful board games for young children.)

The most difficult of co-operative tasks require ongoing co-ordination of behaviour and have no inherently defined roles to guide the actions of individuals in the group. Most of the tasks described in the literature fall into this category. Even in co-operative learning approaches that use roles to facilitate group interaction, group members must constantly adapt their behaviours to one another in order to accomplish the task because it involves many choices about how the group may proceed, and each choice made constrains any subsequent choices of members of the group.

Examples of such tasks at the preschool level include building a house with blocks, or sharing a limited set of materials to create an art project. These types of activity require continuous attention to what other group members are doing, and rely on the group as a whole to achieve co-ordination of interaction. Children must decide for themselves how to divide up the task requirements and combine their efforts. Although it is valuable for young children to experience this type of co-operation, its complexity makes it quite difficult for them to accomplish it. The teachers who were part of CDP generally limited the group size to two when using these types of activities. For a more extensive discussion of the experiences of CDP teachers with co-operative learning, see Dalton and Watson (1997). For an extensive list of suitable collaborative activities for use with young children, as well as guidelines for adapting activities for children's different developmental levels and experience, see Developmental Studies Center (2000).

What to do when children cannot co-operate

Don't give up. While many children of all ages seem intrinsically motivated to engage in co-operative work or play with their peers, others seem to take a coercive stance towards peer interaction (Howes and Ritchie 2002; Watson in press). Children who live in difficult circumstances, or who have had a history of insecure attachment relationships with their caregivers and teachers, are particularly likely to find co-operative learning activities challenging. If children have lived in a highly competitive environment and see their classmates as competitors, if they have poorly developed social and emotional skills, or if they withdraw or become aggressive whenever there is disagreement, co-operative lessons can be very trying indeed. However, children's ability to get along with their classmates is essential for their happiness and for their success in life (Deci and Ryan 1985; Goleman 1995; Sheldon *et al.* 2001). When children cannot co-operate effectively, it is even more important to embark on a programme of co-operative learning.

Just as most students do not grasp academic concepts such as place value or multiplication when they are first introduced, students do not become friendly and collaborative with their peers after one or two co-operative lessons. They have many skills to learn, and many will have to develop trust in both their teacher and their peers before they will be able to work collaboratively with little teacher guidance. Often, we have to work harder to help students develop social and emotional skills and understandings than to teach academic content. The vignette below from Laura Ecken's classroom illustrates the depth and breadth of teaching in the social and emotional domains that is frequently necessary to support students in their struggle to work co-operatively:

Martin and Ella were research partners. They were researching eyes and ears to make a poster and give an oral presentation to the rest of the class. Ella wrote some stuff on the poster and Martin immediately wrote over it, making her words darker. Well, Ella just threw a fit. She slammed the books, she turned her chair away.

So I walked over and said, 'What's the problem here?'

Ella said, 'He's writing over my stuff.'

Martin's explanation was, 'I'm making it better. I can't read what she writes.'

I asked him, 'Why are you writing over this?'

He said, 'Well, look at it. You can hardly read it.'

I said, 'No, I can read that clearly. She doesn't write like you, but it doesn't mean that it can't be read.'

He went, 'Well, I'm making it better.'

I said, 'Martin, how would you feel if you wrote something down and then Ella wrote over it because she said she was making it better?'

He actually thought about it for a minute and said he wouldn't like it. So I asked him how he thought Ella felt.

He said, 'She doesn't like it.'

'Yeah,' I said, 'that's exactly right, Martin. That's what she's telling you. So, what can we do here?'

And he said, 'I don't need to be writing over her stuff.'

I said, 'Exactly. So do you think you two can get to work?' They said yes and then they were fine.

At the end-of-the-day meeting, when I asked the kids to talk about what went well during the day and what were rough spots, Martin raised his hand. 'I learned that you don't write over people's work to make it better, because you wouldn't want somebody doing it to you.'

I thought that was pretty good of him to verbalize that, and to be able to volunteer it.

(Watson in press)

However, Laura's sense of accomplishment did not last long:

The next day during the partner research Martin and Ella were furious and neither one of them was doing any work. I mean, they were literally in a rage. They had their arms folded and their backs to each other. And so I went over and said, 'What's going on here? I know you're both serious learners, but you're not doing any learning like this.'

Martin said, 'She doesn't want me to be her partner.'

Ella said, 'Well, he just wants to write everything down and not let me do anything.'

He said, 'She won't do anything. She was just sitting there.'

And Ella said, 'That's because he was writing it all down.'

So I said, 'Well, how can we solve this?'

Martin started crying and said, 'We can't because she doesn't want me for a partner.'

Ella's also got tears coming down her face, and she said, 'He doesn't want me, either.'

I said, 'You know, this partnership, doing both eyes and ears, you're the only people in the room who are researching two separate things. You've probably got one of the hardest reports to do. That's one of the reasons I put you together. Martin, did you notice how Ella just gets right to work and wants to do a lot, and write a lot, and read a lot?'

He said, 'Yeah.'

Then I said, 'Ella, did you notice that Martin doesn't play around during research? That he also wants to get right into it and learn as much as he can?'

And she said, 'Yeah.'

So I said, 'Well, why do you think I put you two together? This is a great partnership. We've got two people who are such serious learners.'

Then I said, 'Ella, is it true that you don't want to work with Martin?'

She said, 'No, I do want to work with him.'

Then I said, 'Martin?'

And he went, 'Yeah, I want to work with her.'

So I said, 'What can we do?'

Martin said, 'She can draw about the ears and I can draw about the eyes,' and Ella agreed.

(Watson in press)

One week later, on the day that Martin and Ella were preparing to give their presentation, their partnership dissolved again:

They had divided the poster in half and Ella's side about ears was all filled. Martin's side still had some room.

Well, Martin was at counseling when I read the class a book about frogs. Ella asked if she could borrow the book and when Martin came back, she said, 'Martin, I've got something else for the poster.'

Martin immediately said no because he thought it was about ears and there wasn't any room on her side of the poster. Then she got mad because he wouldn't listen. She was trying to talk to him and he wouldn't listen. She put the book down and folded her arms and just sat there. This is when they're supposed to be practicing their presentation, and neither one of them is doing anything.

I said, 'What's the problem?'

Martin said, 'She wants to put stuff from that book on her poster and she doesn't have any room.'

I said, 'Ella, what's going on? What's Martin talking about?'

Ella said, 'You know, you were reading us about the frog that has two eyes up front but then he's got two eye spots in the back that help him scare away predators? I thought Martin would like that and might want to put it on his side of the poster about eyes.'

Martin perked up, 'Oh, I didn't know it was about eyes. I thought it was about ears and you don't have any room.'

So I said, 'You see what's going on here? Martin, you didn't listen and started with an attitude. And then, Ella, when he started with that attitude, what did you do?'

She said, 'Wouldn't talk to him.'

I said, 'Yeah, so he never even knew it was for his side. So that's a lot of time lost with that attitude. And then backing out of the situation and not communicating caused more problems.'

Later, when Ella and Martin made their presentation, Martin seemed pleased to point out that frog information on his side of the poster.

(Watson in press)

Ella and Martin are bright children. They were leaders in Laura's classroom and both were clearly invested in their learning. Yet their defensiveness, lack of trust, combativeness and utter lack of collaborative skills are almost comic. Helping all students to develop the capacities for friendly collaboration is taxing because it requires both patience and perseverance. However, it is time well spent, for if we fail to teach such collaborative skills and interpersonal understanding the classroom is likely to be characterized by conflict, resulting in constant interruptions to academic learning (see Watson in press).

Conclusions

A thoughtful and sequential approach to co-operative learning that attends closely to social interaction skills and prosocial values can do much to contribute to young children's development of social interaction skills, social understanding and concern for others (Watson *et al.* 1988). Although teachers need to keep their students' developmental abilities in mind, good co-operative tasks have the same elements at all age levels: (1) the lesson should be engaging and challenging, (2) it should have a common goal, (3) children should readily see (and/or be helped to understand) the benefits of working together, and (4) all group members should be meaningfully engaged in the task at all times.

Similarly, the teacher's role in co-operative activities is consistent across age levels. He or she has to set clear goals for the activity, monitor groups as they work, intervene as needed, and help children to reflect on their experiences and what they have learned (Watson *et al.* 1988). Under such conditions, even very young children can benefit greatly from working co-operatively with their peers.

References

Ainsworth, M.D.S., Blehar, M.C., Waters, E. and Wall, S. (1978) *Patterns of Attachment*, Hillsdale, NJ: Lawrence Erlbaum.

Battistich, V., Solomon, D. and Delucchi, K. (1993) 'Interaction processes and student outcomes in cooperative learning groups', *The Elementary School Journal*, 94: 19–32.

Baumeister, R.F. and Leary, M.R. (1995) 'The need to belong: desire for interpersonal attachments as a fundamental human motivation', *Psychological Bulletin*, 117: 497–529.

Bloom, P.J., Sheerer, M. and Britz, J. (1991) *Blueprint for Action: Achieving Center-Based Change Through Staff Development*, Lake Forest, IL: New Horizons.

Bowlby, J. (1969) *Attachment and Loss*, Vol. I, New York: Basic Books.

Buzzelli, C.A. (1996) 'The moral implications of teacher–child discourse in early childhood classrooms', *Early Childhood Research Quarterly*, 11: 515–34.

Cohen, E.G. (1987) *Designing Group Work: Strategies for the Heterogeneous Classroom*, New York: Teachers College Press.

Coie, J. D. (1990) 'Towards a theory of peer rejection', in S.R. Asher and J.D. Coie (eds) *Peer Rejection in Childhood*, 17–59, New York: Cambridge University Press.

Dalton, J. and Watson, M. (1997) *Among Friends: Classrooms Where Caring and Learning Prevail*, Oakland, CA: Developmental Studies Center.

Deci, E.L. and Ryan, R.M. (1985) *Intrinsic Motivation and Self-Determination in Human Behavior*, New York: Plenum Press.

Developmental Studies Center (2000) *Blueprints For a Collaborative Classroom*, Oakland, CA: Developmental Studies Center.

DeVries, R. and Zan, B. (1994) *Moral Classrooms, Moral Children: Creating a Constructivist Atmosphere in Early Education*, New York: Teachers College Press.

Dewey, J. (1900) *The Child and the Curriculum and the School and Society*, Chicago, IL: University of Chicago Press.

Goleman, D. (1995) *Emotional Intelligence*, New York: Bantam.

Hildebrandt, C. and Zan, B. (2001) 'Interpersonal understanding in cooperative and competitive games', paper presented at the American Educational Research Association Conference, Seattle, WA.

Howes, C. and Ritchie, S. (2002) *A Matter of Trust: Connecting Teachers and Learners in the Early Childhood Classroom*, New York: Teachers College Press.

Howes, C. and Tonyan, H.H. (1999) 'Peer relations', in L. Balter and C. Tamis-LeMonda (eds) *Child Psychology: A Handbook of Contemporary Issues*, 143–57, Philadelphia, PA: Psychology Press.

Johnson, D.W. and Johnson, R. (1984) *Cooperation in the Classroom*, New Brighton, MN: Interaction Book Company.

—— (1989) *Cooperation and Competition: Theory and Research*, Edina, MN: Interaction Book Company.

—— (1991) *Learning Together and Alone* (3rd edn), Englewood Cliffs, NJ: Prentice-Hall.

Johnson, D.W., Maruyama, G., Johnson, R.T., Nelson, D. and Skon, L. (1981) 'Effects of cooperative, competitive, and individualistic goal structures on achievement: a meta-analysis', *Psychological Bulletin*, 89: 47–62.

Kamii, D. and DeVries, R. (1980) *Group Games in Early Education: Implications of Piaget's Theory*, Washington, DC: National Association for the Education of Young Children.

Noddings, N. (2002) *Educating Moral People*, New York: Teachers College Press.

Orlick, T. (1982) *The Second Cooperative Sports and Games Book*, New York: Pantheon Books.

Piaget, J. (1932/1965) *The Moral Judgment of the Child*, New York: Free Press.

Rogoff, B. (1990) *Apprenticeship in Thinking: Cognitive Development in Social Context*, New York: Oxford University Press.

Sharan, S. (ed.) (1990) *Cooperative Learning: Theory and Research*, New York: Praeger.

Sharan, S. and Shachar, H. (1988) *Language and Learning in the Cooperative Classroom*, New York: Springer-Verlag.

Sheldon, K.M., Elliot, A.J., Kim, Y. and Kasser, T. (2001) 'What is satisfying about satisfying events? Testing 10 candidate psychological needs', *Journal of Personality and Social Psychology*, 80: 325–39.

Slavin, R.E. (1983) *Cooperative Learning*, New York: Longman.

—— (1990) *Cooperative Learning: Theory, Research, and Practice*, Englewood Cliffs, NJ: Prentice-Hall.

Solomon, D., Watson, M., Schaps, E., Battistich, V. and Solomon, J. (1990) 'Cooperative learning as part of a comprehensive classroom program designed to promote prosocial development', in S. Sharan (ed.) *Cooperative Learning: Theory and Research*, 231–60, New York: Praeger.

Sullivan, H.S. (1953) *The Interpersonal Theory of Psychiatry*, New York: Norton.

Vaughan, R. (1996, January) 'Venturing into co-operative learning in the early years of schooling: a classroom teacher's experience', paper presented at the Australian and New Zealand Conference on the First Years of School, Hobart, Tasmania.

Vygotsky, L.S. (1978). *Mind in Society: The Development of Higher Psychological Processes*, ed. and trans. M. Cole, V. John-Steiner, S. Scribner and E. Souberman, Cambridge, MA: Harvard University Press.

Watson, M. (in press) *Learning to Trust: Transforming Difficult Elementary Classrooms Through Developmental Discipline*, San Francisco, CA: Jossey-Bass.

Watson, M., Hildebrandt, C. and Solomon, D. (1988) 'Cooperative learning as a means of promoting prosocial development among kindergarten and early primary-grade children', *The International Journal of Social Education*, 3(2): 34–47.

Youniss, J. (1980) *Parents and Peers in Social Development*, Chicago, IL: University of Chicago Press.

Chapter 3

Structuring co-operative learning experiences in primary school

Robyn M. Gillies

Introduction

Schools are being encouraged to adopt pedagogical practices that promote the active involvement of students in learning (Tapscott 1999). One practice that has received widespread coverage over the past two decades is co-operative, small-group learning. Interest in co-operative learning has developed as schools have become more aware of the academic and social benefits that accrue to students from working together and helping each other. Academic benefits have included enhanced achievements in reading comprehension and vocabulary development, written expression, mathematics understanding and comprehension, and conceptual development in science (Calderon *et al.* 1998; Howe *et al.* 1995; Shachar and Sharan 1994; Whicker *et al.* 1997). Enhanced learning has also occurred when students work in computer-mediated collaborative groups on a range of different topics and subject matter (Zammuner 1995). Furthermore, children with diverse learning and adjustment needs have gained from their participation in co-operative learning (Gillies and Ashman 2000; Ragan 1993). Other benefits include more time on task, increased motivation and perseverance with tasks, and improved communication skills (Hunt *et al.* 1994). In short, achievements have covered a range of subject and curriculum areas and included parallel changes in behaviours, attitudes and interactions.

In the affective area, co-operative learning influences the development of positive attitudes towards peers, including children from diverse cultural and social backgrounds, and children with diverse learning needs (Putnam *et al.* 1996). It has also helped to foster the development of positive attitudes towards learning, a willingness to engage with other children, and to work together to promote each other's learning. In so doing, children have learned how to deal with conflict, consider the perspective of others, negotiate how to proceed with tasks, and share ideas and resources (Johnson *et al.* 1997; McManus and Gettinger 1996). In fact, it has been argued that co-operative learning experiences are crucial to preventing and alleviating many of the social problems related to children, adolescents and young adults (Johnson *et al.* 2000). However, while the benefits of co-operative learning are well acknowledged, many schools and teachers experience difficulties in knowing how to implement this approach to teaching and learning.

Implementing co-operative learning in the classroom

Placing students in groups and expecting them to work together will not necessarily promote co-operative learning. Some children will defer to the more able children in the group who may take over the important roles in ways that benefit them at the expense of other group members. Similarly, other students will be inclined to leave the work to others while they exercise only token commitment to the task.

In co-operative learning, each student is required not only to complete their part of the work but to ensure that others do likewise. The technical term for this dual responsibility is 'positive interdependence', and it is the most important element of co-operative learning (Deutsch 1949). Positive interdependence exists when students perceive that they cannot succeed unless others do and they must learn to co-ordinate their efforts to ensure that this occurs. Cohesiveness develops in the group as a direct result of the perception of goal interdependence and the perceived interdependence among group members (Deutsch 1949). When positive interdependence is understood, each member's efforts are indispensable to the success of the group (Johnson and Johnson 1990). When groups are established where positive goal interdependence does not exist, groups are not truly co-operative.

The second essential element that affects co-operative learning is promotive interaction. Promotive interaction involves individuals encouraging and facilitating each other's efforts as they work together on the group task. Children encourage and facilitate each other's efforts by providing explanations and information to assist understanding, constructive feedback to improve performance with a task, and access to needed materials and resources. In so doing, they exchange ideas and teach each other how to solve problems. One of the benefits of these exchanges is an increased awareness of what other children do not understand and this enables them to provide help that is more easily understood (Webb and Farivar 1994). When this happens, children are likely to feel accepted and valued, less anxious and stressed, and willing to reciprocate and help others in turn. Furthermore, as children interact they are more likely to get to know each other as individuals, and this forms the basis for caring and committed relationships (Johnson *et al.* 1990).

It is this sense of commitment to each other that helps children to feel accountable for their efforts. In fact, the more students perceive they are linked together, the more they feel personally responsible for contributing to the collective effort of the group. Personal responsibility or individual accountability is the third essential element in co-operative learning and it occurs when members accept responsibility for their part of the task and actively facilitate the work of others in the group. Johnson and Johnson (1990) maintain that personal responsibility or individual accountability can be established in two different ways. The first is through structuring for positive interdependence among group members so that they will feel responsible for facilitating each other's efforts. The second is through the teacher establishing requirements for individual accountability so that each student's contribution to the group's efforts can be identified, hence ensuring that each child is responsible for completing their assigned work or task in the group.

Children co-operate and work better together when they have been taught the interpersonal and small group skills needed to facilitate interaction and involvement with each other (Johnson and Johnson 1990). In fact, these skills comprise the fourth essential element in co-operative learning. In a study that examined the effect of training in interpersonal and small group skills on children's interactions and achievement during small group work, Gillies and Ashman (1996) found that the children who were trained to co-operate and help each other used language which was more inclusive of others, and gave more detailed explanations to assist each other than children who had not received explicit training in these skills. Some of the benefits that were evident in the children from the trained groups were increased autonomy and more successful learning outcomes. It may be that as they learned to interact appropriately with each other, they felt more supported in their endeavours and were more willing to work together on their problem-solving activities. Certainly, social support is related to achievement, successful problem-solving, satisfaction, persistence on challenging tasks, more appropriate ways of seeking assistance, and greater compliance with group routines and expectations (Johnson and Johnson 1987). Social support tends to increase group cohesion and, through group norms, affects the pressure to be productive (Deutsch 1949).

The interpersonal skills that facilitate communication include:

- actively listening to each other during group discussions;
- considering the other person's perspective on issues;
- stating ideas freely without fear of derogatory comments;
- being responsible for one's own behaviour;
- constructively critiquing the ideas presented.

The small group skills that facilitate participation in co-operative learning include:

- taking turns to present ideas and share resources;
- sharing tasks equitably among group members;
- resolving differences of opinion and conflict;
- ensuring decisions that affect the group are decided democratically.

These skills are used to promote social interactions and help students deal successfully with conflicts that can arise in small group settings.

In a review of the research on conflict resolution and peer mediation Johnson and Johnson (1996) found that students who were trained in these two areas were able to use these skills effectively in actual conflict situations and generalize them to non-classroom conflict situations, including those in the home. Furthermore, there is additional evidence to show that when these skills are integrated into the school curriculum, students obtain higher academic outcomes. For example, in a study of ninth grade English students who participated in conflict resolution training, Stevahn et al. (1997) found that those who were trained outperformed their untrained peers both in the factual information they learned and the interpretations they made of the novel they reviewed. Moreover, even kindergarten children are able to learn these skills and apply them to different conflict situations. The training they received also helped them to gain a better conceptual understanding of friendship (Stevahn et al. 2000). In effect, there are both social and academic benefits to be derived from training students in the skills needed to manage and resolve conflicts (Johnson and Johnson, 2000).

The last essential element in co-operative learning is group processing. This involves members determining what they have done well and what they will need to do to achieve the group's goals; in other words, giving group members the opportunity to reflect on the learning process has clear academic and social benefits.

Yager et al. (1985) were the first to demonstrate that co-operative small group processing that included summarizing the material being learned and monitoring others' summaries improved group achievements. Later, Johnson et al. (1990) found that when high school students were assigned to a co-operative learning condition with teacher and group processing, they demonstrated greater individual and group problem-solving success than students in the remaining co-operative (no group processing or teacher processing) conditions or the individual condition. In essence, both studies show that students' achievements are enhanced through group processing.

Structural issues in establishing co-operative groups

It has been argued that the academic and social benefits that accrue to students who work co-operatively to achieve a common goal are unequivocal

(Cohen 1994). Johnson and Johnson (1999: 72), for example, believe that 'this is so well confirmed that it stands as one of the strongest principles of social and organizational psychology'. However, establishing productive co-operative groups in classrooms is not easy, as teachers often have to consider how to structure groups, who will be involved and what their task will be. These issues are important because each of these variables will affect the outcomes. Furthermore, with the emphasis on involving children with different learning problems (including both children with learning disabilities and learning difficulties) in mainstream classes, the challenge for teachers is to find ways of drawing them into co-operative group activities so that they can optimize their chances to learn and benefit from the group involvement. Some of the issues that have emerged in establishing co-operative learning in classrooms are training for group members, size of the group, ability groupings and gender composition, type of activity to be undertaken, and the length of time the group should remain together.

Training

Training children to work together is crucial for the success of the group (Johnson and Johnson 1990). In a study of Grade 6 children who worked in either trained or untrained small groups, Gillies and Ashman (1996) found that the children in the trained groups were more co-operative, provided more assistance to each other and obtained higher learning outcomes than the children who worked in the untrained groups. Training involved not only the children in learning the interpersonal and small group skills that would facilitate co-operation, but also ensuring that their teachers understood how to establish co-operative, small group learning activities in their classroom (i.e. understanding the five key elements discussed above). A later study by Gillies and Ashman (1998), involving children in the early and middle years of elementary school, confirmed the importance of training children in the skills they would need to work effectively together. In both studies, the children who had been trained to work co-operatively were more co-operative and helpful to other group members and demonstrated higher learning outcomes than their untrained peers.

The importance of training children in specific interactional skills was also illustrated by Fuchs et al. (1997). In a study conducted in forty general education classrooms in Grades 2, 3 and 4, children were assigned randomly to one of three conditions: peer mediated instruction with training in how to offer and receive elaborated help, peer mediated instruction with training in elaborated help and in how to provide conceptual mathematical explanations, and contrast (i.e. no peer mediated help). Children who received training in elaborated help and how to provide conceptual explanations not only asked more relevant questions but also provided more conceptual explanations to the students they were helping. Furthermore, the achievement of this group was higher than the group of children who had been trained to provide elaborated help only which, in turn, surpassed that of the contrast group. In effect, the study not only demonstrated the importance of training children to provide specific help to each other, but also illustrated that the more explicit this training is (i.e. in the type of help and explanations provided), the higher the achievement gains.

Training teachers in the procedures needed to implement co-operative, small-group learning in their classrooms is also crucial for the success of the groups. In a recent review of fifty-one studies on the effects of small group learning in different classrooms, Lou et al. (2000) found that when teachers were trained to implement small group instructional strategies, they were more able to adapt their instructional strategies to small group instruction, prepare for possible instructional and managerial problems, and achieve success in using these new instructional techniques than teachers who had not been trained. It appears that when teachers have been trained, they may be more prepared to adopt different teaching philosophies, instructional strategies and alternative teaching materials than used previously. Hence training is important in helping them make the transition to small group teaching, learning to use new instructional strategies, and being prepared for possible difficulties in managing this approach.

In short, research indicates clearly that both students and teachers need to be trained to manage the demands of small group work effectively. Students need explicit training in the interpersonal and small group skills that facilitate co-operation and helping, and teachers need to be trained in the strategies required to implement and manage small groups.

Size

Setting the optimal group size is important because, if groups are too large, some students will be overlooked while others will coast at the expense of the workers. Groups of three or four members are preferred to larger groups because members cannot opt out of the activity or loaf at others' expense. A small group ensures that all members are visible and involved. Interestingly, Cohen et al. (1989) found that the more small groups there are operating in the classroom, the more students are likely to talk and work together. In a meta-analysis of sixty-six studies that investigated the effects of grouping practices within classrooms on student achievement, Lou et al. (1996) found that group size was one factor that moderated student achievement. When groups were large (i.e. six to ten), members did not learn significantly more than students in ungrouped or whole classes. In fact, optimally sized small groups for learning seem to be three to four members. It appears that the larger the group, the less likely students are to interact with each other and the more the group is likely to resemble a whole class setting.

Group composition

The ability and gender composition of small groups is another consideration because of the effect they have on interaction among members and achievement. Research by Webb (1985) showed that in mixed-ability groups, high-ability students give more help to their peers than in same-ability groups. In these groups, both high-ability and low-ability students are active in a teacher–pupil relationship while the medium-ability students tend to be ignored. Interestingly, the medium-ability students are more active in uniform or same-ability groups whereas in uniform high-ability groups, students often assumed others knew how to solve the problem and made little effort to explain the material. In uniform low-ability groups, few students understood the problem well enough to explain it to others.

In different gender compositions, Webb (1985) found the achievement of males and females was nearly identical in gender-balanced groups while in majority male or majority female groups, males outperformed their female peers. When groups were gender-balanced, males and females were equally interactive whereas in majority female or male groups this was not so. In majority female groups, the female members directed most of their questions and help to the male member to the detriment of others in the group whereas in majority male groups females were largely ignored.

In a study that examined the effects of mixed ability and gender compositions on Grade 6 students' behaviours and interactions, Gillies and Ashman (1995) found the effect of different ability and gender compositions in the structured co-operative groups was minimal. It appeared that the positive interdependence that had been established with the co-operative group task in conjunction with the training the children had received in facilitating interactions created the momentum to co-operate and help each other. Furthermore, as the students had more time to work together, they became more responsive to the needs of each other and gave more elaborated help to assist each other's learning. It was this help which, in turn, affected the learning that occurred. Groups containing three ability levels (high, medium, low) appeared to adjust earlier to the work context, and those in the groups containing two ability levels also developed co-operative behaviours over the duration of the study.

In a more recent study of group ability composition of students in Grades 7 and 8 who worked collaboratively, Webb et al. (1998) found that group composition had a major impact on the quality of the group discussion and student achievement. Students who participated in mixed-ability groups gave higher quality explanations to assist understanding than did students in uniform-ability groups and this contributed more to their achievement test scores than did their own ability scores, particularly in the case of children with low ability and low to medium ability.

While some previous research has shown that medium-ability students may be left out of the teacher–learner relationships that often develop in mixed-ability groups between high- and low-ability students, this did not happen in the Webb *et al.* (1998) study. They found that medium-ability children were as active in mixed-ability groups as students of high ability or low ability. Furthermore, medium-ability students showed as much high-level participation in their mixed-ability groups as did medium-ability students who worked in homogeneous groups (i.e. all the same ability level) where previous studies had shown they were likely to be more active.

Webb *et al.* (1998) also found that while high-ability students generally performed better in homogeneous groups than in heterogeneous groups, their performance did not suffer when they worked with below-average students. In fact, on balance, the authors reported that heterogeneous grouping with high-ability students working with low-ability students will produce greater achievement gains than restricting high-achievement students to homogeneous groups.

In summary, low-ability students do not benefit from participating in low-ability groups, high-ability students are not adversely affected by working with low-ability students, and medium-ability students appear to do equally well in mixed- or same-ability groups. The effect of gender composition on group interactions is less clear. However, it is clear that when children have been trained to work co-operatively, they are more likely to be responsive to the needs of each other and provide help to assist each other irrespective of gender considerations.

Group task

The type of task students undertake in their groups also affects the discussions that occur. Cohen (1994) argued that in well-structured tasks such as mathematical and computational tasks, there is little need for discussion because there is typically a right answer or a procedure to follow. These tasks require low levels of co-operation because students do not have to discover anything as a group or negotiate any meaning. With this type of task, achievement is consistently related to giving detailed explanations to each other on how to solve the problem. In contrast, in ill-structured tasks such as open-ended and discovery tasks where there are no right answers or procedures to follow, discussion among the members is vital to productivity. Students need to exchange ideas and information if they want to find creative solutions to their assignment or discover the underlying principles to a problem. Under these conditions, achievement depends on task-related interaction.

When students are assigned to either well- or ill-structured group tasks, teachers need to ensure that students understand what type of assistance will be more helpful as they work together. For example, when students are working on well-structured or low-level co-operative tasks where procedures are well defined, the most consistent predictor of achievement is the giving of detailed and elaborated explanations (Webb 1991, 1992). Giving help encourages reorganization and clarification that may enable the explainer to understand the material better, develop new perspectives, and construct more elaborate cognitive understandings than he or she had previously (Wittrock 1990). In other words, students who do the explaining are the ones who benefit. In contrast, being ignored, not receiving an explanation in response to a request for help or being given only the right answer with no explanation is related negatively to achievement (Webb 1991, 1992).

When students work on ill-structured or high-level co-operative tasks in which they are required to interact about the process and discuss how to proceed, interaction is vital to productivity. It might be expected that children would engage in more productive discourse as they worked to resolve the problem or discover the solution. In a study of Grades 3 to 8 students, Hertz-Lazarowitz (1989) found that when the task involved high-level co-operation (i.e. interaction is important for productivity), 78 per cent of the interaction involved applicative or evaluative thinking (higher level thinking), whereas only 44 per cent of the interaction in low-level co-operative tasks involved higher level thinking processes. Cohen (1994) argued that she and her colleagues (Cohen et al. 1989) have consistently found that when students work on tasks requiring high levels of co-operation, it is the frequency of task-related interactions that are related to gains on follow-up content-referenced tests and conceptual development in mathematical and computational tasks. Similarly, Gillies and Ashman (1998) found that task-related interactions, such as providing directives and elaborated help, facilitated the development of higher order thinking among children who worked in small, co-operative groups on discovery-based tasks in social studies.

The findings reported above suggest that high-level co-operative tasks promote higher reasoning interactions which, in turn, affect the learning that occurs. In classrooms, teachers need to be mindful of the different ways of structuring group tasks and the importance of helping students to understand how they can provide help to maximize their own and each other's learning.

Structuring interactions in groups

There are a number of ways of designing group tasks to ensure participants' interactions. In a very early study, King (1991) found that when fifth graders were taught to use a specific, guided questioning strategy with their partners to solve specific computer-based problems, they asked more strategic questions and gave more elaborated explanations than peers who had been told only to ask and answer questions during the problem-solving activities. The questions were designed to guide students' cognitive processing during problem-solving and help them to become aware of their own problem-solving or metacognitive skills.

Under the rubric of planning, monitoring and evaluating (the metacognitive skills), the children were prompted to ask specific questions relevant to each part of the process. For example, typical planning questions included: 'What is the problem?' 'What do we know about the problem so far?' 'Is there another way to do this?' Monitoring questions included: 'Are we using our plan or strategy?' 'Do we need a new plan?' 'Are we on the right track?' Finally, questions that sought to evaluate the success of the task included: 'What worked?' 'What didn't work?' 'What would we do differently next time?' (King 1991: 309).

The results of the study showed that the guided questioners outperformed the unguided questioners on both a follow-up written test of problem-solving and a novel computer task showing that they had achieved generalization by being able to use it on an unprompted task. The guided questioning strategy appeared to teach the children how to be strategic problem-solvers; that is, how to ask for and provide task-appropriate detailed help which their untrained peers were unable to do.

In a follow-up study by King (1994), pairs of fourth and fifth grade children were trained to generate 'thinking' questions as they participated in a unit of work on the biology of the human body. Thinking questions required the children not only to remember information presented but also think about it in some way so they made connections between two or more ideas presented in the lesson. Typical thinking questions were: 'Describe in your own words how the circulatory system works.' 'What is the difference between arteries and veins?' 'Explain how what happens in the heart affects what happens in the arteries' (King 1994: 346). Once again, prompt cards were used to help students remember how to ask questions that encouraged them to think about the material they had studied in class.

In addition to the training in how to generate questions, one group of students was also taught to generate experience-based and lesson-based questions. Experience-based questions explicitly related the lesson material to the children's prior knowledge and experience in a previous lesson or their general knowledge of the world. For example, typical questions that encouraged the children to make connections between ideas presented and previous knowledge were: 'Explain how the circulatory system is similar to a tree.' 'What do you think would happen if our hearts were smaller?' and 'How is the circulatory system related to the digestive system?' A third group of students did not receive any training in questioning; however, they did receive training in how to give explanatory help to enable children to distinguish between describing something and explaining (telling the 'why' and 'how' of it).

Analysis of the questions asked by the children in the different groups showed that those in the training groups asked more questions that required them to integrate knowledge and information than those in the control group who asked more factual questions. Similarly, the children in the trained groups demonstrated significantly more knowledge assimilation than the untrained group. Furthermore, the children who had been trained to generate experienced-based questions generated more knowledge integration statements than the children who had been taught only to generate lesson-based questions and who made more integration statements than the untrained control group.

The findings reported above suggest that when children ask integration and comprehension questions they are more likely to engage in complex levels of knowledge construction, and when they ask factual questions they are more likely to engage in knowledge restating, the lowest form of knowledge construction. When children use questions that guide them to connect ideas within a lesson together or to connect the lesson to prior knowledge, they engage in complex knowledge construction that, in turn, enhances learning. The experience-based questioners learned more than the lesson-based questioners who, in turn, learned more than the controls. The study shows that elementary children can be trained to generate these kinds of question for themselves and to use them to connect ideas within lessons and previous knowledge to enhance learning.

Meloth and Deering (1994) focused on scripting interactions among Grade 4 and 5 students as they worked in a reward condition and a strategic condition. Children in both conditions were provided with think sheets to help guide their discussions during the group activities. In the reward condition, the think sheets contained items that directed discussions towards important task content and required groups to communicate information in an informative manner. For example, a think sheet designed for children in this condition may have required them to read a passage silently and record an inference, prediction, and summary and discuss their recordings with other group members.

In the strategic condition, the think sheets contained similar items; however, these items were followed by prompts for discussing the metacognitive knowledge and skills associated with the tasks. The think sheets for the children in this condition included additional items about declarative (what the lesson was about), conditional (why and when task content should be used), and procedural (how to use task content effectively) knowledge. For example, in addition to the items on the above think sheet, the children in the strategic condition may also have been required to ask at least two group members to comment on the summary each wrote. Questions such as: 'Do they think it was a good one?' 'Why or why not?' 'How could I do it differently?' were designed to encourage metacognitive thinking.

Analyses of students' talk in groups showed that the children in the strategic condition provided more explanations, task-related questions and counter assertions (rebuttals), and that academic talk in general was focused towards the facts, concepts and strategies associated with task content. In essence, these children demonstrated more strategic and metacognitive thinking. Furthermore, they reported greater awareness of specific learning goals, task products and task operations than their peers in the reward condition who did not use this scripted interaction approach. In effect, the strategic condition emphasized the connection between strategy use and learning. The authors concluded that groups are more likely to focus their discussions towards important task content and to improve their awareness of learning goals and task dimensions when discussions are directly oriented towards the metacognitive features of their cooperative tasks.

In summary, the research shows that when children are taught to use specific questioning strategies (i.e. guided questioning or scripted interactions) with their partners as they work on problem-solving tasks, they learn to ask more strategic and thought-provoking questions and provide more elaborated help than peers who had been told only to ask and answer their partners' questions. Furthermore, they engage in more complex knowledge construction and awareness of their own problem-solving or metacognitive skills that, in turn, enhances learning.

Reciprocal teaching

Another means of structuring interactions in groups is through reciprocal teaching, designed to help students develop specific strategies to assist their understanding of written text. Reciprocal teaching is a form of co-operative learning and is based on the premise that expert-led social interactions have a prominent role to play in learning and can provide a major impetus to cognitive growth.

In reciprocal teaching, teachers (as experts) model reciprocal teaching dialogues with their students and, in so doing, provide detailed explanations of the four strategies employed, namely predicting, questioning, summarizing and clarifying, and how they can be used. For example, the teacher may begin by instigating a discussion about the passage to be read by trying to get the children to predict what the story may be about. The children then read a short section and compose a brief summary of the main points or ideas. They then think of a question about the section, make a prediction about what may occur in the following section, and ask for clarification if required. In essence, the strategies of predicting, questioning, summarizing and clarifying encourage children to anticipate information they will encounter, integrate what is presented in the text with prior knowledge, reconstruct prior knowledge to fit in with what they have learned, and monitor for understanding (Palincsar and Brown 1988).

Initially, teachers are involved in extensive modelling of these metacognitive strategies while the students actively answer questions and discuss the passages. Specific feedback is provided for students who attempt to apply any of the four comprehensive strategies to the sections being read. With practice, the students become more adept at applying the strategies and the teacher's support is reduced so that he or she acts more as a coach in providing corrective feedback and encouragement.

As each section of text is discussed, each child, in turn, acts as a dialogue leader. The leader begins by generating a question to which the group members respond. The participants then formulate additional questions based on the information they are reading and share with the rest of the group the questions they have generated. The leader then summarizes the gist of the text that has been read and provides group members with the opportunity to comment and elaborate on the summary offered by the leader. Word meanings and confusing text are clarified before the students predict what may happen in the next paragraph. This process is repeated as each new paragraph is read.

Reciprocal teaching teaches children to mimic the strategies used by successful readers. In essence, strategic readers hypothesize and anticipate what may happen; they rephrase information and seek relationships between key ideas, story lines and characters, and they are alert to breakdowns in their understanding of what they are reading.

During the initial stage of reciprocal teaching, the teacher models the process with the children. The children then practise the strategies and the teacher provides feedback, coaching, modelling and additional help to use the strategies successfully. This process is repeated until the children can use the strategies competently in their interactions with each other. The teacher then increases the demands, requiring the children to participate at a more challenging level.

Reciprocal teaching was developed as a small group instructional activity in which the participants work together as a community of learners to help and support each other's efforts. In an early study, Palincsar and Brown (1988) reported teaching reciprocal teaching strategies to junior high school students in remedial reading classes. The students were adequate decoders but their reading comprehension was two to five years below their grade level. After initial training in reciprocal teaching and twenty days of using these strategies in their reading groups, the students' comprehension levels improved markedly and the strategies learned generalized to other classes and tasks distinctly different from the original training task.

Reciprocal teaching has also been used successfully to enhance the mathematics skills of elementary school children at risk of academic failure. Fantuzzo *et al.* (1992), for example, found that the children who were taught reciprocal teaching strategies coupled with a reward (e.g. act as teacher's helper, messenger, or be permitted time to work on a special project) showed higher levels of accurate mathematical computations than children who were not taught this strategy. Furthermore, when reciprocal teaching was coupled with rewards, the children also showed improved self-control over their behaviours. Fantuzzo *et al.* suggested that successful reward contingencies for academic progress lead to decreases in inappropriate classroom conduct simply because academic productivity is incompatible with disruptive, off-task behaviours.

Reciprocal teaching for enhancing reading comprehension has also been used successfully across diverse situations from elementary to college settings. Lederer (2000) used reciprocal teaching to enhance the reading comprehension of students with learning disabilities during a social studies unit of work in inclusive elementary classrooms. The results showed that the children in the reciprocal teaching group outperformed their peers in their ability to answer questions, generate questions and compose summaries – critical to being able to integrate information from the text and reconstruct prior knowledge to fit in with what they are reading about. Furthermore, the children in the reciprocal teaching condition obtained higher comprehension scores than their peers who were taught traditional methods. The study provides strong support for the notion that scaffolded approaches to learning, such as reciprocal teaching, can improve comprehension for students with learning disabilities.

In another study, Alfassi (1998) investigated whether reciprocal teaching was superior to traditional skill acquisition methods with students in remedial reading high school classes. The results showed that the children who participated in reciprocal teaching instruction showed greater improvements than students exposed to traditional methods of remedial skill acquisition. This study was unusual as it was implemented with large class groups as part of the overall curriculum, making it more economically efficient than has previously been demonstrated.

Hart and Speece (1998) investigated the effects of reciprocal teaching on adults who were at risk of academic failure in a community college setting. Two intact classes of twenty-five students each participated in the study. One class received instruction in the strategies used in reciprocal teaching to enhance reading comprehension while the other class acted as the comparison group. The comparison group focused on interaction and participation (as in reciprocal teaching) but did not include reading strategies specific to remedial teaching. The results showed that the students in the reciprocal teaching group significantly outperformed the comparison group on reading comprehension and strategy acquisition. Furthermore, poorer readers in the reciprocal reading condition still outperformed poorer readers in the comparison condition on both reading comprehension and strategy acquisition. The study documents clearly the benefits of a structured reading comprehension strategy for at-risk college students.

Conclusion

Co-operative learning is a pedagogical practice that promotes socialization and learning across different curriculum areas and classroom settings. However, while the benefits of implementing co-operative learning are widely acknowledged, many schools and teachers still experience difficulties in knowing how to embed this practice into their teaching curricula.

Placing students in groups and expecting them to co-operate will not necessarily promote co-operative learning. It is only when members understand that they are dependent on each other and cannot succeed unless others do that they learn to co-ordinate their efforts and actively work together. Group cohesion develops as a direct consequence of members' perceptions of their interdependence and their willingness to facilitate and encourage each other's learning.

While linking group members together so that they experience task and goal interdependence is a key element of successful co-operative learning, ensuring that they are trained in the interpersonal and small group skills needed to promote positive interactions is also important. Researchers have indicated that children need to be trained in these skills in a purposeful and systematic way if they are to be able to use them effectively in their interactions with their peers.

Another important aspect of successful co-operative group work includes ensuring that group members understand that they are each responsible for contributing to the group's task or goal. Contributions include encouraging others, suggesting ideas and actively promoting the group's efforts. Being willing to help group members reflect on their achievements and evaluate what they need to do as a group is also an important part of successful co-operative learning.

Interestingly, the type of task students undertake in their group affects the interactions that occur. When the task is well structured, students do not need to discuss how to proceed because there is often only a need to find the right answer. In contrast, when the task is more open and discovery-based, discussion is crucial for exchanging ideas and information if students want to find a solution or discover underlying principles to a problem. In essence, teachers need to ensure that students understand the type of assistance that will be more helpful as they work on different types of task in their groups.

There is a considerable body of research which demonstrates that when students are taught to use specific, interactional styles (i.e. guided questioning, scripted interactions, reciprocal teaching), they not only learn to provide more relevant information, but they also demonstrate more strategic and metacognitive thinking. In so doing, the connection between strategy use and learning is emphasized. When this occurs in small, co-operative groups, students learn to scaffold each other's learning, and this results in higher achievement outcomes both for the helpers and the helpees.

References

Alfassi, M. (1998) 'Reading for meaning: the efficacy of reciprocal teaching in fostering reading comprehension in high school students in remedial classes', *American Educational Research Journal*, 35: 309–32.

Calderon, M., Hertz-Lazarowitz, R. and Slavin, R. (1998) 'Effects of bilingual cooperative integrated reading and composition on students making the transition from Spanish to English reading', *The Elementary School Journal*, 99: 153–65.

Cohen, E. (1994) 'Restructuring the classroom: conditions for productive groups', *Review of Educational Research*, 64: 1–35.

Cohen, E., Lotan, R. and Leechor, C. (1989) 'Can classrooms learn?', *Sociology of Education*, 62: 75–94.

Deutsch, M. (1949) 'An experimental study of the effects of cooperation and competition upon group process', *Human Relations*, 2: 199–231.

Fantuzzo, J., King, J. and Heller, L. (1992) 'Effects of reciprocal peer tutoring on mathematics and school adjustment: a component analysis', *Journal of Educational Psychology*, 84: 331–9.

Fuchs, L., Fuchs, D., Hamlett, C., Phillips, N., Karns, K. and Dutka, S. (1997) 'Enhancing students' helping behavior during peer mediated instruction with conceptual mathematical explanations', *The Elementary School Journal*, 97: 223–49.

Gillies, R.M. and Ashman, A.F. (1995) 'The effects of gender and ability on students' behaviours and interactions in classroom-based work groups', *British Journal of Educational Psychology*, 65: 211–25.

—— (1996) 'Teaching collaborative skills to primary school children in classroom-based work groups', *Learning and Instruction*, 6: 187–200.

—— (1998) 'Behavior and interactions of children in cooperative groups in lower and middle elementary grades', *Journal of Educational Psychology*, 90: 746–57.

—— (2000) 'The effects of cooperative learning on students with learning difficulties in the lower elementary school', *Journal of Special Education*, 34: 19–27.

Hart, E. and Speece, D. (1998) 'Reciprocal teaching goes to college: effects for postsecondary students at risk for academic failure', *Journal of Educational Psychology*, 90: 670–81.

Hertz-Lazarowitz, R. (1989) 'Cooperation and helping in the classroom: a contextual approach', *International Journal of Educational Research*, 13: 113–19.

Howe, C., Tolmie, A., Greer, K. and Mckenzie, M. (1995) 'Peer collaboration and conceptual growth in physics: task influences on children's understanding of heating and cooling', *Cognition and Instruction*, 13: 483–503.

Hunt, P., Staub, D., Alwell, M. and Goetz, L. (1994) 'Achievement by all students within the context of cooperative learning groups', *JASH*, 19: 290–301.

Johnson, D.W. and Johnson, F.P. (1987) *Joining Together: Group Theory and Group Skills* (3rd edn), Englewood Cliffs, NJ: Prentice-Hall.

—— (2000) *Joining Together: Group Theory and Group Skills* (7th edn), Boston, MA: Allyn & Bacon.

Johnson, D.W. and Johnson, R. (1990) 'Cooperative learning and achievement', in S. Sharan (ed.) *Cooperative Learning: Theory and Research*, 23–37, New York: Praeger.

—— (1996) 'Conflict resolution and peer mediation programs in elementary secondary schools: a review of the research', *Review of Educational Research*, 66: 459–506.

—— (1999) 'Making cooperative learning work', *Theory into Practice*, 38: 67–73.

Johnson, D.W., Johnson, R. and Holubec, E. (1990) *Cooperative Learning in the Classroom*, Alexandria, VA: Association for Supervision and Curriculum Development.

Johnson, D.W., Johnson, R. and Stanne, M. (2000) *Cooperative Learning Methods: A Meta-analysis*. Online. Available at: <http://www.clcrc.com/pages/cl-methods.html> (accessed 29 January 2001).

Johnson, D.W., Johnson, R., Stanne, M. and Garibaldi, A. (1990) 'Impact of group processing on achievement in cooperative groups', *Journal of Social Psychology*, 130: 507–16.

Johnson, D.W., Johnson, R., Dudley, B., Mitchell, J. and Fredrickson, J. (1997) 'The impact of conflict resolution training on middle school students', *Journal of Social Psychology*, 137: 11–21.

King, A. (1991) 'Effects of training in strategic questioning on children's problem-solving performance', *Journal of Educational Psychology*, 83: 307–17.

—— (1994) 'Guided knowledge construction in the classroom: effects of teaching children how to question and how to explain', *American Educational Research Journal*, 31: 338–68.

Lederer, J. (2000) 'Reciprocal teaching of social studies in inclusive elementary classrooms', *Journal of Learning Disabilities*, 33: 91–106.

Lou, Y., Abrami, P. and Spence, J. (2000) 'Effects of within-class grouping on student achievement: an exploratory model', *Journal of Educational Research*, 94: 101–12.

Lou, Y., Abrami, P., Spence, J., Poulsen, C., Chambers, B. and d'Apollonia, S. (1996) 'Within-class grouping: a meta-analysis', *Review of Educational Research*, 66: 423–58.

McManus, S. and Gettinger, M. (1996) 'Teacher and student evaluations of cooperative learning and observed interactive behaviours', *Journal of Educational Research*, 90: 13–22.

Meloth, M. and Deering, P. (1994) 'Task talk and task awareness under different cooperative learning conditions', *American Educational Research Journal*, 31: 138–65.

Palinscar, A. and Brown, A. (1988) 'Teaching and practising thinking skills to promote comprehension in the context of group problem solving', *Remedial and Special Education*, 9: 53–9.

Putnam, J., Markovchick, K., Johnson, D. and Johnson, R. (1996) 'Cooperative learning and peer acceptance of students with learning disabilities', *Journal of Social Psychology*, 136: 741–52.

Ragan, P. (1993) 'Cooperative learning can work in residential care settings', *Teaching Exceptional Children*, 25(2): 48–51.

Shachar, H. and Sharan, S. (1994) 'Talking, relating, and achieving: effects of cooperative learning and whole-class instruction', *Cognition and Instruction*, 12: 313–53.

Stevahn, L., Johnson, D., Johnson, R., Green, K. and Laginski, A. (1997) 'Effects on high school students of conflict resolution training integrated into English literature', *Journal of Social Psychology*, 137: 302–15.

Stevahn, L., Johnson, D., Johnson, R., Oberle, K. and Wahl, L. (2000) 'Effects of conflict resolution training integrated into a kindergarten curriculum', *Child Development*, 71: 772–84.

Tapscott, D. (1999) 'Educating the net generation', *Educational Leadership*, 56(5): 6–11.

Webb, N. (1985) 'Student interaction and learning in small groups: a research summary', in R. Slavin, S. Sharan, S. Kagan, R. Hertz-Lazarowitz, C. Webb and R. Schmuck (eds) *Learning to Cooperate, Cooperating to Learn*, 5–15, New York: Plenum.

Webb, N. (1991) 'Task-related verbal interaction and mathematical learning in small groups', *Journal of Research in Mathematics Education*, 22: 366–89.

Webb, N. (1992) 'Testing a theoretical model of student interaction and learning in small groups', in R. Hertz-Lazarowitz & N. Miller (eds) *Interaction in Cooperative Groups*, 102–19, Cambridge: Cambridge University Press.

Webb, N. and Farivar, S. (1994) 'Promoting helping behavior in cooperative small groups in middle school mathematics', *American Educational Research Journal*, 31: 369–95.

Webb, N., Nemer, K., Chizhik, A. and Sugrue, B. (1998) 'Equity issues in collaborative group assessment: group composition and performance', *American Educational Research Journal*, 35: 607–51.

Whicker, K., Bol, L. and Nunnery, J. (1997) 'Cooperative learning in the secondary mathematics classroom', *Journal of Educational Research*, 91: 42–8.

Wittrock, M. (1990) 'Generative processes of comprehension', *Educational Psychologist*, 24: 345–76.

Yager, S., Johnson, D. and Johnson, R. (1985) 'Oral discussion, group-to-individual transfer, and achievement in cooperative learning groups', *Journal of Educational Psychology*, 77: 60–6.

Zammuner, V. (1995) 'Individual and cooperative computer-writing and revising: who gets the best results?', *Learning and Instruction*, 5: 101–24.

Chapter 4

Co-operative learning in secondary education

A curriculum perspective

Jan Terwel

Introduction

Co-operative learning has been championed by many advocates. One reason for its popularity lies in the flexibility of the term 'co-operative learning' and, consequently, in the possibility of applying it to different theories and educational contexts. At first sight this flexibility strikes one as positive, and no doubt it is. However, the term is potentially misleading if the conditions it denotes are not seen as being embedded in a particular theory, a specific domain of knowledge or a certain curricular context; for example, a common curriculum or a tracking system.

In co-operative learning contexts students do not learn in what may be called a compositional vacuum; they are members of a class and a small group. I will defend the claim that it is especially such compositional contexts that have consequences for learning opportunities in co-operative learning environments (Resh 1999; Terwel *et al.* 2001; Terwel and Van den Eeden 1994; Webb 1982).

Co-operative learning was designed and implemented to develop social strategies and acceptable social attitudes in students, and to improve social relations within and between groups. In addition, there is a large cluster of co-operative learning models aimed at cognitive development. Sometimes co-operative learning is directed at both the social and the cognitive side of human development.

There is yet a third, more comprehensive perspective, one that is not necessarily in contrast to the social and the cognitive aims of co-operative learning. I would like to call this the curriculum perspective on co-operative learning. This chapter is about that perspective.

If we take the curriculum perspective as a point of departure, then it follows that co-operative learning should be seen as a learning strategy in the mathematics curriculum, in particular, in the common curriculum of the first stage in secondary education. The consequences of this view will be explored in this chapter.

Co-operative learning from a curriculum perspective

But what is a curriculum? Walker (1990) described the curriculum in terms of content and purpose of an educational programme together with its organization.

Purpose

Placing co-operative learning in the context of curriculum theory and practice to me means that co-operative learning is not merely a many-purpose formal technique or model, but rather that it has to be viewed as an integrated part of the curriculum. The latter condition implies that co-operative learning should be evaluated from a curricular point of view. Let me therefore try first to formulate my curricular starting point by describing a general aim of co-operative learning, namely learning how to think for oneself (Dewey 1902, 1922, 1933). Independent thought is a fundamental human desideratum and, in my view, the educational goal for which schools should aim. Co-operative learning is one of the avenues that can lead to that fundamental goal, but only if correctly understood.

Content

The purposes and aims of co-operative learning need to be elaborated within certain domains of study. Co-operative learning is not a technique for its own sake but needs content in order to be useful. The specific content or subject matter is not a result of arbitrary choice, without any consequences for the design of a curriculum in which co-operative learning takes place. Content has its own characteristics, which may be used in the designing process and in the classroom in order to facilitate the development of thinking as a human activity. Mathematics education, for example, offers specific opportunities for co-operative learning with this purpose in view. To put it differently and to make the general idea more specific, the content of mathematics allows for specific models of co-operative learning to accommodate individual differences between students (Freudenthal 1991; Keitel 1987). Mathematical problems can be situated in real-life contexts and designed in such a way that solutions can be reached along different routes and at different levels. This makes co-operative learning in mathematics different from co-operative learning in other domains, such as languages and world orientation. The latter domains have their own opportunities that the teaching and learning process may offer. I will return to the specific opportunities of mathematics later in the context of our empirical research on co-operative learning in mathematics.

Organization

Organization of purpose and content may be summed up in the following composite question: Should all students pursue the same purposes and content or should different programmes be offered to different categories of students? My position has always been that a common curriculum should be offered to all. The question is: How can this be realized in the classroom? Could co-operative learning offer a solution?

My interest in co-operative learning arose especially in the context of these questions. As a teacher in the lowest streams of the traditional Dutch secondary school system I became more and more aware of the limited opportunities for my students in the context of tracking, in which low achievers were separated from their more able peers. This was the result of a classical dilemma in the first stage of secondary education that can be stated as follows: Should we offer a common curriculum to all students between the ages of 12 and 15, or should we present different curricula to different categories of students (Walker 1990)? As is well known, this question has been the subject of intense debate and ongoing research in curriculum studies (Gravemeijer and Terwel 2000; Keitel 1987; Kliebard 1992; Oakes et al. 1992; Page 2000). The intensity and emotionality of the debate can be explained partly by the political, cultural and moral implications of the various viewpoints.

By stating the central question in these terms and by placing co-operative learning in the context of curriculum thinking and practice, we have arrived the heart of one of the above-mentioned dilemmas, which has been described in curriculum literature under the heading of curriculum differentiation versus a common curriculum. Curriculum differentiation – offering different curricula to different categories of students – is common practice in all modern countries. However, for many researchers and scholars co-operative learning entails the promise of avoiding early selection and curriculum differentiation (streaming, tracking) and of promoting learning and social development in a common curriculum for all (Oakes et al. 1992). Can co-operative learning offer a way out of the to track or not to track dilemma?

Curriculum differentiation: research into learning outcomes

Why is it so important to look for alternatives to curriculum differentiation? What do we know from research into curriculum differentiation and, more specifically, group composition (Driessen 2002; Guldemond and Meijnen 2000; Hallinan 1987; Hallinan and Kubitscheck 1999; Kerckhof and Glennie 1999; Orfield and Yun 1999; Pallas 1999; Reay 1998; Resh 1999; Terwel et al. 2001; Van den Eeden and Terwel 1994;

Webb 1982; Westerbeek 1999; Willms 1985; Yates 1966; Yonezawa *et al.* 2002)?

The research literature that covers more than a century may be summarized as follows. In contrast to the views of many policy-makers, as well as administrators and practitioners, curriculum differentiation has no effect on overall (average) learning scores. Students in streamed or tracked schools do not outperform their counterparts in integrated (non-streamed) schools. However, several studies show differential effects for high- and low-achieving students. High-achieving students tend to achieve better results in a system with tracking, while low-achieving students perform better in heterogeneous classes. One of the causal mechanisms behind these research outcomes may be found in classroom interaction processes, to which I will return below. In addition, there are indications that low-achieving students are more sensitive to the quality of their learning environment than high-achieving students, probably because the latter can rely more on personal resources such as prior knowledge, experience, cultural background and habitus. Dar and Resh (1986, 1994) indicated that curriculum differentiation turns out to be especially detrimental in the case of low achievers since they appear to lose more than the high achievers win, compared to a common curriculum for all. Although all students benefit from high-quality learning environments, there are indications that learners need to possess a certain minimum level to be able to profit from an enriched learning environment. To put it differently, there seems to be a limit to the performance interval around the mean in which students can benefit from richer learning environments. Note that generalizations on this point cannot be made, because the interval depends on the instructional models under consideration.

It is precisely at this point that co-operative learning enters the discussion. Many studies on co-operative learning do not specify the conditions in terms of group composition and instructional models as part of the curriculum. Many studies lack information about the interaction processes and the curricular content which may have produced the learning outcomes. I will therefore present the outcomes of a series of projects in which I was involved in the previous decades and in which we tried explicitly to address these points.

Theoretical starting point: mathematics as a human activity

Our empirical studies into co-operative learning were, to a certain extent, inspired by the work of Hans Freudenthal, the well-known Dutch mathematician (Freudenthal 1973a, 1973b, 1980, 1991). Freudenthal, in turn, was influenced by Dewey, Piaget, Vygotsky, and the European progressivists Ovide Decroly and Peter Petersen. Freudenthal's wife, Suus Freudenthal

Lutter, was one of the pioneers who introduced Peter Petersen's Jenaplan School to the Netherlands. The Jenaplan School is well known for its use of various forms of co-operative learning as an integrated part of a curriculum for comprehensive education.

Fortunately, as a well-known mathematician and director of an institute for curriculum research and development and inservice training in mathematics (named the Freudenthal Institute), Freudenthal was able to go beyond his considerable sources of inspiration by making his philosophy more mathematical and therefore more useful to curriculum thinking and classroom practice. Freudenthal was one of the early proponents of co-operative learning in mathematics education. His co-operative learning model consisted of a combination of whole class instruction and working in small heterogeneous groups of four students. What was it that made his proposal for co-operative learning so attractive? It was the particular co-operative learning concept in which he explicitly addressed the fundamental curricular questions starting with Why, How, What and to Whom that inspired so many scholars, researchers and teachers.

My first encounter with Freudenthal took place in the 1970s, when I attended a conference on comprehensive education in the Netherlands (Freudenthal 1973a; Terwel 1990). In his lecture, Freudenthal criticized the German experiments with the middle schools, in which curriculum differentiation by means of tracking, streaming and setting was daily practice. 'Our German colleagues,' he said, 'differentiate students before they integrate them. This differentiation is merely an euphemism for separation' (Freudenthal 1973a). Freudenthal was strongly opposed to early selection and separation of students into different curricular programmes and proposed a new, integrated and common curriculum for all students in the first stage of secondary education. Freudenthal's educational credo was that mathematics should be learned as a human activity and that this could be realized by guided reinvention in co-operative groups of four. Freudenthal strongly advocated mathematics for all. He condemned all forms of streaming and setting by referring to the inevitable Matthew effects. He was convinced that students from different ability levels in the first years of secondary education should not only be in the same classrooms, but should also follow a common curriculum. In this newly designed curriculum students should work together in small heterogeneous groups. Thus Freudenthal's model of co-operative learning was an integrated part of his philosophy of education (Freudenthal 1973a, 1980, 1991; Gravemeijer and Terwel 2000).

Our research projects are based on principles of mathematics teaching and elements from cognitive theories and theories of motivation (Freudenthal 1973a, 1973b; Hoek et al. 1999; Terwel et al. 1994). Since working in small groups is of particular importance in the models under investigation, I will describe below the theoretical background. Samples of the curriculum materials and protocols of interaction processes are given in Terwel (1990) and Hoek *et al.* (1997). In line with theories of cognition it is to be expected that working in groups accelerates the learning process. The dynamics behind the effects of group work may be found in the following five factors inherent in this type of learning environment:

1   Students in small groups are confronted by their fellow students in the group with different solutions and points of view. This may lead to sociocognitive conflicts that are accompanied by feelings of uncertainty. This may cause a willingness in students to reconsider their own solutions from a different perspective. The resulting processes stimulate higher cognitive skills. In principle, students can also conquer the uncertainty caused by different points of view with the help of other members of the group, particularly where difficult or complicated assignments are concerned.

2   Small groups offer group members the opportunity to profit from the knowledge that is available in the group as a whole. This may take the form of knowledge, skills and experiences that not every member of the group possesses. Students use each other as resources under those circumstances (resource-sharing).

3   Collaboration in small groups also means that students are given the opportunity to verbalize their thoughts. Such verbalizations facilitate understanding through cognitive reorganization on the principle that those who teach learn the most. Offering and receiving explanations enhances the learning process. Group members not only profit from the knowledge and insights transmitted through peer tutoring, but they can also internalize effective problem-solving strategies by participating in the collective solution procedures.

4   Positive effects of group work can also be expected on the basis of motivation theory. Co-operation intensifies the learning process. Students in the 12 to 16 age group are strongly oriented towards the peer group and very interested in interaction with their fellow students.

5   From the point of view of teaching methods in mathematics positive effects may be expected from the kinds of assignment that are used in groups. Varied assignments, which appeal to different levels of cognition and experiences, offer students the possibility of applying their strengths in the search for solutions.

Developing a longitudinal multi-level model

Our empirical research into co-operative learning was conducted in a series of studies in the Netherlands and Australia (Brekelmans *et al.* 1997; Hoek *et al.* 2000; Terwel and Mooij 1995; Terwel *et al.* 2001). All studies were field experiments with a pretest-post-test control group design with numbers ranging from about 440 to 810 students in 18 to 33 classes respectively.

In several studies it was found that class composition as measured, for example, by mean class ability in mathematics, has an effect on the development (transformation) of a student's initial knowledge towards his learning outcomes (so-called peer effects). Thus there were once more firm indications that the intellectual resources in a class can facilitate or hinder the learning processes and outcomes of students over and above the effects already explained by initial differences between students (Brekelmans *et al.* 1997; Terwel and Mooij 1995; Terwel *et al.* 2001).

In order to determine the effects of co-operative learning as a learning strategy and at the same time to account for differences in class composition a complex multi-level model was developed. The basic idea behind this model is that students do not learn in a compositional vacuum but are members of a heterogeneous class or small group. It follows that individual learning processes are influenced by the characteristics of the entities at higher levels; that is, the small group and the class. To illustrate these complex relations, we developed a theoretical model (see Figure 4.1). In this model, co-operative learning processes (interaction processes) must to be seen as the primary engines of learning and development. The quality of the interaction processes depends to a certain extent on the available cognitive resources in the classroom and the small group. To put it differently, the individual transformation process from pre-knowledge to learning outcomes is influenced by co-operative group work (interaction processes or experiences). These co-operative activities, in turn, are influenced by students' characteristics and curriculum differentiation

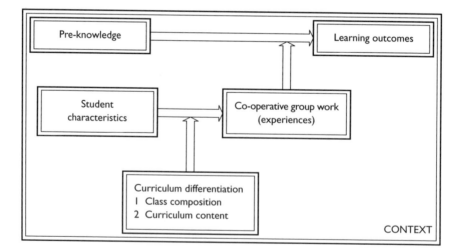

Figure 4.1 Co-operative learning: a longitudinal multi-level model

(consisting of the two main components class composition and curriculum). These processes and structures have to be placed in the context of the school as an institution that is embedded in the broader context of society.

From this model it follows that, in a curricular perspective, the outcomes of co-operative learning are not simply the sum of individual characteristics and social factors. Both factors play an important role in their contribution to the effects of co-operative learning, but always in connection with the purpose, content and organizational context of the curriculum.

Outcomes of co-operative learning: empirical research

First co-operative learning experiment: the ID Project

In an extensive curriculum experiment of the National Institute for Curriculum Development (SLO), Freudenthal's ideas were put to the test by the development, implementation and evaluation of a mathematics curriculum for Dutch secondary schools (Terwel et al. 1988). The evaluation research was conducted by a team of researchers at the University of Utrecht in what was called the ID 12–16 project ($N = 763$). It was in this project that one of the major dilemmas of curriculum differentiation and co-operative learning emerged before our very eyes: Students in the experimental, co-operative learning groups outperformed students in the control group (effect size = 0.22); however, low-achieving students profited less from co-operative learning than high-achieving students (Terwel 1990; Van den Eeden and Terwel 1994).

The outcomes of two of the participating schools in the experimental condition were particularly instructive. The two high-quality schools involved in the research were comparable in terms of student population, teachers, initial mathematics scores, resources and curriculum. Both schools implemented Freudenthal's ideas on co-operative learning in groups of four, working on the same mathematical content but with the possibility of following different paths in the process of problem-solving which Freudenthal referred to as levels in the learning process.

The conditions under which the experimental curriculum was implemented differed on one salient point: whereas the one school, called The Yssel, implemented the Freudenthal curriculum in full as a common, co-operative learning curriculum for all in heterogeneous classrooms, the other school, called The Linge, implemented the same curriculum but in an existing system of separate streams for high-, medium- and low-achieving students. This offered a unique opportunity to test the effects of co-operative learning under two different models for organizing student populations in a real school setting. The results were in line with many other international studies on streaming or tracking. Both schools were comparable in mean results. Thus there was a zero overall effect of streaming as compared to unstreamed classes. However, the experiment produced an intriguing trend: low-achieving students appeared to be better off in the heterogeneous classes at The Yssel, while high-achieving students did a better job at The Linge. This first experiment was the fore-runner of a series of co-operative learning studies in which we also looked for the (differential) effects of class composition on co-operative learning processes and learning outcomes of high- and low-achieving students.

Second co-operative learning experiment: the AGO Project

The experiences and empirical results of the Freudenthal model led to the development of a more elaborate instructional model, the AGO model, which combined whole class instruction, learning in small co-operative groups and individual work. This is a whole class model that allows for student diversity through *ad hoc* remediation and enrichment within small groups on a daily basis. The AGO model consists of the following stages.

1   Whole class introduction of a mathematics topic in real-life contexts.
2   Small group co-operation in heterogeneous groups of four students.
3   Teacher assessments: diagnostic test and observations.
4   Alternative learning paths depending on assessments consisting of two different modes of activity: (a) individual work at individual pace and level (enrichment), in heterogeneous groups with the possibility of consulting other students, or (b) opportunity to work in a remedial group (scaffolding) under direct guidance and supervision of the teacher.
5   Individual work at own level in heterogeneous groups with possi-bilities for students to help each other.
6   Whole class reflection and evaluation of the topic.
7   Final test.

The model provides for diagnostic procedures and special instruction and guidance by the teacher in a small remedial group for low-achieving students.

This cycle is extended through a series of lessons (units) over, for example, three to five weeks, preferably in extended units of uninter-rupted instructional time. Each cycle begins with whole class instruction; for example, in the form of a systematic explanation or a socratic dialogue. The aim of the instruction is to provide an overview of the learning unit and to introduce the most important concepts and solution procedures. The teacher is free to incorporate whole class instruction during other components in the cycle.

After the whole class instruction students work in small, heterogeneous groups of four. The assignments are designed specifically for group work. It is characteristic of AGO that group assignments (where possible or desirable) are presented in real-life contexts. The concepts and solution procedures necessary for the programme's problems are explicitly taught (i.e. in the classroom) before the students start their assignments. The assignments are constructed in such a way that collective solutions in, say, groups of four make sense. Problems can be solved in different ways (depending on levels in the learning process). In view of the support that is devoted to the solution process in the learning materials, as well as the supervision that the class or group receives from the teacher, the group process may be described as guided co-construction. In a whole class inter-mezzo students report on the solutions they have arrived at in the groups and reflect, under the guidance of a teacher, on the differences in solutions and methods of solution.

There then follows a diagnostic test for each individual student. This test may be more or less open depending on the aims of the relevant cycle. It is a means of verifying the level that each student has attained. The teacher marks or grades the test and discusses the results in class. He or she decides – on the basis of the results and his or her personal experiences with the students – how to continue (i.e. whether there should be multiple learning tracks for weaker and stronger students). Students who fall behind, and whose knowledge clearly shows gaps, receive specially adapted instruction from the teacher in groups of, for example, four to six. Other students work independently on individual assignments. Conferring is allowed.

In the next stage, students work independently on assignments in the same heterogeneous groups as for the co-operation component, but the method of working differs in that students work independently on differ-ent assignments. Students are again allowed to ask each other for assis-tance. The teacher supervises individual students. Finally, the teacher ends the classroom cycle. Again, students are allowed to report. The teacher winds up the cycle with a recapitulation of the most important concepts and solution procedures.

In the research project the AGO cycles finished with a final test. This is a research test, but it is also used by the teacher as a means of determining class test marks. The teacher discusses the results after the final test and subsequently introduces a new learning unit.

In this second experiment, the AGO model was put to the test. Stu-dents in the experimental (AGO) condition outperformed their counter-parts in the control group ($N = 582$). In this project an effect size of 0.68 was found. In addition, a significant effect of class composition was found. Students in classes with a higher mean ability outperformed their counter-parts in classes with a lower mean after controlling for initial individual differences in mathematical ability. Also in this project, indications were found that low-achieving students profited less from learning in small groups than high-achieving students (Terwel *et al.* 1994).

Third study: distance to the mean

Inspired by the outcomes of the two earlier projects, a secondary analysis was conducted on the data of the experimental classes in both the ID 12–16 project and the AGO project. This time the main focus was on the relative position of students in their classes. Lower and higher achieving students were defined in relation to their own class mean by using the variable called distance to the classroom mean. In fact, we were looking for the effect of the relative starting position of a student in his class. The outcomes of the analyses were identical in both projects. Students with a pretest score below the mean of their class gained by being in a relative good class and vice versa. This effect of the relative position of a student was over and above the effect of the pretest. To conclude, the classroom makes a difference in co-operative learning. These outcomes were especially convincing because the same effects of distance to the mean were found in both projects. The findings may contribute not only to theory and practice of co-operative learning but also to the frog pond theory. Our answer to the question 'Is it better to be a big frog in a small pond than a small frog in a big pond?' clearly favours the latter (Terwel and Van den Eeden 1994).

Fourth project: training students for problem-solving in co-operative groups

After having determined the positive overall effects of co-operative learning and the effects of the classroom we directed our focus towards the prerequisites of co-operative learning. What kind of pre-knowledge and strategies do students need in order to successfully participate in group-work? In a third project a modification of the AGO model was used (Hoek *et al.* 1997). Students were trained in social or cognitive strategies for realistic problem-solving contexts in co-operative groups (with $N = 144$ and 172 respectively and $N = 195$ for the control group). Special attention was given to the analysis of differential effects for high- and low-achieving students. The outcomes show the expected positive effects (effect sizes 0.32 and 0.52 for, respectively, the social strategies programme and the cognitive strategies programme as compared to a control group). In addition to this main effect, the low-achieving students in the experimental condition outperformed their counterparts in the control group, indicating that the special training and remedial instruction of low-achieving students had a compensating effect. This was the first time we were able to show that low-achieving students benefited from co-operative learning!

Fifth experiment: combining training in social and cognitive strategies

The aim of the fifth study was to assess the effects of the social and cognitive training as combined in one programme ($N = 222$ for the experimental group and $N = 222$ for the control group). It was hypothesized that integration of programmes would be more powerful than the separate social or cognitive programme in the third study (Hoek et al. 1999). The outcomes showed an overall effect of the experimental programme ($ES = 0.21$). It turned out that combining the two strategies benefited the high achievers rather than the low achievers. This last outcome was not expected but, with hindsight, seems reasonable in view of the high cognitive demands made by the integrated programme. Low achievers in particular seem to profit from strategy training as long as the instruction is not too complex and as long as the student composition of the small group allows for a rich learning environment, in which high-achieving students can serve as role models.

Conclusions and discussion

The overall conclusion from these co-operative learning experiments is that, in comparison with the control programmes, the experimental programmes produced positive outcomes. In all experiments, students in the co-operative learning programme outperformed their counterparts in the control condition. In some of the experiments differential effects for high- and low-achieving students were found. This warrants the conclusion that special attention to low achievers is necessary. Training in the use of social and cognitive strategies would seem to be an attractive avenue for further development and research, particularly in the area of support for low-achieving students. In addition, from the multi-level analyses, clear indications were found that the student composition of the small group and the class promotes or hinders learning processes and outcomes. These positive experiences and outcomes of co-operative learning are in line with other studies (e.g. Cohen 1994; Cohen and Lotan 1995; Webb and Farivar 1994).

More specifically, the outcomes regarding the effects of group and class composition are not only in line with the work of Dar and Resh (1986, 1994) but also with other recent studies in The Netherlands, in which cognitive and sociocultural differences in classroom composition were also taken into consideration. These effects can, to a large extent, also be explained by differences not so much in the colour of a classroom (black or white) as in its cognitive resources. Such resources can, in turn, be traced back to the categorically differentiated experiences of the students in their socio-economic home backgrounds and in their local communities (Driessen 2002; Tilly 1998; Westerbeek 1999).

The findings revealed what many parents already know intuitively: student composition counts, whether in a school, a class or a small group. Students in classes with a higher mean ability tend to give each other higher quality help and feedback than do their counterparts in lower classrooms (Terwel *et al.* 2001). Not only teachers, but fellow students as well, can really make a difference. These findings are a challenge to curriculum theorists, and especially to scholars and teachers involved in discussions about co-operative learning. Furthermore, the study of co-operative learning strategies can contribute to the to track or not to track debate in the first stage of secondary education. However, co-operative learning is not a panacea and we need to be aware that, just because of its flexibility, it can be applied in ways and in classroom contexts that might be detrimental, especially to the interests of low-achieving students. In our research projects the focus became more and more on the prerequisites of co-operative learning and on the group composition. What kinds of pre-knowledge and strategies do students need in order to participate successfully in group work? And since we know that students in co-operative learning depend on their fellow students, what kind of group composition is necessary to evoke high-quality interaction processes? To profit from co-operative learning low-achieving students, in particular, need to be prepared and guided over an extended period of time in the use of social and cognitive strategies in heterogeneous classrooms.

References

Brekelmans, M., Van den Eeden, P., Terwel, J. and Wubbels, T. (1997) 'Student characteristics and learning environment interactions in mathematics and physics education: a resource perspective', *International Journal of Educational Research*, 27: 283–92.

Cohen, E.G. (1994) 'Restructuring the classroom: conditions for productive small groups', *Review of Educational Research*, 64(1): 1–35.

Cohen, E.G. and Lotan, R.A. (1995) 'Producing equal-status interaction in the heterogeneous classroom', *American Educational Research Journal*, 32: 99–120.

Dar, Y. and Resh, N. (1986) *Classroom Composition and Pupil Achievement: A Study of the Effects of Ability Based Classes*, New York: Gordon & Breach.

—— (1994) 'Separating and mixing students for learning: concepts and research', *Pedagogisch Tijdschrift*, 19: 109–26.

Dewey, J. (1902) *The Child and the Curriculum*, Chicago, IL: University of Chicago Press.

—— (1922) 'Education as politics', *New Republic*, 32: 139–41.

—— (1933) *How We Think. A Restatement of the Relation of Reflective Thinking to the Educative Process*, Boston, MA: Houghton Mifflin.

Driessen, G. (2002) 'Sociaal-etnische schoolcompositie en onderwijsresultaten: effecten van positie, concentratie en diversiteit', *Pedagogische Studien*, 79: 212–30.

Freudenthal, H. (1973a) 'De niveaus in het leerproces en de heterogene leergroep met het oog op de middenschool', in *Gesamtschule Conferentie 1973*, Amsterdam/Purmerend: APS/Muuses.

—— (1973b) *Mathematics as an Educational Task*, Dordrecht: Reidel.

—— (1980) *Weeding and Sowing*, Dordrecht: Reidel.

—— (1991) *Revisiting Mathematics Education, China Lectures*, Dordrecht: Kluwer Academic.

Gravemeijer, K. and Terwel, J. (2000) 'Hans Freudenthal: a mathematician on didactics and curriculum theory', *Journal of Curriculum Studies*, 32: 777–96.

Guldemond, H. and Meijnen, G.W. (2000) 'Group effects on individual learning achievement', *Social Psychology of Education*, 4: 117–38.

Hallinan, M.T. (1987) 'Ability grouping and student learning', in M.T. Hallinan (ed.) *The Social Organization of Schools: New Conceptualizations of the Learning Process*, 41–69, New York: Plenum.

Hallinan, M.T. and Kubitschek, W.N. (1999) 'Curriculum differentiation and high school achievement', *Social Psychology of Education*, 3: 41–62.

Hoek, D.J., Terwel, J. and Van den Eeden, P. (1997) 'Effects of training in the use of social and cognitive strategies: an intervention study in secondary mathematics in cooperative groups', *Educational Research and Evaluation*, 3: 364–89.

Hoek, D.J., Van den Eeden, P. and Terwel, J. (1999) 'The effects of integrated social and cognitive strategy instruction on the mathematics achievement in secondary education', *Learning and Instruction*, 9: 427–48.

Hoek, D.J., Terwel, J. and Van Hout-Wolters, B.H.A.M. (2000) 'Effecten van een didactische interventie bij het leren in kleine groepen in de basisvorming', *Pedagogische Studiën*, 77: 222–40.

Jackson, P.W. (ed.) (1992) *Handbook of Research on Curriculum*, New York: Macmillan.

Karstanje, P.N. (1996) *Beleidstheorie Basisvorming: Een Proeve van Reconstructie*, SCO-rapport 412, Amsterdam: SCO-Kohnstamm Instituut.

Keitel, C. (1987) 'What are the goals of mathematics for all?', *Journal of Curriculum Studies*, 27: 13–30.

Kerckhof, A.C. and Glennie, E. (1999) 'The Matthew effect in American education', in A.M. Pallas (ed.) *Sociology of Education and Socialization*, 35–66, Stamford, CT: JAI Press.

Kliebard, H.M. (1992) 'Constructing a history of the American curriculum', in P.W. Jackson (ed.) *Handbook of Research on Curriculum*, 157–84, New York: Macmillan.

Mickelson, R.A. (2001) 'Subverting Swann: first- and second-generation segregation in the Charlotte-Mecklenburg schools', *American Educational Research Journal*, 38: 215–52.

Oakes, J., Gamoran, A. and Page, R.N. (1992) 'Curriculum differentiation: opportunities, outcomes and meanings', in P.W. Jackson (ed.) *Handbook of Research on Curriculum*, 570–608, New York: Macmillan.

Orfield, G. and Yun, J.T. (1999) *Resegregation in American Schools*, Cambridge, MA: Harvard University, The Civil Rights Project. Online. Available at: <http://www.civilrightsproject.harvard.edu/research/deseg/reseg_schools99.php> (accessed 9 December 2002).

Page, R.N. (2000) 'The tracking show', in B.M. Franklin (ed.) *Curriculum and*

Consequence: Herbert Kliebard and the Promise of Schooling, 103–27, New York: Teachers College Press.

Pallas, A.M. (1999) 'James S. Coleman and the purposes of schooling', in A.M. Pallas (ed.) *Sociology of Education and Socialization*, 35–66, Stamford, CT: JAI Press.

Reay, D. (1998) 'Setting the agenda: the growing impact of market forces on pupil grouping in British secondary schooling', *Journal of Curriculum Studies*, 30: 545–58.

Resh, N. (1999) 'Injustice in schools: perception of deprivation and classroom composition', *Social Psychology of Education*, 3: 103–26.

Terwel, J. (1990) 'Real maths in cooperative groups', in N. Davidson (ed.) *Cooperative Learning in Mathematics*, 228–64, Menlo Park, CA: Addison-Wesley.

Terwel, J. and Mooij, T. (1995) 'De relevantie van sociale contexten: klas en groepjes als sociale hulpbronnen bij het wiskunde onderwijs', *Sociologische Gids*, XLII: 301–17.

Terwel, J. and Van den Eeden, P. (1994) 'Effecten van klassensamenstelling and kwaliteit van instructie bij wiskunde [Effects of class composition and quality of instruction in mathematics education]', *Pedagogisch Tijdschrift*, 19: 155–73.

Terwel, J., Gillies, R.M., Van den Eeden, P. and Hoek, D. (2001) 'Cooperative learning processes of students: a longitudinal multilevel perspective', *British Journal of Educational Psychology*, 71: 619–45.

Terwel, J., Herfs, P., Dekker, R. and Akkermans, W. (1988) *Implementatie en Effecten van Interne Differentiatie: Een Empirisch, Vergelijkend Onderzoek naar de Realisering en de Effecten van Interne Differentiatie in Heterogene Groepen in de Eerste Fase Voortgezet Onderwijs bij Wiskunde*, 's-Gravenhage, The Netherlands: Instituut voor Onderzoek van het Onderwijs, SVO.

Terwel, J., Herfs, P.G.P., Mertens, E.H.M. and Perrenet, J.C. (1994) 'Cooperative learning and adaptive instruction in a mathematics curriculum', *Journal of Curriculum Studies*, 26: 217–33.

Tilly, C. (1998) *Durable Inequality*, Berkeley, CA: University of California Press.

Van den Eeden, P. and Terwel, J. (1994) 'Evaluation of a mathematics curriculum: differential effects', *Studies in Educational Evalution*, 20: 457–75.

Walker, D. (1990) *Fundamentals of Curriculum*, San Diego, CA: Harcourt.

Webb, N.M. (1982) 'Group composition, group interaction, and achievement in cooperative small groups', *Journal of Educational Psychology*, 74: 475–84.

Webb, N.M. and Farivar, S. (1994) 'Promoting helping behavior in cooperative small groups in middle school mathematics', *American Educational Research Journal*, 31: 369–95.

Westerbeek, K. (1999) *The Colors of My Classroom: A Study Into the Effects of the Ethnic Composition of Classrooms on the Achievement of Pupils from Different Ethnic Backgrounds*, Florence, Italy: European University Institute.

Willms, D.J. (1985) 'The balance thesis: contextual effects of ability on pupils' O-grade examination results', *Oxford Review of Education*, 11: 33–41.

Yates, A. (ed.) (1966) *Grouping in Education. A Report Sponsored by the UNESCO Institute for Education, Hamburg*, Stockholm: Almqvist & Wiksell.

Yonezawa, S., Wells, A.S. and Serna, I. (2002) 'Choosing tracks: "freedom of choice" in detracking schools', *American Educational Research Journal*, 39: 37–67.

Chapter 5

From co-operation to collaboration

Helping students become collaborative learners

Katherine McWhaw, Heidi Schnackenberg, Jennifer Sclater and Philip C. Abrami

College and university students are increasingly being asked by faculty to work co-operatively and learn collaboratively. This increased emphasis on group learning is partly a reaction to societal changes including a new emphasis on team work in the business sector (Millis and Cottell 1998) coupled with a realization that in a rapidly changing information society (Hansen and Stephens 2000) communication skills are increasingly important. At the tertiary level of education, the reasons include an increasingly diverse student population who need to develop ways of learning together in order to achieve (Millis and Cottell 1998), the increased use of teaching and learning that emphasize learner-driven approaches such as peer learning (Hansen and Stephens 2000), the growth of online courses (Carlson 2000) that may include a computer-mediated conferencing component requiring online dialogue, and student projects that often require a team approach because of their scope, depth and type (Puntambekar 1999).

Researchers have shown that group learning leads to academic and cognitive benefits. Group learning promotes student learning and achievement (Cockrell *et al.* 2000; Hiltz 1998; Johnson *et al.* 2000; Slavin 1992), increase the development of critical thinking skills (Brandon and Hollingshead 1999; Cockrell *et al.* 2000), and promote greater transfer of learning (Brandon and Hollingshead 1999). Group learning also aids in the development of social skills such as communication, presentation, problem-solving, leadership, delegation and organization (Cheng and Warren 2000).

For all its demonstrated benefits, students are often apprehensive about group learning, especially those who have had previous experience with learning in groups. Students fear that other team members will not pull their weight or that they will waste their time explaining the material to be learned to slower team mates (Felder and Brent 1996; Salomon and Globerson 1989). Students are also resistant to student-centred approaches to learning because of its novelty; they are accustomed to teacher-centred, direct instruction where students are provided with the content they need to know (Felder and Brent 1996). Another major reason for apprehension is that college and university students often do not know how to work together and are not given any help in making their groups functional (Phipps *et al.* 2001).

Equally important is the impact of group learning on faculty. Faculty face myriad instructional and institutional challenges when implementing group learning into their classrooms. These include the changing role of the instructor from lecturer to facilitator or coach, the shift in authority from the individual instructor to shared authority with the group of learners, careful planning of the instructional setting such as timing and efficiency concerns, and assessment issues such as group versus individual grades.

Traditionally, the instructor has been the source of knowledge in the classroom (Hansen and Stephens 2000). As a result of the nature of this role, instructors adopted what they considered to be the most efficient instructional method for imparting information – lecturing. While lecturing is still the most common teaching method in higher education (Gamson 1994), it simply does not occupy a very major role in the collaborative learning context. As the onus for knowledge construction, information researching and product creation rests increasingly with student groups, the role of the teacher changes from 'the sage on the stage' to 'the guide on the side'. In this way, faculty become individuals who facilitate students in the learning process. They assist with knowledge discovery and investigation, subtly steer learning activities and group processes, and coach students along in the educational experience.

In group learning, the relationships between students and teachers are different from more traditional educational contexts. Both learners and instructors share the responsibility for the learning experience. Students become participants who use social skills to create knowledge, and undertake and complete tasks (Matthews *et al.* 1995). For the teacher-as-lecturer to become the teacher-as-facilitator, a shift in authority within the classroom must occur. This can be disconcerting for many teachers. However, with careful planning, flexibility, self-confidence and practice, a shift in the role of the teacher from the traditional lecturer to a facilitator/mentor can be accomplished successfully (Hanson 1995).

Group learning imposes a steep learning curve on everyone involved (Felder and Brent 1996). The key to making group learning successful is to understand the process and to take precautionary steps to ensure success (Felder and Brent 1996). In this chapter we begin by explaining how the process operates using several theoretical perspectives and then present some recommendations, based on the latest research, to ensure a successful and productive group learning experience for students.

Co-operative learning versus collaborative learning

The terms 'co-operative learning' and 'collaborative learning' are often used interchangeably but, according to some, there are major differences between the two (Bruffee 1995; Panitz 1997; Roschelle and Teasley 1995).

Co-operative learning is considered to be the most structured approach to learning in groups while collaborative learning is less structured (Panitz 1997). In co-operative learning, the structure is imposed by the teacher (Abrami et al. 1995) and is designed to achieve a specific goal or end-product (Panitz 1997). Collaborative learning represents a different philosophy of interaction whereby students are given more power over their learning than in traditional instruction (Abrami et al. 1995).

While many would agree that what distinguishes co-operative learning from collaborative learning is the degree of structure used (Abrami et al. 1995; Panitz 1997), others propose that co-operative and collaborative learning differ profoundly on a number of other issues (Bruffee 1995). These differences are by no means accepted by all and remain somewhat controversial.

Bruffee (1995) proposed that co-operative learning is more appropriate for use with elementary schoolchildren while collaborative learning is better suited for adults including college and university students. With co-operative learning, it is assumed that elementary schoolchildren do not have the social skills required to work effectively together (Matthews et al. 1995). In collaborative learning, it is assumed that the students already have the necessary social skills and the motivation to reach their joint learning goals (Matthews et al. 1995).

Moreover, in collaborative learning environments students should be responsible for the governance and evaluation of their group. For example, Bruffee (1993) stated that use of collaborative learning activities involves a re-acculturation process for the teacher and the students. This occurs because collaborative learning experiences allow delegation of decision-making to the students whereas it has been traditionally placed with the teacher. Proponents of collaborative learning advocate a more democratic process, giving students more power than in traditional instruction (Pradl 1991).

Finally, co-operative learning is seen as more appropriate for knowledge that is foundational such as learning facts and formulas, while collaborative learning is seen as being better suited for learning non-foundational higher order knowledge, which requires a critical approach to learning (Bruffee 1995).

Which of the two approaches to learning in groups is most appropriate for college and university students? According to Johnson and Johnson

(1993), faculty should structure group work carefully at the tertiary level to make it productive. All the elements that are included in co-operative learning with elementary schoolchildren should be included in group work at the college and university levels. These include positive interdependence, individual accountability, promotive interaction, social skills and group processing. Slavin (1993) believed that co-operative learning can be adapted for higher education settings by taking into account students' ages, curricular goals and practical matters. However, he stressed the importance of assessing individual accountability to ensure that all group members participated. In contrast, Bruffee (1995) emphasized the collaborative approach for college and university students whereby students are responsible for the governance and evaluation of their groups and faculty did not intervene in the functioning of those groups.

How should faculty decide which approach is appropriate? First, faculty should understand that these recommendations stem from different theoretical perspectives on learning in groups. Second, they need to refer to the latest research on co-operative and collaborative learning with college and university students before implementing either approach. In the following section, we consider three major theoretical perspectives on group learning followed by a summary of the latest research into co-operative and collaborative learning with college and university students.

Theories of co-operative and collaborative learning

Abrami *et al.* (1995) summarized several motivational and learning explanations of the positive effects of co-operative learning. Motivational explanations concentrate on explaining student interest in, involvement with and persistence at learning. Slavin (1992) argued that both co-operative incentive and co-operative task structures increase performance when they lead to encouragement among members to perform the group task and help one another to do so. Johnson and Johnson (1994) used the social interdependence theory to explain how the perception of interdependence among students motivates them to engage in promotive interactions that facilitate the realization of mutual goals. Ames (1984) suggested that a morality-based motivational system underlies co-operative goal structures such that students are motivated by the desire to help others and place special emphasis on individual and group efforts to achieve, thus making causal ascriptions to effort more salient than attributions to ability. Social cohesion explanations (Cohen 1994; Sharan and Sharan 1992) argue for the pre-eminent role of group cohesion that arises from care and concern for the group and its members.

Learning explanations focus on how the interactions among students affect their understanding and cognitive processes. Cognitive elaboration perspectives (Dansereau 1985; Webb 1989) suggest that the learner must engage in cognitive restructuring if information is to be retained and related to information already in memory, particularly by giving and receiving elaborated explanations. Johnson and Johnson (1992) described several ways whereby the promotive interactions affect student thinking including oral rehearsal, perspective-taking, peer monitoring, feedback and cognitive controversy. Damon (1984) highlighted the cognitive-developmental perspectives of Piaget and Vygotsky who both emphasized how interaction among students around cognitively appropriate tasks increases the mastery of critical concepts via discovery, idea generation, argumentation, verification and criticism. Other explanations focus on practice effects, time on task and classroom organization explanations.

Vygotsky proposed that learning is a naturally social act in which participants talk among themselves. It is through talk that learning occurs (Gerlach 1994). Learning also occurs because individuals interact with others who have different backgrounds, knowledge and experience. By engaging with others who may be more capable, learners operate within their zone of proximal development, defined as the distance between their actual and their potential development (Dillenborg et al. 1996).

According to Piagetian theory, learning occurs when an individual experiences a cognitive conflict or disequilibrium while learning with peers (Dillenborg et al. 1996). They must wrestle with the conflicting information they receive from their peers and incorporate it into their current understanding. The idea that group learning involves conflict supports Bruffee's (1995) assertion that collaborative learning should include different opinions and dissent. The developmental theory of group learning also seems more appropriate for college students who have a diversity of backgrounds and are learning non-foundational knowledge.

An alternate explanation for group learning is based on social loafing theory. Situated within the social psychology literature, social loafing theory proposes that individuals exert less effort when their efforts are pooled than when these efforts are exerted individually (Latané et al. 1979). Social loafing research has been undertaken on cognitive and physical tasks and with different age groups (Karau and Kipling 1993).

There are three sources for low productivity in groups according to social loafing theory (Sheppard 1993). First, group members believe there is no value associated with contributing to the group. They believe the group product is unimportant or because their own efforts are unnoticed, and thus go unrewarded. Second, group members do not perceive a contingency between performance and outcome. This is because they believe the group product is unattainable or their own contributions are perceived as unnecessary or dispensable. Third, group members perceive that the physical or psychological demands required from the group are excessive.

One of the major and consistent findings from the social loafing literature is that individuals exert effort when they perceive it to be indispensable and loaf when they see their efforts as dispensable (Sheppard and Taylor 1999). Individuals will also work hard when their efforts and contributions are being evaluated even when there are no rewards for participation.

Research evidence

Group learning has been explained from a variety of theoretical perspectives – motivational (Slavin 1992), social interdependence (Johnson and Johnson 1994), learning (Dansereau 1985, Webb 1989), cognitive-developmental (Damon 1984) and social loafing (Sheppard 1993). Moreover, the extensive research conducted on group learning has shown it to be a more effective instructional method over competitive and individualistic approaches (Johnson et al. 2000).

In studies conducted on co-operative learning with elementary and secondary school students, 78 per cent found a significant positive effect on achievement (Slavin 1995). While these studies showed definite benefits, it does not mean that co-operative learning is appropriate or effective for college and university students. These students may already have the social skills and experience of working in groups and may not need the highly structured learning environment to succeed. The non-foundational nature of learning in which college and university students engage may also not lend itself easily to co-operative learning because it focuses on problems or questions with dubious or ambiguous answers (Bruffee 1995).

Following this theme, Johnson et al. (2000) completed a meta-analysis of 158 studies on co-operative learning from elementary to post-secondary settings. Of these, 21 per cent were conducted at the post-secondary level. The meta-analysis investigated eight co-operative learning methods from direct co-operative learning methods that teachers are required to follow in an exact, lock-step way to conceptual co-operative learning methods that teachers use as a template to fit their particular circumstances. All these methods were found to be effective in increasing achievement for all groups, including post-secondary students. However, this meta-analysis neither investigated which of these two approaches, direct and conceptual, was more appropriate for college and university students; nor did it compare the effects of structured co-operative groups with unstructured collaborative groups. There are, however, a number of recent studies that have examined the effects of structured co-operative groups and unstructured collaborative groups on college and university students' achievement, motivation and attitudes.

Research conducted with college and university students in structured co-operative groups found that this population of students benefits academically and socially when faculty structure group activities to include positive interdependence, individual accountability, promotive interaction, social skills and group processing.

A recent study with university students examined the experiences of students in groups when co-operative learning principles were incorporated into classroom-based learning activities (Phipps *et al.* 2001). In this study, 210 freshmen, sophomore and junior university students were asked about their experiences in classrooms where the faculty had incorporated five elements of co-operative learning. These elements were positive interdependence, individual accountability, face-to-face promotive interaction, interpersonal and small group skills, and group processing. Students perceived the inclusion of individual accountability, interpersonal and small group skills, and group processing as the most effective for learning, while positive interdependence and face-to-face promotive interaction were perceived as the least effective. In this study, positive interdependence was defined as shared grades for exams and projects. In general, only 18 per cent of students perceived co-operative learning as positively affecting learning while 48 per cent perceived it to have a positive effect on motivation. Some general comments made by students were that they did not know how to work together, and this resulted in problems with keeping focused and inequalities in responsibilities in sharing the work. Students did not like the idea of shared grades for exams but were more accepting of shared grades for projects. The goals students had for learning had profound effects on the co-operative learning experience. Groups in which students had very different goals for learning such as achieving an 'A' or just getting by did not function as well as groups in which students shared similar goals.

Research conducted with college and university students in unstructured collaborative learning groups demonstrated that students can organize themselves to work productively by sharing roles and tasks (Colbeck *et al.* 2000; Harasim 1993; Oliver and Omari 2001) and by encouraging each other to actively construct knowledge together (Harasim 1993). However, there was great variability among the groups that were studied with some groups working very effectively together while others struggled with how to share roles and co-ordinate and manage tasks.

One study looked at how groups structured themselves in a web-based environment (Oliver and Omari 2001). Students were assigned at random to groups of four or five in a problem-based approach to learning. The study showed that there was a range of structure within the groups from unstructured with no obvious leadership or co-ordination to highly structured groups managed and co-ordinated by a single student. Most groups had role interdependence whereby one student synthesized the various suggestions to a problem and posted it online. Some groups did not engage in task-sharing, and this occurred mostly in groups where only one person acted as the co-ordinator rather than sharing the role of co-ordinator.

In terms of group assignments, there were mixed results with some groups performing extremely well and others poorly. It should be noted that students' grades were based on their group's performance rather than on their individual contributions to the group. At the end of the study, 89 per cent of the students stated they were satisfied by what they had learned from the activities. However, 50 per cent of the students said they would prefer to work alone rather than in a group. The authors of this study (Oliver and Omari 2001) have recommended that students be provided with more structure and guidance in the organization and management of their groups given the variability in behaviour and performance within each of the groups.

A study with undergraduate students in engineering looked at the conditions that contributed to a positive group experience for students when faculty did not structure the groups (Colbeck et al. 2000). Positive results from this study were that students' previous experience with group projects helped to foster positive interdependence because the students had good communication, planning and technical skills. Out-of-class experiences such as employment also helped students develop positive interdependence. Resource interdependence evolved when group members had prior group experience. However, there were negative findings as well. The researchers found that when there was little goal interdependence, role interdependence failed to develop. Two major roles emerged in the groups: leader and slacker. This occurred when there was only one single group product that was rewarded. Furthermore, without faculty guidance only a few teams developed positive goal and role interdependence.

In a study with graduate and undergraduate students in an online environment students took on specific roles in each of the groups such as presenting and moderating a seminar and conducting and presenting a group research project (Harasim 1993). The learning tasks were formal for core curricular activities and informal for learner-supported activities. Students were expected to post messages to their online conferencing group at least three to four times per week. These individual weekly messages were graded for quantity and quality. The results of this study were a high level of student participation and students found the group interaction to be highly motivating. The quality of the interactions was high in that students engaged in active questioning, elaboration and debate. One of the reasons the author attributes to the high level of participation and quality of the work and interactions was that students' work was visible to their peers. However, students commented that organizing and co-ordinating the tasks was difficult and expressed the need for active moderation of the online conferencing environment.

Social loafing theorists have studied the sources of low productivity in unstructured groups. While they have proposed three sources of low productivity in such groups (Sheppard 1993), only two of these have been examined consistently with college and university students.

The first source of low productivity stems from student beliefs that there is no value associated with contributing to a group; either the group product is unrewarded or their own efforts are not noticed, and therefore not rewarded. Sheppard and Taylor (1999) found that students worked hard in a group if they valued the reward highly even when their own efforts were not evaluated individually. Gagné and Zuckerman (1999) found that when students believed that their contribution to a group was anonymous and could not be evaluated, they were more likely to engage in social loafing. One of the ways this can be remedied is through informal evaluations or formal evaluations. Faculty observing groups in the class-room can do informal evaluations. However, many group activities often occur outside the classroom at college or university level as when students work on group projects together. In this case, it may be difficult for faculty to observe how the group is functioning and faculty may need to rely on student peer evaluation.

The second source of low productivity stems from students' perceived lack of contingency between performance and outcome; the group product is unattainable or their own contributions are seen as unnecessary or dis-pensable. Researchers have shown that when students believe their contri-butions to a group are unique, they are less likely to free-ride on the efforts of their team mates (Kerr and Bruun 1983).

The social loafing research demonstrated that low productivity in groups occurs when individuals do not value the rewards for participating in the group or do not feel that their contributions to the group are unique. This coincides with the view expressed by co-operative learning theorists (Johnson and Johnson 1992; Slavin 1995) that students require both group rewards or goals (i.e. positive interdependence) and individual accountability for effective group functioning. However, group rewards are not effective unless they are highly valued by the students (Sheppard and Taylor 1999). Students are resentful of having to share grades with other students for evaluations such as tests but less so for group projects (Phipps *et al.* 2001). This may be because the complexity, scope and type of projects that students are asked to work on require a team approach (Puntambekar 1999). Therefore, students believe that their individual con-tributions to the group are both indispensable and unique.

The studies reviewed above with college and university students in co-operative structured groups and unstructured collaborative groups demonstrated that both approaches have positive and negative outcomes on achievement and productivity and on motivation and attitudes (Colbeck *et al.* 2000; Harasim 1993; Oliver and Omari 2001; Phipps *et al.* 2001; Sheppard and Taylor 1999).

One consistent finding that emerged from these studies done with both types of group learning is the need for training and ongoing monitoring by faculty to make group learning a productive and motivating experience (Colbeck et al. 2000; Harasim 1993; Oliver and Omari 2001). Our own experience with training students in how to work collaboratively suggests that though it is helpful, training alone will not ensure a productive or motivating experience for students especially if training is given as a one-time workshop rather than as a process scaffolded and monitored across a semester.

Training

Two of the authors were involved in a project to train two classes of graduate students in a human performance technology course within the Educational Technology Program at Concordia University in Montreal. One of the authors who taught the students decided that they would benefit from participating in a workshop on co-operative learning since they did a substantial amount of group work in their courses and this experience was not always motivating or productive. This faculty member also believed that since, on graduation, these students would be working as instructional designers they would need the skills to work effectively in groups.

Near the beginning of the first semester, the first author gave a two-hour workshop to each of the classes on how to work and learn in a team based on the co-operative learning principles of positive interdependence and individual accountability. Specifically, students were taught how to set group goals, share roles, divide tasks, and communicate face-to-face and virtually.

Ten students agreed to be interviewed about their experience working in their groups about halfway through the semester. The interviews revealed that most of the students discussed and agreed upon their roles for the group, shared roles or assigned specific roles in their teams, and divided up tasks equitably. Six of the students reported that overall they felt their experience of working in a team to be a mostly positive experience and four found it to be a mostly negative experience. The reasons given for the negative experiences were that there was a lack of trust and communication among the group members in one group, one person was always dominating the conversations in a second group, and goals were not set from the beginning in another group. Six students reported that participating in the workshop on co-operative learning helped to make their group experience a positive one.

This study shows that training was not effective for all the students. It may be more beneficial to combine training with structured group tasks in the beginning as students learn to work together and then give students the opportunity to assume more of the management of their groups as they gain experience. Abrami et al. (1995) proposed that group learning follows a developmental progression from teacher-imposed structures in the early stages when students may not have the desire to act co-operatively towards one another to students internalizing the value of co-operation in the later stages and acting autonomously to help others learn.

Although training and ongoing monitoring by faculty can help students learn to work and learn in groups successfully, group work can still prove to be problematic if additional steps are not taken to ensure that all members of the group are contributing equally. According to social loafing theory, individuals will loaf if they do not value the rewards or goals associated with participating in the group. Individuals must value the activity to which they are contributing. These rewards can be tangible such as a group grade or intangible such as the intrinsic satisfaction of working with different individuals to co-construct knowledge together. However, assigning a group grade may also promote social loafing unless individuals believe their contributions to the group are indispensable and unique (Sheppard 1993; Sheppard and Taylor 1999).

One way to encourage this perception of indispensability is to make the task sufficiently difficult for students to come to believe that their group cannot function without everyone's contribution (Meyers 1997). Another way is to assess students' individual contributions to the group. In a recent study on social loafing, students who were involved in brainstorming activity exerted high effort when they thought the experimenter could assess their individual input whether or not they anticipated a reward for their efforts (Sheppard and Taylor 1999).

In the following section we discuss the different ways that individual contributions to a group can be assessed.

Assessment

The dynamics of evaluating group learning activities can be quite intricate, and therefore challenging for faculty. In one sense, it is consistent with the tenets of collaborative learning that students assess (at least in part) their own learning outcomes. However, many faculty feel a sense of responsibility to have a hand in assessment. As grading has been an area of some subjectivity and discomfort for many faculty, the addition of new grading structures has not been met with much enthusiasm. Commonly, collaborative learning uses some combination of at least two types of grading activities: the more traditional product evaluation and a newer form of assessment – peer evaluation.

Peer evaluation is a process in which group members assess each other's contribution towards the learning process, product outcome and/or group functioning. In collaborative learning, since group work often takes a large portion of time in a course, fairness often dictates that group evaluation become a component of the grading system (Hansen and Stephens 2000).

Peer evaluation can contribute to a percentage of a student's overall course grade, a group's overall grade, or it can be simply a form of feedback dissociated with grades. Studies on peer evaluation have shown that students are reasonably competent at evaluating their own performance and their peers' performance (Falchikov 1993; Freeman 1995; Sullivan and Hall 1997).

Instructors need to consider that peer evaluation is a structure which is quite unlike any grading systems traditionally used in education, where the only authority equipped for assessment was the faculty member. This can cause students to be quite uncomfortable with peer evaluation. They may refrain from contributing critically to the group for fear of reprisals at the time of evaluation. This may affect adversely the collaborative learning process. It is important that faculty structure peer evaluation be a supportive, consistent reflection of a group's functioning rather than a final litmus test of collaborative efforts. Instructors can do much to foster positive feedback structures, such as modelling appropriate ways to offer critique and analysis, participating in peer evaluation, and sensing the amount of peer evaluation with which a particular student group would be comfortable. Peer evaluation, like many aspects of teaching, is a dynamic structure that can be tailored to individual class personalities in order to attain the richest benefits from its implementation.

The second type of evaluation used most commonly in collaborative learning is end-product evaluation. End-product evaluation is quite familiar to virtually all students and instructors. However, for students, if only an end-product of a group collaboration is assessed, an instructor has failed to consider the entirety of the educational experience, especially where collaborative learning is concerned, for fear that students will learn to ignore the learning process and focus only on the learning outcome.

A third way to evaluate students' contributions to their groups is to involve them in computer-supported collaborative learning (CSCL) activities in which the instructor can evaluate in an online environment the contributions and level of participation of each member of a group.

Computer-supported collaborative learning

Computer supported collaborative learning (CSCL) may be defined as the educational use of computer technology to facilitate group learning. Brandon and Hollingshead (1999) further characterized CSCL as the union of theory and research on classroom-based collaborative learning and computer-mediated communication (CMC) in the pursuit of understanding how CMC-based group projects can enhance learning. The benefits of using CSCL include increased student responsibility, initiative, participation, learning and higher grades, as well as increased communication with peers through discussion of course concepts (Brandon and Hollingshead 1999; Feather 1999).

An important aspect of group learning dynamics is the understanding and awareness of who is contributing to the group process and product. This speaks to the feelings many learners have in dysfunctional groups that certain members are just free-loaders and not doing their share. The use of asynchronous communication is a step towards alleviating these feelings since there is a record of each individual's contributions to be judged by peers and the instructor. Ongoing discussion by a group about how it is functioning is helpful for the group to be successful. This involves learners in goal-setting prior to commencement of a collaborative group activity, ongoing discussion during the activity on how to proceed and reflection at the end of each activity on what went on, what to continue and what to do differently during future collaborative activities. Open dialogue between group members creates a deeper group dynamic which encourages all group members to be active participants. Including peer and self assessment not only provides some kind of quantitative assessment of each member's individual performance and the contributions of their peers, but also provides a detailed assessment of what transpired over the course of the activity.

However, posting a group's process for all to see, including the instructor, may not be enough to give learners sufficient motivation to be contributing members of a group. Some learners still need the extrinsic motivation which only grades can provide. By grading the learner's process, either through self- and peer assessment or by including an instructor assessment, students are provided with tangible recognition for their work towards group process and product and contrariwise penalized for not contributing.

Commitment to the group, sharing resources, providing feedback and a sense of trustworthiness are all characteristics of promotive interaction. When these activities take place in an asynchronous learning environment, students who participate in these positive activities can be given credit for their contributions.

A strong emphasis is placed on social skills, especially within a CSCL environment. Brandon and Hollingshead (1999) believed that this reality is due to the fact that collaboration and communication are social activities, which are natural influences on learning, and that an online learning environment offers a stronger sense of context than the traditional classroom. To facilitate the introduction of CSCL, it is good practice to begin small and work up to more complex, less structured activities. Getting-to-know-you or ice-breaker activities, such as simple introductions, can be a good place to start especially if these activities are conducted in the online learning environment (Abrami et al. 1995; Towns 1998).

Conclusion

As with any instructional strategy, the science of teaching must meet the art of practice. Faculty need time to learn the science and refine the craft of using co-operative and collaborative learning. This includes knowing when and how to use positive interdependence, individual accountability, promotive interaction, social skills development and group processing.

In addition, students should receive training in collaborative learning (Colbeck *et al.* 2000; Oliver and Omari 2001) such as how to set goals, share roles and communicate in a way that promotes deeper understanding of the material to be learned. However, training should not be restricted to a one-time workshop. Students may also need the experience of practising these skills in structured groups whereby the instructor can monitor and give feedback on how the groups are functioning. Once students have internalized the skills and the ethos of working together they will be more likely to be successful working collaboratively with less faculty-imposed structure.

During student collaboration, faculty must also allow students to communicate freely and explore through dialogue. While answers and directions commonly are at hand readily for most instructors, the insertion of these types of information from traditional figures of authority generally will alter the collaborative dynamic and stifle the natural processing of the group. In addition, it is important that faculty allow for a certain amount of disagreement, controversy or conflict within groups. As with any collective situation, there are bound to be differences of vision and opinion. Traditionally, faculty were the ones to provide the answers in areas of dispute. In collaborative learning, it is the job of the instructor to monitor that disagreement is voiced productively, but not to stifle controversy by stepping in prematurely and settling disputes without promoting learning.

In addition to providing training and ongoing monitoring, faculty should include group rewards valued by the students and ensure that individual contributions to the groups can be assessed as indicated by social loafing theory (Sheppard 1993). First, group members should believe that there is value associated with contributing to a group. They should believe the group product to be important or that their own efforts are noticed and will be rewarded. Second, group members should perceive a contingency between performance and outcome. They should believe the group product is attainable and that their own contributions are perceived as necessary or indispensable. Third, group members should perceive that the physical or psychological demands required in the group are not excessive. Recommended ways of assessing individual contributions to a group include peer and self-evaluation and having students work in computer-supported collaborative learning (CSCL) environments.

Finally, one might ask why it is important to move students along a continuum from structured co-operative learning to unstructured collaborative learning. Research on self-regulated learning has shown that successful learners are motivationally, cognitively and behaviourally active participants in their own learning (Pintrich and De Groot 1990; Zimmerman 1986). While self-regulated learning has focused on the individual learner, this research also suggests that successful learners should take responsibility for their own learning in different contexts such as those encountered in collaborative learning environments. We propose that when students learn how to assume responsibility for developing motivating and effective collaborative learning experiences for themselves as well as for their group members, they will be on their way to becoming truly self-regulated learners.

References

Abrami, P.C., Chambers, B., Poulsen, C., De Simone, C., d'Appolonia, S. and Howden, J. (1995) *Classroom Connections: Understanding Cooperative Learning*, Toronto: Harcourt Brace.

Ames, C. (1984) 'Competitive, cooperative, and individualistic goal structures: a cognitive-motivational analysis', in R.E. Ames and C. Ames (eds) *Research on Motivation in Education*, Vol. 1, Orlando, FL: Academic Press.

Brandon, D.P. and Hollingshead, A.B. (1999) 'Collaborative learning and computer supported groups', *Communications Education*, 48: 109–26.

Bruffee, K.A. (1993) 'Collaboration, conversation, and reacculturation', in K.A. Bruffee (ed.) *Collaborative Learning: Higher Education, Interdependence, and the Authority of Knowledge*, Baltimore, MD: Johns Hopkins University Press.

—— (1995) 'Sharing our toys: cooperative learning versus collaborative learning', *Change*, January/February: 12–18.

Carlson, S. (2000) 'Campus-computing survey finds that adding technology to teaching is a top issue', *Chronicle of Higher Education, Online Edition*. Available at: <http://chronicle.com/free/2000/10/200010120.htm> (accessed 15 July 2002).

Cheng, W. and Warren, M. (2000) 'Making a difference: using peers to assess individual students' contributions to a group project', *Teaching in Higher Education*, 5, 243–55.

Chui, M.M. (2000) 'Effects of status on solutions, leadership, and evaluations during problem solving', *Sociology of Education*, 73: 175–95.

Cockrell, K.S., Hughes-Caplow, J.A. and Donaldson, J.F. (2000) 'A context for learning: collaborative groups in problem-based learning environment', *Review of Higher Education*, 23: 347–63.

Cohen, E. (1994) 'Restructuring the classroom: conditions for productive small groups', *Review of Educational Research*, 64: 1–35.

Colbeck, C.L., Campbell, S.E. and Bjorklund, S.A. (2000) 'Grouping in the dark', *Journal of Higher Education*, 71: 60–83.

Damon, W. (1984) 'Peer education: the untapped potential', *Journal of Applied Developmental Psychology*, 5: 331–43.

Dansereau, D.F. (1985) 'Learning strategy research', in J.W. Segal, S.F. Chipman and R. Glaser (eds) *Thinking and Learning Skills: Vol. 1. Relating Instruction to Research*, Hillsdale, NJ: Erlbaum.

Dillenborg, P., Baker, M., Blaye, A. and O'Malley, C. (1996) 'The evolution of research on collaborative learning', in E. Spada and P. Reiman (eds) *Learning in Humans and Machines: Towards an Interdisciplinary Learning Science*, Oxford: Elsevier.

Falchikov, N. (1993) 'Group process analysis: self and peer assessment of working together in a group', *Educational & Training Technology International*, 30: 275–84.

Feather, S. (1999) 'The impact of group support systems on collaborative learning groups' stages of development', *Information Technology, Learning, and Performance Journal*, 17(2): 23–34.

Felder, R.M. and Brent, R. (1996) 'Navigating the bumpy road to student-centered instruction', *College Teaching*, 44(2): 43–7.

Freeman, M. (1995) 'Peer assessment by groups of group work', *Assessment & Evaluation in Higher Education*, 20: 289–99.

Gagné, M. and Zuckerman, M. (1999) 'Performance and learning goal orientation as moderators of social loafing and social facilitation', *Small Group Research*, 30: 524–41.

Gamson, Z.F. (1994) 'Collaborative learning comes of age', *Change*, 26(5): 44–9.

Gerlach, J.M. (1994) 'Is this collaboration?', in K. Bosworth and S.J. Hamilton (eds) *Collaborative Learning: Underlying Processes and Effective Techniques, New Directions in Teaching and Learning, 59*, San Francisco, CA: Jossey-Bass.

Hansen, E.J. and Stephens, J.A. (2000) 'The ethics of learner-centered education: dynamics that impede the process', *Change*, 33(5): 40–7.

Hanson, M.G. (1995) 'Joining the conversation: collaborative learning and bibliographic instruction', *Reference Librarian*, 51/52: 147–59.

Harasim, L. (1993) 'Collaborating in cyberspace: using computer conferences as a group learning environment', *Interactive Learning Environments*, 3: 119–30.

Hiltz, R.S. (1998) 'Collaborative learning in networks: building learning communities', in *Proceedings from Web 98, Orlando, Florida*. Available at: <http://eies.njit.edu/~hitlz/collaborative_learning_in_asynch.htm> (accessed 15 July 2002).

Johnson, D.W. and Johnson, R. (1992) *Positive Interdependence: The Heart of Cooperative Learning*, Edina, MN: Interaction Books.

—— (1993) 'What we know about cooperative learning at the college level', *Cooperative Learning*, 13(3): 17–18.

—— (1994) *Learning Together and Alone: Cooperative, Competitive and Individualistic Learning* (4th edn), Boston, MA: Allyn & Bacon.

Johnson, D.W., Johnson, R. and Stanne, M. (2000) *Cooperative Learning Methods: A Meta-analysis*. Available at: http://www.clcrc.com/pages/cl-methods.html (accessed 15 July 2002).

Karau, S.J. and Kipling D.W. (1993) 'Social loafing: a meta-analytic review and theoretical integration', *Journal of Personality and Social Psychology*, 65: 681–706.

Kerr, N.L. and Bruun, S. (1983) 'The dispensability of member effort and group motivation losses: free rider effects', *Journal of Personality and Social Psychology*, 44: 78–94.

Latané, B., Williams, K. and Harkins, S. (1979) 'Many hands make light the work: the causes and consequences of social loafing', *Journal of Personality and Social Psychology*, 37: 822–32.

Matthews, R.S., Cooper, R.L., Davidson, N. and Hawkes, P. (1995) 'Building bridges between cooperative and collaborative learning', *Change*, 27(4): 34–7, 40.

Meyers, S.A. (1997) 'Increasing student participation and productivity in small-group activities for psychology classes', *Teaching of Psychology*, 24: 105–15.

Millis, B.J. and Cottell, P.G. (1998) *Cooperative Learning for Higher Education Faculty*, Phoenix, AZ: Oryx Press.

Oliver, R. and Omari A. (2001) 'Student responses to collaborating and learning in a web-based environment', *Journal of Computer Assisted Learning*, 17: 34–47.

Panitz, T. (1997) 'Collaborative versus cooperative learning: comparing the two definitions helps understand the nature of interactive learning', *Cooperative Learning and College Teaching*, 8(2): 5–7.

Phipps, M., Phipps, C., Kask, S. and Higgins, S. (2001) 'University students' perceptions of cooperative learning: implications for administrators and instructors', *Journal of Experiential Education*, 24: 14–21.

Pintrich, P.R. and De Groot, E. (1990) 'Motivational and self-regulated learning components of classroom academic performance', *Journal of Educational Psychology*, 82: 33–40.

Pradl, G.M. (1991) 'Collaborative learning and mature dependency', in M. Brubacher, R. Payne and K. Richette (eds) *Perspectives on Small Group Learning*, Oakville, ON: Rubicon.

Puntambekar, S. (1999) 'An integrated approach to individual and collaborative learning in a web-based learning environment', in C. Hoadley and J. Roschelle (eds) *Proceedings of the Computer Support for Collaborative Learning (CSCL) 1999 Conference*, Mahwah, NJ: Lawrence Erlbaum Associates.

Roschelle, J. and Teasley, S. (1995) 'The construction of shared knowledge in collaborative problem solving', in C.E. O'Malley (ed.) *Computer-supported Collaborative Learning*, Heidelberg, Germany: Springer-Verlag.

Salomon, G. and Globerson, T. (1989) 'When teams do not function the way they ought to', *International Journal of Educational Research*, 39: 70–9.

Sharan, S. and Sharan, Y. (1992) *Expanding Cooperative Learning through Group Investigation*, New York: Teachers College Press.

Sheppard, J.A. (1993) 'Productivity loss in performance groups: a motivation analysis', *Psychological Bulletin*, 113(1): 67–81.

Sheppard, J.A. and Taylor, K.M. (1999) 'Social loafing and expectancy-value theory', *Personality and Social Psychology Bulletin*, 25: 1147–58.

Slavin, R.E. (1992) 'When and why does cooperative learning increase achievement? Theoretical and empirical perspectives', in R. Hertz-Lazarowitz and N. Miller (eds) *Interaction in Cooperative Groups: The Theoretical Anatomy of Group Learning*, Cambridge: Cambridge University Press.

—— (1993) 'What can post-secondary cooperative education learn from elementary and secondary research', *Cooperative Learning and College Teaching*, 4(1): 2–3.

Slavin, R.E. (1995) 'Cooperative learning among students: theory, research, and implications for active learning', paper written for the Centre for Educational Research and Innovation, Organization for Economic Cooperation and Development.

Sullivan, K. and Hall, C. (1997) 'Introducing students to self-assessment', *Assessment and Education in Higher Education*, 22: 289–305.

Towns, M.H. (1998) 'How do I get my students to work together? Getting cooperative learning started', *Journal of Chemical Education*, 75: 67–9.

Webb, N. (1989) 'Peer interaction and learning in small groups', *International Journal of Educational Research*, 13: 21–39.

Zimmerman, B.J. (1986) 'Becoming a self-regulated learner: which are the key subprocesses', *Contemporary Educational Psychology*, 11: 307–13.

Chapter 6

Peer mediation and students with diverse learning needs

Adrian F. Ashman

The intent of this chapter is to discuss several issues within the framework of peer-mediated learning. Comments and observations are made on topics including inclusion and teacher training, the value of peer mediation for students with special learning needs, the implementation of new teaching-learning approaches, and effective student collaboration.

For several decades, educators around the world have been concerned about students who do not learn as much, or as effectively, as their peers. The focus of much attention has commonly been the assessment of individual needs, the provision of the most appropriate teaching programmes to enhance individual capabilities, and the evaluation of outcomes within a prescribed instructional setting. How teachers and school systems have addressed these issues differs greatly. In some countries, meeting needs has a political and legislative imperative. In the United States and the United Kingdom, for example, community responsibility has been affirmed through the passage of laws such as PL 94-142 and the Education Act respectively. In Australia and New Zealand, the provision of special education has always been considered to be more of a professional responsibility than legislative prescription.

Providing assistance to students with special learning needs would seem to be a relatively straightforward task if appropriate assessment, remedial or supplementary educational programmes, and adequate personnel and physical resources were available. However, it is arguable whether this has ever been the case and, in addition, there are many pressures on schools and staff that make the inclusion in mainstream education of students with special learning needs a difficult task and, in some cases, a questionable practice.

While many teachers support the principle of inclusion, the practicalities associated with its implementation find many teachers ill-prepared in terms of their knowledge of the students, their difficulties and appropriate teaching strategies. This appears to stem from inadequate training at the pre- and inservice levels and continues to be a universal concern (see e.g. Goodlad and Field 1993; McIntosh *et al.* 1993). Some teachers argue that the education of students with high support needs is the province and responsibility of others who have appropriate training. These arguments have been supplemented with counter-claims that schools have not gone far enough to cater for students with special needs and that more effort is needed to restructure classrooms, curricula and instructional methods to cater for students with diverse learning needs (Johnson 1999).

The issue of teacher training raises an additional concern: namely, the nexus between what is taught theoretically during teacher training and what occurs practically in the classroom. Many newly credentialed teachers leave their training institutions with a general understanding of curriculum requirements and a broad view of educational practices and strategies. However, their new school colleagues often confront them with a pervasive ethos that 'what you've learned in the ivory tower will not work in the real world'. New teachers quickly learn the value of accommodating the current school or staff room philosophy of educational practice. However, the division between the ideals instilled in them during training and those expressed by experienced colleagues can be a source of internal conflict, especially when this relates to students with special needs and their inclusion in mainstream classes.

Peer mediation and special need groups

There have been many educational innovations introduced into industrialized countries over the past twenty to twenty-five years. The growth in the number of teaching and learning approaches based upon models of human cognition, for example, has supported the belief that all students (with the possible exception of those with the most serious intellectual impairment) can develop intellectually and socially to an unprecedented level. In some countries, cognitive education has become a common foundation for many programmes in which the focus is the development of students' thinking skills and maximizing opportunities for learning using all available resources inside and outside the classroom. Cognitive approaches to education include specific programmes designed to address a single curriculum area such as reading or mathematics, more general approaches that assist students who experience a range of learning difficulties as well as a variety of teaching-learning settings. One of the more common pedagogical approaches employed over the past decade draws on peers as facilitators within the teaching-learning context.

There are consistent similarities among most peer-mediation models but also some subtle, and not so subtle, differences between them. The most common generic labels that cover the diversity of such approaches include co-operative learning, peer-mediated learning, peer tutoring and student team learning.

Researchers and educational practitioners who support peer-mediated learning have directed their attention primarily towards improving the academic achievement and social development of students who were performing appropriately for their age and grade. In addition, they have also tested the effectiveness of peer mediation with higher and lower performing students including those who are especially gifted and those displaying a variety of impairments and disabilities. Co-operative learning has now been used to support the learning and social acceptance of a broad range of students from kindergarten through high school across the breadth of the curriculum (see e.g. Ammer 1998; Fuchs *et al.* 2001; Lederer 2000). It is not within the scope of this chapter to review each of the areas in great depth. Here, I am more concerned with what has been achieved generally, provide a number of examples of work that has shown the success of peer mediation, and consider its potential and some limitations.

As will be evident from the expansive body of research cited in this book, peer-mediation models and approaches have been employed for more than thirty years, beginning with a modest volume of developmental psychology research on the helping behaviours of children (see e.g. Bryan and London 1970). In the 1980s, educators began to recognize the value of harnessing the powerful influence that children can have on each other's intellectual and social development.

During the 1970s and 1980s it is, perhaps, not surprising that the movement towards enhancing students' facilitation in classroom activities and the reported successes of peer-mediated learning methods created a perception of co-operation as a panacea for most, if not all, instructional ills (see e.g. Cohen *et al.* 1982; Devin-Sheehan *et al.* 1976; Ehly and Larsen 1980; Greenwood *et al.* 1988; Johnson and Johnson 1981, 1987; Sharan 1990). One outcome of this was the development and application of teaching-learning models for specific academic areas (reading in particular) and their eventual application to other curriculum areas. These included reciprocal teaching (Palincsar and Brown 1984), classwide peer tutoring (CWPT) (Delquadri *et al.* 1986), and a later adaptation of CWPT, peer-assisted learning strategies (PALS) (Simmons *et al.* 1994), team accelerated instruction, student teams achievement divisions, jigsaw, and teams-games-tournaments (see Goor and Schwenn 1993; Olson and Platt, 1993; Valletutti and Dummett 1992).

Gifted students

The quality of education for gifted and talented students in regular classes has often been questioned (Braggett 2002), and in this context co-operative learning models and mixed ability groupings have attracted their share of criticism. Some writers have argued that peer-mediation models fail to consider the needs of gifted and talented students, especially in terms of flexibility, variety, curiosity and independent learning (Gallagher and Gallagher 1994; Robinson 1991). Robinson, for example, described the role often given to a gifted student as the 'explainer', the teacher's helper, and that such a responsibility constituted exploitation of brighter students.

Needless to say, advocates of peer-mediated learning do not view the interactions and experiences that occur in mixed-ability groups as exploitation of the brighter students. Indeed, both Slavin (1986) and Johnson and Johnson (1985) reported that gifted and talented students benefit just as much as their lower ability counterparts from peer-mediated learning experiences.

Melser (1999), for example, found that fourth and fifth grade gifted students gained in self-esteem in heterogeneous groups and lost self-esteem in homogeneous groups although, in both contexts, they gained in the targeted academic area, namely reading. Opposite affective and academic results were reported by Sheppard and Kanevsky (1999), and Ramsay and Richards (1997) extended the complexity of the topic by reporting that gifted students were less positive about co-operative learning than their average-ability peers although their disposition did not affect their attitude towards school subjects. More recently, Garduno (2001) found that seventh and eighth grade gifted students made some limited gains academically within co-operative learning settings but lost motivation when they were required to explain content and process to their peers. Overall, participants had a more positive attitude towards mathematics in whole group, competitive settings than in co-operative settings.

Individual differences among students may account for equivocal results across peer-mediation studies that involve gifted and talented students. In their cluster and factor analytic study, Feldhusen et al. (2000) found that gifted students generally were not negative about competitive *or* co-operative learning conditions. They could discriminate between situations when each was an appropriate learning context and were aware of their own preferred learning circumstances. Many also knew that they could be turned off or turned on to peer mediation depending upon their personal learning preference.

Students with learning disabilities

Co-operative learning appeals to teachers because it can provide opportunities for feedback to students that may not be readily available in other teaching-learning events such as during didactic instruction or individual work. Numerous studies have shown that peer mediation fosters academic achievement among students with learning disabilities – used here to refer to the US special education classification – and promotes social acceptance (see e.g. Fuchs et al. 1997; Kuntz et al. 2001). However, as with the equivocal outcomes of research with gifted students, there have also been mixed results reported when peer-mediation approaches have been used to enhance the learning outcomes of students with learning disabilities.

Several research teams have reviewed collections of published peer-mediation studies and have drawn attention to those in which appropriate research methods and analyses have been successfully employed (see Erlbaum *et al.* 2000; Lloyd *et al.* 1988; Maheady *et al.* 2001; McMaster and Fuchs 2002). McMaster and Fuchs, for example, drew several significant conclusions from research published between 1990 and 2000. They reported that when co-operative learning programmes are used as one aspect of multi-component interventions, it is difficult to separate the influence of co-operative learning from other intervention elements. They emphasized the need for ensuring that students accepted responsibility for learning outcomes and stressed the importance of raising the achievement level of students with learning disabilities to that of their normally achieving peers, not simply improving it, but still maintaining the relative discrepancy between them and their peers' achievement. Of note was their finding that more such positive outcomes were found in regular classrooms than in special education settings.

Vaughn and her colleagues (Erlbaum *et al.* 1999; Vaughn *et al.* 2001) also summarized the reading achievement outcomes of group work for students with learning disabilities. They argued that the literature supported the view that small groups were as effective as one-to-one instruction for students with mild to severe learning disabilities with benefits being derived from the effective use of the teacher's time and instruction time, the advantages of peer interactions, and opportunities for the participants to generalize newly acquired skills. They also indicated that these benefits were about the same for students with and without learning disabilities.

Notwithstanding the findings of Vaughn *et al.* (2001), other writers have claimed that students with learning difficulties have not fared consistently better in co-operative learning conditions than in individualized instruction. Bryant and Bryant (1998), for example, argued that adaptations are necessary to the teaching-learning context and instructional approach because these students do not have the necessary skills to perform appropriately in co-operative activities. They suggested that modifications are needed to usual classroom procedures and organizations to accommodate students with learning disabilities to allow them to compensate for the challenges they face when working with others. These included changes to the teaching procedure, classroom management practices and the physical environment, plus adaptation of the curriculum and availability of appropriate materials and technology.

Students with severe disabilities

A number of research teams have reported using peer mediation approaches with students with severe intellectual disability, severe behavioural problems, acquired brain injury, and physical, hearing and vision impairments. Many have involved case studies or have used small sample designs. Several investigators, for example, have drawn attention to positive outcomes with students who have sense impairment and moderate to severe intellectual disability (Englert *et al.* 2001; Liberman *et al.* 2000; McDonnell *et al.* 2001; Morgan *et al.* 1999). Less impressive results have been reported with students who have a language impairment (e.g. Brinton *et al.* 1998, 2000).

A small number of studies have been conducted in which the effectiveness of peer mediation with students with autism has been examined. Most of these have focused on social responsiveness. Weiss and Harris (2001), for example, reported on the placement of socially competent students with peers with autism, the training of peers to manage autistic behaviour and the initiation of interactions with autistic students. These and other skills such as answering questions, turn-taking and looking at others when they speak are basic skills necessary for the success of co-operative learning activities. In some studies, researchers have suggested that simply having normally achieving students interact with autistic peers will positively affect both participant groups. However, Weiss and Harris suggested that proximity alone does not bring about enduring social change, and generalization of any skills beyond the training context is uncommon.

Of significance in this discussion are the benefits that derive from the use of the more well-known peer-mediation programmes for students with severe disabilities. Gains for this group of students appear similar to those of normally achieving students. Specifically, all students can benefit from an increase in the amount of instructional time, effective pacing of the learning activity, relevant feedback on performance, error correction and the coverage of all material appropriate to the task. Gains are commonly reported in targeted curriculum areas although the main emphasis of programmes introduced with children with autism appears to have been the promotion of social interactions, especially increased engagement time with, and responsiveness to, others.

While optimism has been expressed by some writers who have employed peer-mediation models with students who have severe disabilities (e.g. Ryan and Paterna 1997), others have expressed reservations. In a short review of co-operative learning methods, again with students with autism, Harrower and Dunlap (2001) drew attention to investigations in which class-wide peer tutoring and co-operative learning models were employed successfully. In these, the authors referred to improvement in targeted academic skills and engagement. There were also increased interactions between children with autism and their classmates who learned to cue and prompt the autistic students successfully to facilitate achievement in the target areas. Notwithstanding these positive outcomes, Harrower and Dunlap cautioned that, while these approaches may seem to work quite effectively in inclusive classrooms, increasing the rate of social interaction among children with disability through peer mediation may not lead to enduring changes outside of the programme settings.

Some general conclusions

Has peer-mediated learning achieved researchers' and practitioners' expectations? Twenty-plus years has seen advocacy for peer mediation grow to the extent that most teachers are, at least, familiar with the general concepts if not with specific details of any approach. Certainly, advocates claim that peer mediation is capable of facilitating large-scale inclusion of students with special needs in regular classes although evidence of district-wide or regional applications is largely missing. Many reports of peer mediation with students with special education needs to be found in the literature involve predominantly small sample applications up to classroom size. Several examples of these have been cited (e.g. Englert *et al.* 2001; McDonnell *et al.* 2000, 2001; Ryan and Paterna 1997). The most consistent outcomes result from applications of the more refined programmes (such as class-wide peer tutoring), but even in these researchers have acknowledged outcome variability.

Any instructional approach, didactic or otherwise, is applied on the assumption that all learners will benefit from the teaching-learning process in the same way. And, of course, this is no more the case for peer mediation as for the traditional 'chalk-and-talk' approaches. While several writers have drawn attention to less than ideal research outcomes (e.g. Allsopp 1997; Brinton *et al.* 1998), few seem to have considered matching teaching method with individual students' preferred learning styles. Clearly, this is a tough request of any regular classroom teacher but there remain underlying assumptions in many research projects that students should find peer tutoring equally beneficial despite different abilities or impairments (see e.g. Pomplun 1997; Prater *et al.* 1998). Notwithstanding the apparent value of any new instructional approach, the initial challenge is acceptance by the classroom practitioner.

Implementing new teaching-learning approaches

For at least fifty years, if not for much longer, new teaching-learning approaches and methods, including peer-mediation models, have been introduced with the expectation that they are more effective than existing teaching practices. A complication has often arisen, however, when claims are made of success without empirical validation. Ashman and Conway (1997) reviewed the major cognitive interventions that had received exposure in the professional literature over the previous decade and found that most did not have a research foundation to substantiate widespread application. Even where there was research support for an approach, effecting widespread use was a serious challenge. King-Sears (2001) claimed that many of the teaching methods which have the potential to improve the learning outcome of students with and without disabilities, and that have been appropriately researched, do not find their way into school curricula. She claimed that five conditions must exist before any innovation can be achieved at the institution or system levels. These included a well-defined enduring problem, a practice or programme that will deal with the problem, correct implementation of the practice or programme, measurable outcomes to demonstrate effectiveness, and evidence that circumstances in the future will still require implementation of the practice or programme.

The extent to which teachers will be encouraged to adopt promising techniques, such as peer mediation, depends upon the existence of competing priorities and instructional objectives. In some situations, teachers are motivated by pressures to prepare students for assessments that are considered high stakes for the school. In such circumstances, there appears to be little room to manoeuvre around the traditional, or the tried and trusted, teaching practices. Two significant obstacles are the teachers' perception that the new method has questionable practical relevance and that its adoption involves an increased workload. In many cases, especially when there is no systemic support, trials are often assigned a relatively low priority when compared with other factors that influence the teachers' professional life. At the system level, for example, there are requirements to accommodate new curriculum policies and administrative guidelines (such as inclusion), and to reflect system requirements concerning accountability.

At the school level there might be pressures associated with management or administrative reorganizations that require accountability for financial and educational decisions. These especially affect classroom practices if additional human and physical resources are needed to support students with diverse abilities. For the teacher, there are also abstract pressures associated with changes in the professional status of teaching and contradictions between the ideals and values one might have been taught in the training institution and the realities of the classroom.

Perhaps the most significant of all are the practicalities of the working classroom that involve determining the appropriate classroom organization, student management procedures, planning and presenting learning experiences for children with mixed abilities and ages in the same classes, undertaking appropriate assessment, and providing effective feedback to students.

Any new technology must be evaluated in the light of the time available for teachers to adapt their current procedures or strategies and to implement changes that are consistent with the curriculum requirements. Implementing the curriculum requires teachers and other school or system personnel to make judgements about how it can be taught and learned efficiently. New initiatives and technologies are evaluated in relation to current teaching practices and the underlying philosophies held at the time.

While there is an implicit (and sometimes explicit) demand on teachers to keep abreast of current trends and the latest terminology, they are understandably often reluctant to implement new programmes. The antagonism of teachers towards new technologies mirror those expressed towards imposed curriculum changes and perceived as an additional burden if the reason for considering the new method is associated with the inclusion of an often unwanted student with a disability. In this regard, Allsopp's (1997) conclusions were particularly telling. In his study, he examined the effectiveness of class-wide peer tutoring (CWPT) on algebra problem-solving skills. He compared the performance of students at risk of failure with those who were achieving at age and grade level. His results showed that both CWPT and independent student practice were equally effective. However, Allsopp also undertook interviews with the participating teachers who indicated that implementing student collaboration was too demanding in terms of the planning process and physically exhausting due to the energy spent monitoring students during the tutoring activity. Three out of the four teachers involved indicated that they would only use CWPT again in a limited way, as a review activity.

The factors listed above suggest that those who seek to change existing classroom practices must take into account the teachers' needs and workloads. While many teachers may know of peer tutoring and co-operative learning methods, their widespread application will still depend largely upon the context and pressures that classroom teachers perceive and experience.

Some final comments on effective student collaborations

There are several matters that affect students with special education needs who attend regular education classes more than their normally achieving peers. All have an impact on teaching-learning outcome generally and will limit the effectiveness of student collaborations.

Students with special learning needs can be educationally short-changed through involvement in general school activities that take them away from scheduled academic engagements within the classroom. In some schools, for example, students with intellectual disability can be assigned 'helper' duties that include guiding visitors and delivering parcels or papers to their destination within the school. Setting aside such instances of flagrant wastage of learning time, these students can also be disadvantaged inadvertently through participation in withdrawal programmes (e.g. for reading or mathematics), participation in therapy or behaviour management programmes, or ultimately counselling or assessment sessions.

While some withdrawal activities may be advantageous, other education and socialization goals can be achieved effectively through involvement in planned peer-mediation programmes. For example, students who display challenging behaviour are sometimes kept away from class to resolve a disagreement with a teacher or spend a period in a time-out space. These and other consequences of a behaviour disorder may cause the student to miss the teacher's comments or directions at the beginning of a lesson that would be detrimental especially when the student has difficulties processing information, staying on task, or ascertaining the critical information.

Being out of class is especially significant when student collaboration is occurring. Malmgren (1998) stressed that one appealing aspect of peer-mediated learning is the development of social skills that all students learn from relating to each other through teacher-guided structured activities. Along with these social skills and related interactions come opportunities for further gains as a consequence of the interdependence that exists among group members and sharing a successful outcome. When the student with a special learning need is missing from the lesson or otherwise engaged, it is likely that the reward and group affiliation will be substantially reduced or missing altogether.

Groups containing students with physical or sense impairments generally operate like other groups, but the interactions between students with behavioural disorders and intellectual disability and their non-disabled peers are different as students with disability tend to listen and participate less. Pomplun (1997) reported that this was probably a function of the open-ended and non-routine nature of the task that students were asked to perform. She indicated that if the task was well structured with prescribed goals, the student with a disability may be less dependent and supported more by peers without a disability. In her conclusion, she suggested that some exceptional students need more social and group skills training to increase the chance of successful inclusion.

Many writers have drawn attention to the social and interaction skills that develop during student collaborations. Putnam et al. (1996) went further to claim that co-operative learning was the most promising method of instruction for encouraging positive interactions between regular education and students with special learning needs. In their study, they were concerned about the stability of students' perceptions of their peers and the impact of including students with learning disability in regular education classrooms and how this affected peer perceptions over time.

Putnam *et al.* (1996) found that regular students in traditional classes in which co-operative learning was not employed formed negative views of their classmates who had a learning disability and maintained these perceptions over the eight-month duration of their study. Putnam *et al.* stated that co-operative learning did not guarantee that every student with special learning needs would be more accepted, but it did promote greater acceptance than found in traditional classes. In the co-operative learning condition, changes to the regular students' perceptions of their peers with a learning disability were almost always positive with only one special education student being more negatively evaluated at the end of the study. Two hypotheses were suggested for the negative perceptions of students with special education needs. First, their low intellectual capabilities may be perceived unfavourably, and second, these students behave in ways that hinder other students' progress, regardless of the setting. It is notable that Putnam *et al.*'s study did not include students with seriously disruptive behaviour.

Other researchers, such as Prater *et al.* (1998) and Gut (2000), have supported the application of newly acquired social skills in role-play and co-operative learning activities. Gut, for example, claimed that co-operative learning programmes can reduce the social isolation some students experience by providing opportunities to help classmates make friends with each other. She reported that when students in her study who had previously been excluded from social grouping were included, students generally listened, questioned, encouraged and engaged in problem-solving activities with, and for, each other during group time.

However, other writers have not reported results as heartening as those of Putnam *et al.* (1996) and have drawn attention to the failure of student collaborations due to the seriously disruptive behaviour of students with disabilities. When working with children with language impairment, for example, Brinton *et al.* (1998, 2000) suggested that social-interactional difficulties (e.g. withdrawal, aggression and low impulse control) undermine the success during group interactions. In their 2000 study, two students displayed few sociable behaviours towards their partners, were often off-task, appeared to prefer to work alone, and engaged in activities that were unrelated to the group goal. Moreover, instructions given to the six children with language impairments about working co-operatively did not always facilitate successful collaboration. Indeed, the possession of an appropriate level of social interaction skills appears to be crucial if students with special learning needs are to be integrated successfully within regular classrooms and in peer-mediated learning situations in particular.

I have also been attracted by the underlying assumptions of the apprenticeship process and scaffolding metaphors introduced by Englert *et al.* (2001). In their paper, they list four apprenticeship features that related specifically to their work on collaborative writing. These are summarized in a more general way as follows:

1   Students participate fully in activities and it is the teacher's responsibility to ensure that opportunities are provided to enable this to occur.
2   Collaborations must bring together students in ways that encourage them to learn about the thinking and problem-solving process.
3   Performance must be mediated and supported (scaffolded) so that skills are acquired and lead towards independent learning and problem-solving.
4   Education practitioners (i.e. teachers, researchers) must consider the cultural, historical and dynamic aspects of the learning environment.

There is a corollary to these four points. It may be inappropriate and disadvantageous to involve some students with a disability in peer collaborations if they do not have the necessary social skills to interact successfully in a regular education class. Indeed, over the years, I have been mindful of the many recommendations that have been made about the importance of ensuring that appropriate preparation is undertaken when students with a disability are to be enrolled into regular schools and regular education classrooms. This includes not only briefing teachers and regular education students about their soon-to-be classmate but also ensuring that the student with special education needs has the requisite social skills to interact with classmates (and the teacher) appropriately.

Finally in this chapter, I have given a mixed impression of the value or benefits of student collaborations. The intention was not to suggest that peer-mediated learning or co-operative learning approaches (or the many other student collaboration models) are ineffective with students who experience learning problems. Clearly they are not. My concern is more about the way in which student collaborations are conceptualized and implemented.

References

Allsopp, D.H. (1997) 'Using classwide peer tutoring to teach beginning algebra problem-solving skills in heterogeneous classrooms', *Remedial and Special Education*, 18: 367–76.
Ammer, J.J. (1998) 'Peer evaluation model for enhancing writing performance of students with learning disabilities', *Reading and Writing Quarterly*, 14: 263–82.
Ashman, A.F. and Conway, R.N.F. (1997) *An Introduction to Cognitive Education: Theory and Applications*, London: Routledge.

Braggett, E. (2002) 'Gifted and talented children and their education', in A.F. Ashman and J. Elkins (eds) *Educating Children with Diverse Abilities*, 286–348, Frenchs Forest, NSW: Pearson Education Australia.

Brinton, B., Fujiki, M. and Higbee, L.M. (1998) 'Participation in cooperative learning activities by children with specific language impairment', *Journal of Speech, Language and Hearing Research*, 41: 1193–206.

Brinton, B., Fujiki, M., Montague, E.C. and Hanton, J.L. (2000) 'Children with language impairment in cooperative work groups: a pilot study', *Language, Speech, and Hearing Services in Schools*, 31: 252–64.

Bryan, J.H. and London, P. (1970) 'Altruistic behaviour in children', *Psychological Bulletin*, 73: 200–11.

Bryant, D.P. and Bryant, B.R. (1998) 'Using assistive technology adaptations to include students with learning disabilities in cooperative learning activities', *Journal of Learning Disabilities*, 31: 41–54.

Cohen, P.A., Kulik, J.A. and Kulik, C. (1982) 'Educational outcomes of tutoring: a meta-analysis of findings', *American Educational Research Journal*, 19: 237–48.

Delquadri, J.C., Greenwood, C.R., Whorton, D., Carta, J.J. and Hall, R.V. (1986) 'Classwide peer tutoring', *Exceptional Children*, 52: 535–42.

Devin-Sheehan, L., Feldman, R.S. and Allen, V.L. (1976) 'Research on children tutoring children: a critical review', *Review of Educational Research*, 46: 355–85.

Ehly, S.W. and Larsen, S.C. (1980) *Peer Tutoring for Individualized Instruction*, Boston, MA: Allyn & Bacon.

Englert, C.S., Berry, R. and Dunsmore, K. (2001) 'A case study of the apprenticeship process: another perspective on the apprentice and the scaffolding metaphor', *Journal of Learning Disabilities*, 34: 152–71.

Erlbaum, B., Vaughn, S., Hughes, M. and Watson Moody, S. (1999) 'Grouping practices and reading outcomes for students with disabilities', *Exceptional Children*, 65: 399–415.

Erlbaum, B., Vaughn, S., Hughes, M.T., Watson Moody, S. and Schumm, J.S. (2000) 'A meta-analytic review of the effects of instructional grouping format on the reading outcomes of students with disabilities', in R. Gersten, E. Schiller, J.S. Schumm and S. Vaughn (eds) *Issues and Research in Special Education*, 10–135, Hillsdale, NJ: Erlbaum.

Feldhusen, J.F., Dai, D.Y. and Clinkenbeard, P.R. (2000) 'Dimensions of competitive and cooperative learning among gifted learners', *Journal for the Education of the Gifted*, 23: 328–42.

Fuchs, L.S., Fuchs, D. and Karns, K. (2001) 'Enhancing kindergarteners' mathematical development: effects of peer-assisted learning strategies', *Elementary School Journal*, 101: 494–510.

Fuchs, D., Fuchs, L.S., Mathes, P.G. and Simmons, D.C. (1997) 'Peer-assisted learning strategies: making classrooms more responsive to diversity', *American Educational Research Journal*, 34: 176–206.

Gallagher, J.J. and Gallagher, S.A. (1994) *Teaching the Gifted Child* (4th edn), Boston, MA: Allyn & Bacon.

Garduno, E.L.H. (2001) 'The influence of cooperative problem solving on gender differences in achievement, self-efficacy, and attitudes toward mathematics in gifted students', *Gifted Child Quarterly*, 45: 268–82.

Goodlad, J.I. and Field, S. (1993) 'Teachers for renewing schools', in J.I. Goodlad and T.C. Lovitt (eds) *Integrating General and Special Education*, 229–52, New York: Merrill.

Goor, M.B. and Schwenn, J.O. (1993) 'Accommodating diversity and disability with cooperative learning', *Intervention in School and Clinic*, 29(1): 6–16.

Greenwood, C.R., Carta, J.J. and Hall, R.V. (1988) 'The use of peer tutoring strategies in classroom management and educational instruction', *School Psychology Review*, 17: 258–75.

Gut, D.M. (2000) 'We are social beings learning how to learn cooperatively', *Teaching Exceptional Children*, 32(5): 46–61.

Harrower, J.K. and Dunlap, G. (2001) 'Including children with autism in general education classrooms', *Behavior Modification*, 25: 762–84.

Johnson, D.W. and Johnson, R. (1981) 'Effects of cooperative and individualistic learning experiences on interethnic interaction', *Journal of Educational Psychology*, 73: 444–9.

—— (1985) 'Internal dynamics of cooperative learning groups', in R. Slavin, S. Sharan, S. Kagan, R. Hertz-Lazarowitz, C. Webb and R. Schmuch (eds) *Learning to Cooperate, Cooperating to Learn*, 103–24, New York: Plenum Press.

—— (1987) *Learning Together and Alone*, Englewood Cliffs, NJ: Prentice-Hall.

Johnson, G.M. (1999) 'Inclusive education: fundamental instructional strategies and considerations', *Preventing School Failure*, 43: 72–81.

King-Sears, M. (2001) 'Institutionalizing peer-mediated instruction and interventions in schools', *Remedial and Special Education*, 22: 89–98.

Kuntz, K.L., McLaughlin, T.F. and Howard, V.F. (2001) 'A comparison of cooperative learning and small group individualized instruction for math in a self contained classroom for elementary students with disabilities', *Educational Research Quarterly*, 24: 41–56.

Lederer, J.M. (2000) 'Reciprocal teaching of social studies in inclusive elementary classrooms', *Journal of Learning Disabilities*, 33: 91–102.

Liberman, L.J., Dunn, J.M., van der Mars, H. and McCubbin, J. (2000) 'Peer tutors' effects on activity levels of deaf students in inclusive elementary physical education', *Adapted Physical Activity Quarterly*, 17: 20–39.

Lloyd, J.W., Crowley, E.P., Kohler, F.W. and Strain, P.S. (1988) 'Redefining the applied research agenda: cooperative learning, prereferral, teacher consultation, and peer-mediated interventions', *Journal of Learning Disabilities*, 21: 43–52.

Longwill, A.W. and Kleinert, H.L. (1998) 'The unexpected benefits of high school peer tutoring', *Teaching Exceptional Children*, 30: 60–74.

McDonnell, J., Thorson, N. and Allen, C. (2000) 'The effects of partner learning during spelling for students with severe disabilities and their peers', *Journal of Behavioral Education*, 10: 207–21.

McDonnell, J., Mathot-Buckner, C., Thorson, N. and Fister, S. (2001) 'Supporting the inclusion of students with moderate and severe disabilities in junior high school general education classes: the effects of classwide peer tutoring, multielement curriculum, and accommodations', *Education and Treatment of Children*, 24: 141–60.

McIntosh, R., Vaughn, S., Schumm, J., Haager, C. and Lee, O. (1993) 'Observations of students with learning disabilities in general education classrooms', *Exceptional Children*, 60: 249–61.

McMaster, K.N. and Fuchs, D. (2002) 'Effects of cooperative learning on the academic achievement of students with learning disabilities: an update of Tateyama-Sniezek's review', *Learning Disabilities Research and Practice*, 17: 107–17.

Maheady, L., Harper, G.F. and Mallette, B. (2001) 'Peer-mediated instruction and interventions and students with mild disabilities', *Remedial and Special Education*, 22: 4–14.

Malmgren, K.W. (1998) 'Cooperative learning as an academic intervention for students with mild disabilities', *Focus on Exceptional Children*, 31: 1–8.

Melser, N.A. (1999) 'Gifted students and cooperative learning: a study of grouping strategies', *Roeper Review*, 21: 315.

Morgan, R.L., Whorton, J.E. and Turtle, L.B. (1999) 'Use of peer tutoring to improve speech skills in a preschooler with a severe hearing impairment', *Educational Research Quarterly*, 23: 44–55.

Olson, J. and Platt, J. (1992) *Teaching Children and Adolescents with Special Needs*, New York: Merrill.

Palincsar, A.S. and Brown, A.L. (1984) 'Scaffolded instruction of listening comprehension with first graders at risk for academic difficulty', in A. McKeough and J.L. Lupart (eds) *Towards the Practice of Theory-Based Instruction: Current Cognitive Theories and Their Educational Promise*, 50–65, Hillsdale, NJ: Erlbaum.

Pomplun, M. (1997) 'When students with disabilities participate in cooperative groups', *Exceptional Children*, 64: 49–58.

Prater, M.A., Bruhl, S. and Serna, L.A. (1998) 'Acquiring social skills through cooperative learning and teacher-directed instruction', *Remedial and Special Education*, 19: 160–71.

Putnam, J., Markovchick, K., Johnson, D.W. and Johnson, R.T. (1996) 'Cooperative learning and peer acceptance of students with learning disabilities', *Journal of Social Psychology*, 136: 741–52.

Ramsay, S.G. and Richards, H.C. (1997) 'Cooperative learning environments: effects on academic attitudes of gifted students', *Gifted Child Quarterly*, 41: 160–8.

Robinson, A. (1991) 'Cooperation or exploitation? The argument against cooperative learning for talented students', *Journal for the Education of the Gifted*, 14: 9–27.

Ryan, S. and Paterna, L. (1997) 'Junior high can be inclusive: using natural supports and cooperative learning', *Teaching Exceptional Children*, 30(2): 36–41.

Sharan, S. (ed.) (1990) *Cooperative Learning: Theory and Research*, New York: Praeger.

Sheppard, S. and Kanevsky, L.S. (1999) 'Nurturing gifted students' metacognitive awareness: effects of training in homogeneous and heterogeneous classes', *Roeper Review*, 21: 266–75.

Simmons, D.C., Fuchs, D., Fuchs, L.S., Hodge, J.P. and Mathes, P.G. (1994) 'Importance of instructional complexity and role reciprocity to classwide peer tutoring', *Learning Disabilities Research & Practice*, 9: 203–12.

Slavin, R.E. (1986) *Using Student Team Learning* (3rd edn), Baltimore, MD: Johns Hopkins University Press.

Valletutti, P.J. and Dummett, L. (1992) *Cognitive Development: A Functional Approach*, San Diego, CA: Singular Publishing.

Vaughn, S., Hughes, M.T., Watson Moody, S. and Erlbaum, B. (2001) 'Instructional grouping for reading for students with LD: implications for practice', *Intervention in School and Clinic*, 36: 131–50.

Weiss, M.J. and Harris, S.L. (2001) 'Teaching social skills to people with autism', *Behavior Modification*, 25: 785–802.

Chapter 7

Who gains what from co-operative learning

An overview of eight studies

Hanna Shachar

The question is often asked in academic and inservice training settings how to teach in the heterogeneous classroom (Oakes 1985; Rich 1993; Slavin *et al.* 1996). The reference is to classrooms with ethnically, socio-economically and culturally diverse populations, resulting in multiple levels of academic achievement among students. Teachers frequently and justifiably comment, 'every class is heterogeneous, and you have to find the appropriate method for each level'. In all classes with an average size of thirty students, including classes considered to be homogeneous from a cultural and socio-economic point of view we can identify students who are high, middle and low achievers. There will also be a range of problems with which teachers must cope to form a productive pedagogic relationship with their students.

One of the relatively comprehensive replies offered thus far to the question of instruction in the heterogeneous classroom is the view that classroom learning should be designed to promote co-operation and interdependence among pupils. That approach makes it possible for students to serve as learning resources for one another as they engage in discussions and debates, asking questions of one another, and providing explanations (Thelen 1981; Vygotsky 1978). The latter approach has developed since the 1970s and produced a range of instructional methods known collectively as co-operative learning (CL) (Sharan 1999). Research on co-operative learning conducted during the past three decades in several countries has consistently documented the positive effects of co-operative learning and its contribution to the improvement of students' skills in reading, arithmetic, the acquisition of a second language, and the study of the social and natural sciences (Foley and O'Donnell 2002; Shachar and Sharan 1994; Slavin and Madden 1999; Slavin *et al.* 1996). Quite surprisingly very few studies published thus far assessed if CL affects all students equally, or if students of different levels of achievement are affected differentially. There is evidence that high-achieving students respond differently to CL than do low-achieving students, as related in the following episode.

An experiment was conducted with CL in ninth grade classrooms in a very prestigious school, serving a high socio-economic-level population. The seventh grade of that school admits one-third of its students from an area where most inhabitants are of low socioeconomic status (SES). The school makes an effort to compose heterogeneous classrooms with identical numbers of students from the various levels of academic achievement.

One classroom with students who varied from different SES and achievement levels undertook a group investigation project. Three weeks into the project some students told the teacher that they did not wish to continue working together in groups, but rather as individuals. During the conversation that followed it became clear that all the 'rebels' were high-achieving students with impressive abilities who did not want to work in groups because group work would lower their grades due to the low-achieving students in the group. They indicated that they were unwilling to do the work for the other members of the group whose grades were lower than theirs. Apart from the fact that the teacher and the researcher were surprised by their attitude, it was an instructive experience to learn how students understood the idea of school success. In this case school success obviously excluded co-operating with their classmates, offering them assistance or other social values. The problem was solved when the students were convinced that the evaluation of their work in groups would not detract from their individual grades.

Research has shown that, in addition to students' self-reports about their experience with CL, their academic achievements and a variety of perceptions of which they are not always aware are distinctly affected by the different methods of co-operative learning (Cohen 1994; Mevarech and Kramarski 1997; Shachar and Sharan 1994; Slavin 1990). However, the nature of these effects appears to vary as a function of students' level of academic achievement. Consequently, the nature of the relationship between the effect of CL and students' social and academic status deserves detailed examination. The primary goal of such an examination is to determine who gains the most from CL and also what is gained by which group of students. Do some students lose out when studying with these methods? Finally, what educational implications may be derived from a closer examination of the CL methods?

The following exploration of the effects of CL methods is based on seven studies conducted in Israel and one reported in Singapore. These studies compared various effects of CL with those generated by traditional whole class instruction on students with different levels of academic achievement and from different SES levels. After presenting the details of, and findings from, all the studies, their specific implications will be discussed.

What was studied and how?

The studies examined here investigated students' academic achievement and social behaviour. Table 7.1 presents each of the studies and the variables assessed at given levels of academic achievement. The eight studies encompassed 2,837 students who studied in classrooms that ranged from fifth to eleventh grade. The researchers assessed academic achievement in seven different disciplines including mathematics, students' attitudes towards three disciplines, as well as students' quality of life at school and their social relations with other students. Tables 7.2 and 7.3 present the results obtained for each of the variables evaluated in the studies for each level of student achievement.

Table 7.1 List of research projects, variables and data concerning the number of students and achievement levels in each study

Researchers and date	Variables examined	Grade and number of students	Number of achievement levels
Sharan *et al.* (1984)	Academic achievement in English language and literature.	781 seventh grade	3 (high, medium and low)
Shachar and Sharan (1994)	Verbal behaviour and turn-taking in a group discussion. Use of cognitive categories. Social interactions.	351 eighth grade	2 (high and low)
Leiter (1997)	Academic achievement in science, students' attitudes towards studying science.	199 fifth and sixth grade	3 (high, medium and low)
Mevarech and Kramarski (1997)	Mathematical reasoning, information processing.	247 7th grade 265 7th grade	3 (high, medium and low)
Fischer (1996)	Achievement in chemistry.	168 eleventh grade	3 (high, medium and low)
Shachar and Eitan (2000)	Quantity of students' writing.	197 eighth grade	2 (high and low)
Lilach (2002)	Students' perception of the quality of life in school.	281 ninth grade	2 (high and low)
Lee *et al.* (2002)	Achievement in social studies. Attitudes towards social studies. Classroom inventory.	595 fifth grade	3 (high, medium and low)

Table 7.2 Summary of results from five studies that compared three levels of students' achievement

Variables	Co-operative learning			Whole class instruction		
	Low	Middle ability	High	Low	Middle ability	High
Achievement in English	++[a]	++	++	+	+	+
Achievement in science	+	+	0	0	+	0
Mathematical reasoning and information processing	+	0	0	−	−	−
Achievement in chemistry	+	+	0	+	−	−
Achievement in social studies[b]	+	+	−			
Perceptions of classroom climate	+	0	−	0	0	+
Attitudes towards social studies	+	0	+	−	0	−

Notes
0 No significant difference.
+ Difference in favour of CL.
− Difference in favour of WC instruction.

a First + for the GI method, second + for the STAD method.
b No pre-test was administered in this study. The +/− signs indicate differences between two teaching methods, each for high-, middle- and low-ability students.

Table 7.3 Summary of results from three studies that compared two levels of students' achievement

Variables	Difference between CL and WC instruction (high achievers)	Difference between CL and WC instruction (low achievers)	Interaction between method and group
Quantity of speech in a discussion	0	+	0
Number of turns taken to speak	0	+	+
Use of high-order thinking categories in a discussion	+	+	0
Social interactions	+	+	0
Quantity of writing in a test	+	+	0
Perception of quality of life in school			
1 Liking for teachers	−	+	+
2 Liking for home-room teacher	−	+	+
3 Liking for school	−	+	+
4 Social satisfaction	+	0	+

Notes
0 No significant difference.
+ Difference in favour of CL.
− Difference in favour of WC instruction.

Methods used

The studies reviewed here were school-based experiments which compared classes that studied with co-operative learning methods versus classes that were taught with the traditional whole class instruction (WC) method. Each of the experiments was preceded by a period of teacher training for the acquisition of the skills and concepts needed to implement the CL method. The amount of time devoted to teacher training ranged from three to eight months. Only upon completion of the pre-experimental training period did teachers conduct their classrooms with CL. The data were obtained from evaluations of the students' experiences over the course of the academic year.

Data were gathered at the beginning and again at the end of the experiment for all seven variables assessed in both the experimental and the control groups, at two or three levels of student achievement. For three additional variables data were gathered for the experimental and the control groups at two or three levels of achievement, but without repeated measures at the beginning and at the end of the experiment. The comparison of the students' scores in different disciplines between studies was made possible by the fact that a uniform scale of scores was employed in all the studies, namely from 0 to 100.

Table 7.1 shows that the different investigators employed five methods of co-operative learning. The duration of time students studied in co-operative groups varied. In some studies CL took place twice a week for ninety minutes per session, in other studies four times a week for ninety minutes per session. The number of months over which experiments were conducted also varied from two to six. All the studies included one or more observations for the purpose of determining how teachers implemented the CL method they had studied. They all had the benefit of a consultant or a team of consultants with whom they could discuss their work.

Academic achievement of students after using CL methods

The independent variable in the study by Sharan et al. (1984) comprised three instructional methods: group investigation (GI), STAD and whole class instruction (Sharan and Sharan 1992; Slavin 1990). The second independent variable comprised three levels of students' academic achievement: high, middle and low. An analysis of the results shows that high achievers from classrooms conducted with the GI method registered an improvement of 5.6 points in their achievement scores from the pre-test to the post-test. High achievers in classes conducted with the STAD method displayed an improvement of 4.3 points. High-achieving students in the whole class method improved their scores by 1.9 points. The STAD method proved most effective for middle-achieving students, who improved their scores by 11.1 points compared to WC (7.9 points) and to GI (6.54 points). Students at the low level of academic achievement improved their scores by 7.7 points in GI classes, 7.2 points in STAD classes and 6.5. points in WC instruction classes.

In sum, students who derived the greatest benefit from CL in both GI and STAD were of middle-level academic achievement (8.8 points on average). Somewhat less benefit accrued to students of low-level academic achievement in the CL classes (7.45 points). The least amount of benefit from CL was derived by high-achieving students (4.5 points).

Students' achievement in science studies in GI classes versus WC instruction classes was reported by Leiter (1997). Students with a previously low academic achievement improved their scores from pre- to post-test by 8.54 points. Middle-level achievers advanced 2.0 points in their scores while high-level achievers registered a decline of one point from the pre-test to the post-test. In another study (Mevarech and Kramarski 1997), low-level achievers in CL classrooms displayed a 10.5 point improvement in their achievement on an algebra test and the middle-level achievers improved fully 13.06 points in their algebra achievement scores, whereas high-level achievers improved their scores by 1.9 points only. On scores related to a second variable in this study, called mathematical reasoning, the academically slowest students showed an improvement of 3.6 points while middle students' grades declined by 2.5 points and high-achieving students' scores declined by 11.6 points, compared to the control group where low achievers declined by 7.6 points, middle achievers declined by 15.9 points, and high achievers declined by 12.4 points from the pre- to the post-test. The researchers' explanations as to the reason for the decline had to do with the fact that mathematical reasoning deals with word problems only which are more challenging than an introduction to algebra. Nevertheless, it seems that the CL method used in this experiment was of substantial help for the low achievers.

A study of eleventh grade students' achievement in chemistry in classes conducted with the GI method (Fischer 1996) found that the low achievers improved their pre- to post-test scores by 10.6 points, middle achievers improved by 6.2 points while high achievers' scores fell by 1.8 points. The Singapore study (Lee *et al.* 2002) did not have pre- and post-test measures. Nevertheless, results were consistent with those reported by other investigators to the effect that high achievers in both CL and traditionally taught classes did not reveal any difference in achievement. Once again, middle-achieving students in CL classrooms displayed superior scores (5.4 points) compared to peers in the WC instruction classrooms. A marked difference of 13.4 points emerged to the benefit of low achievers in the CL classes compared to their peers in the traditional WC instruction classes.

It is noteworthy that low-achieving students in traditional classrooms received the lowest scores of all six groups assessed in the Singapore study. Clearly, the low-achieving students consistently emerged as those who derived maximum benefit from studying in classes with CL compared to students from the other two levels of academic achievement, above and beyond the students' age or the discipline studied. Students of middle-level academic achievement also derived significant benefit from CL. Students of high-level academic achievement did not receive significant benefit from the CL approach to instruction. Based on the five studies reviewed thus far, the average benefit for students of each of the achievement levels appears as follows: high-level achieving students improved their scores by 1 per cent, middle-level achievers improved by 7.5 per cent, and low-achieving students improved by 9.3 per cent.

Perceptions, attitudes and verbal behaviour of high and low achievers

Students' attitudes towards the significance of their studies in social science were investigated by Lee *et al.* (2002). The specific variables evaluated were liking for social science (SS), liking for teachers, and liking for co-operative group work. The study reported more positive students' perceptions of their study of SS by high and low achievers in the classes that studied with CL, whereas middle-level achievers did not register any change. There were no changes in the scores of middle-level achievers in the WC instruction classes. However, both high and low achievers in the WC classes showed a decline in their perceptions of the quality of school life over the course of the study. The decline indicated by low achievers was almost twice that of high achievers.

Lilach (2002) assessed ninth grade students' perceptions of the quality of life in their school both prior to and following a five-month co-operative learning project. The variables of quality of school life assessed were liking for teachers, liking for the home room teacher, liking for school, and satisfaction with social life in school. Contrary to expectations, high achievers in the CL classes registered a decline at the conclusion of the project in the extent of their liking for teachers and for the school. High achievers in the WC classes showed an improvement in their perceptions of these variables. A different picture emerged for the low achievers. Those in CL classes did not show any decline in their perceptions in the CL classes, while those in WC classes revealed a sharp decline in their perceptions. In fact, these low achievers registered the lowest scores of all four groups on measures of their perception in this study. These results are consistent with those reported in Singapore. In both cases the low-achieving students in the WC classes emerged at the lowest level on both achievement test and evaluation of their perceptions regarding the quality of school and classroom life.

A six-month experiment with the GI method assessed students' quantity of speech during a thirty-minute discussion (Shachar and Sharan 1994). In general, students from the CL classes spoke more than their peers from the WC classes. The more salient change in the quantity of students' speech was observed among low-achieving students from the GI classes. On the other hand, high achievers from the WC classes dominated the speaking privileges in the discussion groups and expressed themselves twice as frequently as did low achievers in these groups. Moreover, in the discussion groups comprised of students from the GI classes high achievers and low achievers expressed themselves with almost equal quantity of speech. Regarding the second variable of students' speech, namely the number of times students took a turn to speak, high achievers from the WC classes took twice as many turns as did their low-achieving peers, while both high and low achievers from the GI classes took almost an equal number of turns. A similar finding emerged in the study of students' writing (Shachar and Eitan 2000). After students had studied for seven months in classes conducted with the GI method they wrote more words on an examination than did their peers who studied with the WC instruction method. A point of particular interest is that the low achievers from the GI classes used as many or even a somewhat larger number of words than did their high-achieving peers. In contrast, low-achieving students from the WC classes used half the number of words on the test than did the high-achieving students. Once again, in writing as in speaking, low-achieving students from the WC classes were on the lowest rung of the achievement ladder.

What about gifted children?

Clearly, CL affects high-achieving students differently from low-achieving students. How then does CL affect gifted students? Investigators have assessed the effects of CL on gifted compared to regular students in Grades 6, 7 and 8. Teachers in a study by Ramsay and Richards (1997) employed the CL methods known as STAD, TGT and TAI (Slavin 1990), or learning together (Johnson and Johnson 1994). The methods were used in a flexible fashion, not always according to their authors' recommendations. It was found that the gifted students complained that CL did not offer them any challenge and was even boring. In general, they responded to CL less positively than did the regular students. An important question arising from this study is why the teachers chose those CL methods intended to assist low-achieving students (Slavin 1990), which were not appropriate for the needs of gifted students. CL is a general term. Teachers must have the professional knowledge needed to differentiate between the various CL methods to employ them successfully with different student populations (Sharan 2002).

The picture portrayed thus far by the data about students who studied in WC classrooms indicates that this form of instruction does a disservice to low-achieving students. That conclusion is supported by results obtained across all the variables evaluated in the different studies. The slow students in the traditional WC classes occupied the lowest rung on the ladder of scores obtained on all the measures employed in all the studies reviewed here.

In contrast, CL impacted positively on the slow students. They showed significant improvement on all measures over the course of the studies reported here, thereby limiting the gap between their scores and those of the high-achieving students from the CL classrooms. Findings reported by Ramsay and Richards (1997) regarding the attitude of gifted versus regular students towards CL may be interpreted as consistent with some of the findings reported here, to the effect that high-achieving students evaluated CL less positively than did low-achieving students.

Conclusions from each of the two methods

The whole class method

Table 7.2 reveals that traditional WC methods contribute almost equally to all students' academic progress, whether they be of high, middle or low academic achievement. Traditional WC methods in English and chemistry contributed positively to lower achieving students' progress. No improvement was noted in the latter students' scores in science or in terms of their liking for their classes. These same students registered a decline in their scores over the course of the experiments reported here in the study of mathematics and in their attitudes towards the study of social science.

Traditional WC methods had different effects on students of middle academic achievement. On two findings assessing achievement in English and science there was a positive effect. On two other variables, namely liking for the classroom and for the study of science, there was no change, whereas findings regarding achievement in maths and chemistry registered a decline from the pre- to post-test scores. Traditional WC methods had a positive effect on high-achieving students in English and in respect to their classroom climate, but did not affect their achievement in science studies. However, their scores in maths and chemistry, and their attitudes towards social studies, indicated a decline. Noteworthy is the fact that low and middle achievers in the traditional classes made a certain progress in their academic achievement, but showed a decline in their perceptions regarding their classroom climate and studies.

The co-operative learning method

Low-achieving students from the CL classes advanced significantly on all seven variables assessed in these studies. Middle-level achievers showed improvements on four variables, while high-level achievers made significant progress on two variables only (Table 7.2). The conclusion from the description of the studies reviewed here is that traditional WC instruction perpetuates, and perhaps even accentuates, the learning gaps and lack of academic equality among students. Readers may recall that WC instruction involves teacher talk for a high portion of classroom time and students are required to follow teachers' instruction uniformly during a given amount of time. The reason for the varying progress of students at different academic levels stems from the fact that there are thirty to forty students in each class and the teacher is expected to have them all progress uniformly according to a given curriculum. This kind of organizational structure does not allow for individualized attention to students. Indeed, teachers' efforts succeed in all students making a reasonable degree of progress in their studies, but they do not and cannot respond to students' special needs. Other findings obtained from studies of CL lead to the conclusion that it provides significant support to students who are slow learners. CL allows these students to participate in discussions where their peers do not necessarily agree with one another, to plan their studies in conjunction with others, and to think out loud. These processes are regulated by group members' ability to progress in their studies and not by the teachers' impression of the mean ability level in a given class. A large number of investigators and educational philosophers have discussed these matters at length and support this perspective (Dewey 1938; McCarthy 1994; Piaget 1970; Thelen 1981; Wells 1998; Vygotsky 1978). In short, in comparison to the WC approach, CL reduces the academic gap between students. It thereby creates conditions for greater equality among students in terms of the access to learning experiences enjoyed by low-level achievers (Cohen 1994).

CL and high-achieving students

Additional conclusions reached on the basis of the evidence presented here indicate that high-achieving students do not derive any significant benefit from CL. The data from Singapore and Israel also reveal that they are not particularly enamoured of this style of learning. As mentioned above, high achievers did not particularly like to study with the CL method. What is it about CL that does not appeal to high-achieving students? One possible reply to this question is that they have completely adjusted to the WC method that constantly compares students with one another in terms of their academic achievement. They have also succeeded in acquiring considerable competence in coping with standardized tests. The rules of the game in the arena of academic achievement are well known to these students and they are completely in tune with them (Ames 1992). Obviously those who succeed with a given method will perceive any change in this method as a threat to their success. CL requires students to assist others in their group, to offer explanations, and to be dependent to some extent on other students in their group who may have lower grades. One of the weaknesses of CL may be the fact that the instructional method employed in the classroom changed, but the system of evaluating students did not. Student evaluation remained as it was and did not provide any of the students with some recognition of the help they afforded others in their group, nor were they given recognition for improvement in their organizational skills or in their thinking. Moreover, there was no formal acknowledgement of any kind regarding the development of the group process and manner of inter-action. Under such conditions it was no wonder that high-achieving students were not eager to risk, as they saw it, their personal grades by participating in an unknown form of classroom learning whose rules and regulations differed significantly from those to which they were accustomed.

Traditional WC and low-achieving students

I noted previously that the traditional WC method does a disservice to low-achieving students. Their scores on typical tests do not improve by comparison to their classmates when studying in a traditional classroom. But several of the studies reviewed here revealed noteworthy findings about the perceptions of low-achieving students in the WC classrooms regarding their teachers, their class and their school. The values attached to these perceptions were so low that they allow for one interpretation only. Low-achieving students felt that they were rejected, almost abandoned, by the system in which they studied. Data obtained by Lilach (2002) demonstrated unequivocally that low-achieving students in the ninth grade taught by the WC method evaluated the quality of their school life at the lowest level ($M = 2.2$, $SD = 0.76$ on a 4-point scale) compared to all other groups and compared to the scores of the high achievers ($M = 2.8$, $SD = 0.85$). Lilach's study focused on two high schools (previously one school that was divided into two institutions due to its large size). One of the two schools (School A) served as the experimental site and the second school (School B) served as a control school. School A decided to change its instructional methods in an effort to improve students' motivation to learn. Teachers participated in an inservice project devoted to CL according to the group investigation method (Sharan and Sharan 1992). Teachers also decided to adopt a multidisciplinary approach to the curriculum in order to formulate broad and interesting problems that groups could investigate.

The principal of School B adopted a series of special projects to assist a larger group of students to improve their academic achievement and be able to take the national graduation examinations. Success in these examinations is the popular criterion for determining the success rate of schools. It should be noted that success on these external examinations is one of the central political goals of the Israel Ministry of Education. High schools make a significant effort to prepare the largest possible number of students for these examinations and to increase their scores on these exams as much as possible. The project adopted by School B included preparing students to take examinations, intensive studies in maths and English language and so forth. Each of the two high schools had five ninth grade classes. In both schools these classes were divided in such a way that there were three classes of high achievers and two of low achievers.

Rather unexpectedly, results of the research reviewed here regarding the low-achieving students in School B were somewhat distressing. These students' perceptions regarding their teachers, the school, and their studies in general declined sharply over the course of the year. This finding testifies to the extent to which the students felt that the school had written them off. They felt they were not important to the school because their chances of undertaking the national examinations and succeeding were very low. In contrast, the classes of high achievers in this school constituted the only group in this study whose scores on perception of quality of school life showed positive progress. The school devoted many hours to providing these students with assistance that would help them succeed in the examinations and it seems that the high-achieving students responded to this effort with satisfaction. Two distinct populations of students evolved in School B; namely, those who were important and those who were not. Not surprisingly, the gap in perceptions between the two groups of students widened considerably over the year.

Effects of the experiment on high-achieving students

Completion of the GI project in School A took the form of group presentations of their work to their classmates and other classes. The presentation displayed a high level of students' creativity. The activity demanded by the research project, preparing summaries, and the actual presentations generated much excitement and satisfaction in the school. Many parents participated in their children's presentations. The impression made by these activities during the project was that the students were very gratified by their work on the project, but the results of the research do not fully confirm this conclusion.

In light of the results presented above, it may be observed that the high-achieving students in School A evaluated their teachers and studies at the conclusion of the project less positively than they had at the beginning. The high-achieving students in School B who had received assistance to achieve high scores on the national examinations, however, displayed an improvement in their perceptions of their teachers and their studies.

The experiment with the GI method of co-operative learning was interesting and satisfying for high-achieving students, even though they felt that this form of learning did not increase their chances of getting high grades in the final examinations. At this stage in their high school careers, high grades in the exams were more important than having creative or interesting studies. Support for this interpretation is found in the study by Fischer (1996), who gathered letters from eleventh grade students who studied chemistry with the GI method. Twenty-five per cent of these students said, 'If we were studying only for intellectual challenge, this would be a good method. But we are studying for the exams, so it's not appropriate.' In other words, the traditional WC method successfully eradicates students' intellectual gratification and interest and turns school studies into a mechanical process aimed exclusively at a specific target. High-achieving students use their ability to succeed in the system that evaluates achievement on the basis of standardized tests. In School A, the gap between high- and low-achieving students in regard to their perceptions of the quality of school life was closed significantly over the course of the project.

Do high-achieving students gain from CL?

Many educational systems proclaim equal educational opportunity and equal access to learning experiences as their major goal (Cohen and Lotan 1997; Shachar and Amir 1996; Slavin 1990). CL is widely considered to be one of the means to this end. However, the question arises as to whether low-achieving students benefit from CL at the expense of high achievers. This question will be raised by any educational system that examines research results as a basis for making a policy decision on this matter. For many systems, encouraging and promoting students who excel in school is also an educational goal that requires long-term investment in this important human resource.

The studies reviewed here testify to the improvement of high-achieving students in both cognitive and social-emotional domains of learning. Their thinking demonstrated in various ways the positive effect of their membership in groups that engaged in studying and discussing the method and content of their studies. A distinctly superior form of cognitive behaviour on the part of these students was closely associated with more effective patterns of peer interaction in their groups. Drucker (1996) was of the opinion that, at least from the point of view of an economist, the proper education for the future should emphasize students' ability to express ideas clearly both orally and in writing, their ability to collaborate and work together as a team, and the ability to plan their careers. It seems reasonable to observe that CL affords students opportunities to experience and cultivate these three domains and offers high-achieving students an opportunity to learn and function effectively as group leaders. We understand, of course, that goals of that nature are beyond the horizon of the students themselves. As young people they are not yet able to envisage such long-term goals and values. They are aware of what the existing system typically demands of them and, while they succeed within this system, they will not be enthusiastic about any change to the system.

Still another approach to interpreting the results of the studies reviewed here focuses on the need to change the academic norms and social behaviour of teachers and students in order to implement CL. Implementation of such a change ordinarily requires an extended period of time, whereas the studies of CL referred to here were carried out in a short period of time – too short to expect teachers and students to internalize the new norms of behaviour, academic goals, evaluation and so forth. The norms prevailing in schools are part of a broad institutional culture (Sarason 1996) whose criteria for students' academic success or failure have been part of the organizational norms of schools in the Western world for many decades. A short experiment for a few months cannot conceivably alter deeply rooted views. Quite the contrary, the academic constraints placed on educational research in the field of instructional methods can result in decidedly misleading conclusions precisely because they reflect students' pre-existing conceptions and attitudes and not their responses to any new form of learning they had experienced. We may assume that if and when a relatively large number of schools adopt CL with its appropriate approach to students' evaluation as an accepted set of norms, the perceptions of high-achieving students regarding the nature of success in school will also change.

A perspective on co-operative learning

Traditional whole class instruction in its various manifestations is a product of the industrial revolution, which sought to provide literacy skills to masses of people who crowded into the cities in search of work. For this purpose it seems to have been relatively successful. Today's world and society are totally different, demanding new forms of thinking and acting (Banathy 1991, 1992; Drucker 1997; Sarason 1997). Continued use of antiquated views about instruction harms students. Lower achieving students are harmed because they cannot learn according to their abilities, and they grow up with a sense of being second-rate citizens with all the negative implications of that idea. High-achieving students are harmed by the constriction of their range of values to a narrow individualism and competition for high grades. The net result is a serious loss to society of a richer quality of life and values. CL reflects a far more appropriate pattern of thought about teaching and learning than does the traditional WC instruction approach. The results of research presented in this chapter appear to support this position.

References

Ames, C. (1992) 'Classrooms: goals, structures and student motivation', *Journal of Educational Psychology*, 84: 261–71.

Banathy, B. (1991) *A Systems View of Education*, Englewood Cliffs, NJ: Educational Technology Publications.

—— (1992) *Systems Design of Education*, Englewood Cliffs, NJ: Educational Technology Publications.

Cohen, E. (1994) *Designing Group Work: Strategies for the Heterogeneous Classroom* (2nd edn), New York: Teachers College Press.

Cohen, E. and Lotan, R. (1997) *Working for Equity in Heterogeneous Classrooms*, New York: Teachers College Press.

Dewey, J. (1938) *Experience and Education*, New York: Macmillan.

Drucker, P. (1996) *Management of Yesterday and the Leadership of Tomorrow*, San Francisco, CA: Jossey-Bass.

—— (1997) 'Introduction: toward the new organization', in F. Hesselbein, M. Goldsmith and R. Beckhard (eds) *The Organization of the Future*, 1–5, San Francisco, CA: Jossey-Bass.

Fischer, S. (1996) 'Effects of cooperative learning on achievement and motivation of 11th grade chemistry students', unpublished Masters dissertation, School of Education, Bar Ilan University, Israel.

Foley, K. and O'Donnell, A. (2002) 'Cooperative learning and visual organizers: effect on solving mole problems in high school chemistry', *Asia Pacific Journal of Education*, 22: 38–51.

Johnson, D.W. and Johnson, R. (1994) 'Learning together', in S. Sharan (ed.) *Handbook of Cooperative Learning Methods*, Westport, CT: Praeger.

Lee, C., Ng, M. and Phang, R. (2002) 'Effects of cooperative learning on students' outcomes', *Asia Pacific Journal of Education*, 22: 3–16.

Leiter, T. (1997) 'Effects of cooperative learning and whole-class instruction on 5th and 6th grade science students' achievement and attitudes', unpublished Masters dissertation, School of Education, Bar Ilan University, Israel.

Lilach, C. (2002) 'Studying interdisciplinary curriculum with group investigation and 9th grade students' perception of quality of life in school', unpublished Masters dissertation, School of Education, Bar Ilan University, Israel.

McCarthy, S. (1994) 'Authors, text, and talk: the internalization of dialogue from social interaction during writing', *Reading Research Quarterly*, 29: 201–31.

Mevarech, Z. and Kramarski, B. (1997) 'IMPROVE: a multidimensional method for teaching mathematics in heterogeneous classrooms', *American Educational Research Journal*, 34: 365–94.

Oakes, J. (1985) *Keeping Track: How Schools Structure Inequality*, New Haven, CT: Yale University Press.

Piaget, J. (1970) *Science of Education and the Psychology of the Child*, New York: Penguin Books.

Ramsay, S. and Richards, H. (1997) 'Cooperative learning environments: effects of academic attitudes of gifted students', *Gifted Child Quarterly*, 41: 160–8.

Rich, Y. (1993) *Education and Instruction in the Heterogeneous Class*, Springfield, IL: Charles C. Thomas.

Sarason, S. (1996) *Revisiting 'The Culture of the School and the Problem of Change'*, New York: Teachers College Press.

—— (1997) *How Schools Might Be Governed and Why*, New York: Teachers College Press.

Shachar, H. and Amir, Y. (1996) 'Training teachers and students for intercultural cooperation in Israel: two models', in D. Landis and R. Bhagat (eds) *Handbook of Intercultural Training* (2nd edn), 400–13, Thousand Oaks, CA: Sage.

Shachar, H. and Eitan, T. (2000) 'Group investigation and the quantity of students' writing in heterogeneous junior-high school classrooms', unpublished manuscript, School of Education, Bar Ilan University, Israel.

Shachar, H. and Sharan, S. (1994) 'Talking relating and achieving: effects of cooperative learning and whole class instruction', *Cognition and Instruction*, 12: 313–53.

Sharan, S. (ed.) (1999) *Handbook of Cooperative Learning Methods* (2nd edn), Westport, CT: Praeger.

—— (2002) 'Differentiating methods of cooperative learning in research and practice', *Asia Pacific Journal of Education*, 22: 106–17.

Sharan, S., Kussell, P., Hertz-Lazarowitz, R., Bejarano, Y., Raviv, S. and Sharan, Y. (1984) *Cooperative Learning in the Classroom: Research in Desegregated Schools*, Hillsdale NJ: Lawrence Erlbaum.

Sharan, Y. and Sharan, S. (1992) *Expanding Cooperative Learning Through Group Investigation*, New York: Teachers College Press.

Slavin, R. (1990) *Cooperative Learning: Theory, Research and Practice*, Englewood Cliffs, NJ: Prentice-Hall.

Slavin, R. and Madden, N. (1999) 'Effects of bilingual and second language adaptations of Success For All on the reading achievement of students acquiring English', *Journal of Education for Students Placed At Risk*, 4: 393–416.

Slavin, R., Madden, N., Dolan, L., Wasik, B., Ross, S., Smith, L. and Dianda, M. (1996) 'Success for All: a summary of research', *Journal of Education for Students Placed At Risk*, 1: 41–76.

Thelen, H. (1981) *The Classroom Society*, London: Croom Helm.

Vygotsky, L.S. (1978). *Mind in Society: The Development of Higher Psychological Processes*, ed. and trans. M. Cole, V. John-Steiner, S. Scribner and E. Souberman, Cambridge, MA: Harvard University Press.

Wells, G. (1998) 'Some questions about direct instruction: why? to whom? how? and when?', *Language Arts*, 76: 27–35.

Chapter 8

Student assessment practices in co-operative learning

John A. Ross and Carol Rolheiser

Introduction

Student assessment in co-operative learning (CL) constitutes a substantial challenge for instructors. Teachers who have evaluated students as isolated learners have to figure out how to evaluate students working in groups, at a time when standards for appraisal are escalating. Guidelines for giving students feedback on group work abound in CL manuals but little is known about the effectiveness of these strategies. In this chapter we will review previous research on student assessment in CL, with particular attention to the practical issues that teachers face. We will reframe the practical issue as a set of research questions and report the results of research. Finally, we will suggest practical actions teachers might take based on the research findings.

Teacher cognitions about student assessment

Teachers devote substantial time to student assessment, yet give themselves low proficiency ratings on assessment tasks (Impara *et al.* 1993), even when they have experienced fairly lengthy training (Bennett *et al.* 1992). Feedback from researchers about the quality of teachers' assessment practices is often negative because few teacher-developed tests measure higher order objectives, and item writing guidelines are frequently violated (Wilson 1996).

New expectations for student assessment practices escalate demands on teachers (Joint Advisory Committee 1992). Assessment must now be transparent (Fredericksen and Collins 1989), meaning that the criteria for appraisal, the population from which tasks are drawn, the scoring key and interpretive schemes must be visible to students. Asking teachers to engage students in setting assessment criteria (Bellanca and Berman 1994) intensifies demands. The new assessment standards require precise specification of what will be measured, identification of multiple levels of attainment, and descriptions of opportunities to learn (Linn 1994). The moral dimension of assessment (e.g. Wiggins 1998) requires that teachers support due process, allowing students to be assessed at an appropriate level of difficulty and when ready. Pitfalls abound when teachers attempt to implement these prescriptions (Briscoe 1994).

Although the new assessment paradigm challenges all teachers, the impact is especially acute for CL teachers. First, they have to disentangle individual from collective performances because students who coast on the work of others must be identified, parents want reports focused on their child, and administrators are legally obliged to promote individuals not groups. Second, CL involves teachers sharing control of assessment with students through procedures such as peer- and self-assessment. Such strategies open grading to a new source of bias, making it more difficult for teachers to defend the grades they assign. Third, most of the advice (and instruments) for assessing CL students addresses social or collaborative skills, but accountability expectations emphasize the measurement of cognitive growth.

An interview study of thirteen exemplary users of CL methods (Ross *et al.* 1998) found that, although the collective assessment knowledge of the group was substantial, anxiety, guilt and uncertainty permeated these teachers' talk about evaluation. They felt they were not assessing often enough, that they failed to balance individual and group accountability appropriately, that their appraisals were imprecise and unsystematic, and that they were using unreflective and unsophisticated procedures. There was a belief that rigorous assessment excludes the intuition and subjectivity that often characterize CL teaching. They saw assessment as distinct from and less important than teaching. Assessment was coupled loosely with teaching; it was done after the important issues had been decided. Some teacher uncertainty was based on having limited discussion with other CL teachers regarding assessment practices, but was also based on their perception that CL theorists contradict one another on assessment issues. In addition, recommended assessment strategies often conflicted with other goals they held dear: 'I hesitate [with peer evaluation] sometimes, I think because we work so much on team-building and having people feel good about themselves. I hate to put anybody in a critical mode with their peers' (Ross *et al.* 1998: 306). In summary, teachers in this study were aware of their assessment limitations and articulated their desire to improve their practices.

In a recent study, seventy-nine participants attending the Great Lakes Association for Cooperation in Education's (GLACIE) Annual Conference, held in Toronto, Canada in May 2002, responded to the prompt: 'Challenges and concerns I experience in the assessment of Cooperative Learning ...'. Three broad categories emerged: what to measure (e.g. 'differentiating between assessing the skills of working cooperatively versus the knowledge of curriculum content'); how to measure (e.g. 'what guidelines do I use to assess when I'm observing groups interact'); and translating assessments into grades (e.g. 'how to translate a child's performance in a cooperative group to a letter grade on a report card').

Distinguishing individual from group performance

Teacher concerns

This was the top concern of teachers and administrators at every educational level in the GLACIE survey. For example, 'differentiating between what a student knows and can do when assessed independently on a task versus what they know and can do when working cooperatively on a task'; knowing when the student's work is really the student's work; worrying that one person may take over the group; tracking how much work each student has put into a team project; and, distinguishing individual and group performance for purposes of evaluation and reporting.

Research evidence

Is it appropriate to assign group grades for curriculum content learning in CL activities?

Group grades are generally less controversial (both in research and practice) for assessing group processes than for measuring academic achievement. Although a thorough discussion of grading practices is often missing in CL texts, there are exceptions. Bennett *et al.* (1991), for example, generated questions and principles to guide teachers' grading in CL. One of the options included team-mates sharing a single group grade. Johnson and Johnson proposed three bases for distributing grades to students: 'equity (the person who contributes the most or scores the highest receives the greatest reward), equality (every person receives the same reward), and need (those who have the greatest need receive the greatest reward)' (1996: 2).

Another contributor to the research discussion of grading in CL is Robert Slavin. Slavin (1980) initially offered a motivational theory for why CL contributed to achievement. When the teacher offers a group reward, it changes the classroom goal structure from competition (i.e. students compete with one another in a zero-sum game) to co-operation (i.e. individuals can accomplish their goals only if peers do). Slavin argued that when a co-operative goal structure prevails, students become social reinforcers of task efforts: it is through success for all that success for each is achieved. In contrast, high achievers in classrooms governed by competitive reward structures are decried as rate-busters because their success diminishes goal attainment opportunities of other students. Slavin (1977) and others (e.g. Johnson *et al.* 1981) conducted meta-analyses demonstrating that co-operative goal structures have positive effects on achievement. These data suggest that assigning group grades is appropriate, for example, by assigning a group score to a group product, randomly selecting one member's paper to score, or totalling/averaging members' individual scores (see Johnson and Johnson (1996) for additional options).

Studies of collaborative assessment that are emerging from mandated testing programmes which include collaborative tasks in their assessment batteries suggest that assigning a group grade has benefits but it is insufficient on its own. Collaborative assessments tend to inflate the scores of lower and average-ability students (Fuchs *et al.* 1998; Webb *et al.* 1998). Weighing against the loss of accuracy is the contribution that collaborative assessment makes to student learning. For example, Fall *et al.* (2000) found that Grade 10 students benefited from discussing answers among themselves prior to completing an individual assessment measuring comprehension of a story. Students who misunderstood the story benefited the most but even those who had understood it initially crystallized their views and added details during the discussion. Billington (1994) found that the positive effects of collaborative assessment continued on retention tests individually administered a week later. Collaborative assessment also provides information about students' content learning that is not visible in individual tests. Webb *et al.* (1995) compared performance on an individual test to what students said when the same task was undertaken in a group of three. Some students revealed concept understanding in the collaborative assessment that was not visible in their individual tests while other students demonstrated misconceptions in the collaborative assessment that were not apparent in the individual test.

Evidence from collaborative assessments support Slavin's conclusion that the essence of effective CL is the combination of individual and group accountability. Slavin (1995) validated his claim with a meta-analysis of seventy-seven studies in which CL was compared to a control group. The meta-analysis found that CL treatments which included both individual and group accountability had medium effects (ES = 0.32) while those that lacked one or more of the elements had negligible impact (ES = 0.07 to 0.16).

Slavin's argument and empirical validation provide a persuasive rationale for assigning group grades, provided they are balanced with individual assessments. However, Slavin included in his analysis only studies using standardized tests of student achievement (Slavin 1986). For example, he excluded a study which found that a whole class treatment was more effective over a twelve- to fifteen-week period than STAD in promoting various kinds of problem-solving because it used performance measures particularized to the concepts to be learned rather than generalized measures of achievement (Ross 1988). In addition, extrinsic rewards impact negatively on intrinsic motivation (Deci *et al.* 2001). D'Apollonia *et al.* (1996) found that a CL treatment based on group rewards produced higher achievement than a control but also produced lower expectations of future learning, less cohesiveness and lower self-concept.

The culminating argument for including individual accountability with collaborative assessment is that there is consistent evidence of social loafing in group tasks. Karau and Williams (1993) reviewed seventy-eight studies which found a reduction in motivation and effort of individuals (mostly college students) when working in groups. This review found that social loafing could be eliminated by increasing evaluation potential – if students knew they could be evaluated by peers, researcher or themselves, they did not loaf. Evaluation has its greatest impact when combined with other tactics for increasing participation such as appropriate levels of task difficulty, gender-balanced group composition and various strategies for creating positive interdependence.

The research evidence suggests that group grading alone is unwise. Combining individual and group accountability is appropriate, for example, by assigning individual scores plus bonus points based on all members reaching a criterion, individual scores plus bonus points based on the lowest score in the group, or individual scores plus the group average. We will explore collaborative assessment issues further below, focusing on high- and low- ability learners.

Are high-ability learners exploited in collaborative assessments?

Robinson (1990) argued that co-operative mixed-ability groups exploit high-ability learners, making them junior teachers. She argued against assigning gifted learners to CL activities because (1) no studies have examined the impact of CL on populations that have been defined as gifted through a credible identification procedure, (2) there have been no comparisons of co-operative learning to well-designed programmes for gifted learners, and (3) most of the evidence about CL effects is based on low-level content objectives – Robinson argued that co-operative learning is ineffective when high-level objectives are examined (a view not supported by evidence marshalled by CL researchers such as Sharan and Shachar (1988)). The advent of high-stakes testing accentuated student and parent concerns about exploitation of high-ability learners in CL. If group grades are assigned, they are likely to be lower than what the high-ability student would have achieved on his or her own.

However, having high-ability students participate in collaborative assessments is likely to have a positive impact on their achievement because it provides opportunity to give help to peers, particularly explanations. Learning occurs because giving explanations requires the reorganization of the material to be learned (Bargh and Schul 1980); it makes unconscious thoughts explicit (King 1990), and it contributes to cognitive conflict that can lead to restructuring (Yackel *et al.* 1991). Current research suggests that CL activities involving mixed-ability groups tend to favour high- and low-ability learners (who give and receive help respectively) over middle-ability learners. The effects are moderated by the nature of the instructional task. For example, Hooper and Hannafin (1988) found that the achievement of high-ability students declined if they were placed in mixed-ability grouping in Grade 8 mathematics, probably because the tasks provided insufficient challenge to high-ability learners.

Clearly, the evidence to date is inconclusive about the effects of collaborative assessment on high-ability learners. For example, Webb *et al.* (1998) found that the performance of high-ability students was not affected by group composition. They performed equally well in all groups and when working alone. The result suggests that collaborative assessment had no impact on their grades but one cannot rule out ceiling effects.

Are the contributions of low-ability learners recognized in collaborative assessments?

Low-ability students' participation rates tend to be lower than those of other students in CL activities. Dale (1993) observed that peers marginalized students who were perceived to have weak task-relevant skills. King (1993) found that when low-ability students were assigned leadership positions, more able group members usurped their roles; the contributions of lower performers to group decisions were limited to minor procedural suggestions. The dominance of co-operative group work by more capable students is particularly strong when the goal is to produce a single group product (Matthews 1992), which is frequently the case in collaborative assessments. In these circumstances, students who feel their offerings are of little value respond by withdrawing from the task (Karau and Williams 1993). Lower ability student passivity and upper ability dominance in small groups have been observed across a range of samples (evidence is summarized in Ross and Cousins (1995b)).

Several factors may reduce the engagement of lower ability students in collaborative assessments. Past failures may create negative expectations or depressed feelings of self-efficacy: students with low self-efficacy are less likely to persist on a task (Bandura 1997). Pressure from high-ability students to complete tasks quickly (observed in Ross and Cousins (1993)) may create a helper/helpee caste system that reduces participation by the less able. The response of more able students to low-ability student requests for help may also depress participation. For example, help-givers in elementary mathematics tend to give poor explanations because they are uncertain about the intended performance, lack a language for describing their thoughts, have deficient teaching skills, and tend to be insensitive to seekers' learning needs (Ross and Cousins 1995a, 1995b). These findings suggest that in the absence of intervention, assigning a single grade to a group is likely to exclude the contributions of lower ability students.

Cohen (1994) generalized these findings, arguing from expectation states theory that high-status individuals will dominate CL activities and that status characteristic can be specific to the task (i.e. ability) or general (i.e. race, culture, gender). Cohen and colleagues (e.g. Cohen and Lotan 1995) reduced status gaps in heterogeneous groups through two strategies: multiple abilities (telling students that the task requires multiple abilities possessed by different group members) and assigning competence to low-status individuals (praising low-status students who demonstrate a particular skill and linking that ability to task requirements).

Another strategy for reducing status discrepancies is to train low-ability students in particular skills required by the task prior to the CL activity. A related strategy is to increase the learning capacity of the group. King and colleagues found that providing students with generic prompts stimulated conceptual talk and contributed to improved achievement (e.g. King et al. 1998). More extensive approaches consist of teaching those who need help how to ask for it, and showing those who have knowledge to share how to give good explanations. Although the effects have been mixed, there is evidence that such treatments improve student achievement (e.g. Gillies and Ashman 1996), especially if the help-giving training is specific to subject content (Fuchs et al. 1997). These strategies for reducing status discrepancies between high- and low-ability learners have not been tested in collaborative assessments. The findings, however, suggest that implementation of status-equalizing treatments is likely to increase inclusion of contributions of lower ability students in CL activities.

A final strategy is to implement Slavin's (1995) fair scoring procedure. This approach combines individual and group accountability by basing the contribution of each individual to the group score on that individual's prior achievement. The calculation of the group score gives students of all ability levels equal opportunity to contribute to the group grade. Slavin has assembled impressive evidence of the effects of treatments that use fair scoring, although his team has never attempted to disentangle the effects of the assessment procedure from the impact of other treatment elements.

How do students feel about collaborative assessment?

Unsystematic anecdotal evidence suggests that high-ability students are uneasy when teachers assign a single grade for content achievement to a group. More systematic attempts to survey students about their feelings towards collaborative assessment indicate that students are generally positive (Griffin *et al.* 1995; Morgan 1999; Stuart 1994), although none of these studies distinguished student views by ability.

Summary

The research evidence should discourage teachers from assigning only group grades. Doing so inflates the scores of lower ability students, may be unfair to higher ability students, and may encourage dysfunctional processes such as social loafing (students who allow others to do the work), resentment (on the part of the workers), division of labour (individual students addressing only a portion of the task) and copying (by those unable to keep up).

What to measure

Teacher concerns

Balancing individual and group accountability was the dominant concern of all groups of GLACIE respondents. Considerably lower in second place were concerns about how to link assessments of CL activities to achievement standards established by governing curriculum documents. The GLACIE teachers were especially concerned with such perennial assessment issues as how to integrate into a single grade scores generated in diverse assessment formats, that measure different aspects of the curriculum, that employ tasks of varying difficulty and which address a range of performance rubrics. These concerns are not unique to assessment in CL and for that reason we will not discuss them here but refer readers to other sources (e.g. Wilson 1996). Of greater relevance to assessment in CL are concerns about individual accountability – what kinds of individual contributions to group activities should be measured?

Research evidence

Can individual contributions to group processes and product be measured with the same instrument?

Product and process must be distinguished because group productivity and learning from group work may be in conflict. Co-construction of ideas, stimulation of conceptual controversy, giving help, encouraging help-seeking and ensuring equal participation of all group members increase individual learning in a group but they may also inhibit group productivity. As Webb *et al.* (1995) argued, if the task is a linear one (e.g. building a model of a bridge), group productivity is highest when the most capable person generates the solution alone. In non-linear tasks (e.g. students developing a school dress code), individual learning and group productivity may be highly correlated. Process and product scores can be aggregated into a single grade for report cards, just as the results of tests measuring different topics can be combined, but accurate measurement requires separate assessment of the components.

What individual behaviours contribute to learning of group members?

There is consistent evidence from process-product studies that the frequency and quality of help-seeking and help-giving influence how much students learn from group work. These studies indicate that it is sequences of dialogue (requests and responses) that need to be measured, not isolated utterances.

Researchers have examined the effect of different types of help-seeking on the help-seeker's learning: (1) asking for simple information contributes to learning if an answer is received; if not, the effect is negative; (2) asking for evaluations, although occurring frequently, is unrelated to achievement, and (3) asking for explanations is potentially the most powerful learning strategy, but the results have been mixed. Some researchers have found a positive effect; others have not. When an explanation-seeker is given no response or an unelaborated factual reply, the effects are negative. (For reviews of the evidence see Ross and Cousins 1995b; Webb 1989.)

These findings from process-product studies demonstrate the effectiveness of particular tactics. But the quantitative approach might miss dimensions discernible in a qualitative analysis of the data, such as the strategy for making requests (Wilkinson and Spinelli (1983) found that effective requests are explicit, focused, repeated and directed towards an individual) or the purpose for help-seeking (Nelson-Le Gall (1990) found that requests emerging from a mastery orientation were more likely to be productive than those that issued from dependency). Especially important is whether the help requested is necessary: for example, many students do not know when they need help (Markman 1979).

All forms of academic help-giving contribute to the help-givers' learning, including giving (1) unelaborated information (facts and procedures), (2) evaluations, and especially (3) explanations. (For review of the evidence see Webb 1989.) Additional dimensions of help-giving emerge from qualitative explorations of student talk in context. The quality of explanations which students give is crucial. A high-quality explanation may consist of a peer modelling the correct performance while providing a verbal commentary that describes how the performance was generated, using language and ideas familiar to the learner. A quality explanation is one that provides the specific answer required by the immediate task while offering the student sufficient procedural knowledge to solve future problems of a similar type on his or her own. The quality of peer explanations is typically poor (e.g. Ross and Cousins 1993). Explanation-givers' procedures for monitoring the results of their help affect its utility. Student help-givers tend to be insensitive to the needs of help-seekers and rarely assist in testing their understanding of the help given. Although some researchers observed effective student monitoring (e.g. Hooper 1992), others who looked for such evidence failed to find it (e.g. Ross and Cousins 1993).

In summary, research on group interactions indicates that dialogue is central. There is great consistency in the types of talk that contribute to learning in CL activities. The findings indicate that although giving help contributes more to learning than receiving it, both forms of involvement can be productive. Less optimistically, the research indicates that the most powerful contributors to learning are relatively rare, although their frequency can be substantially increased through training programmes and by manipulating task and reward structures. From the standpoint of assessment, what should be measured are patterns of requests and responses, not isolated utterances.

What individual behaviours contribute to group productivity?

There is much less researcher consensus around what behaviours contribute to group productivity. Researchers have taken two approaches: generalized conceptions of argument development and subject-specific conceptions.

The first approach is represented by Woodruff (1995). He proposed that CL groups be viewed as micro-communities that use argument as a form of enquiry, developing shared knowledge through constructive conflict. Woodruff proposed an argumentation hierarchy for assessing the contributions made by undergraduates developing a shared interpretation of a text. Level 1 arguments consisted of building a set of collectively valid statements; for example, students expressing unelaborated agreement with a proposition. Level 2 arguments were statements that elaborated an idea by suggesting warrants, evidence or ways to test the idea. Level 3 arguments identified discrepancies between a proposed idea and conventional belief (e.g. identifying misconceptions). Level 4 contributions challenged an idea by presenting contrary evidence, thereby suggesting an alternative hypothesis. Ross (1996) used Woodruff's scheme and added three new codes to measure intellectual leadership among graduate students working on a collaborative writing task:

1   Procedural leadership referred to students giving directives to others (e.g. assigning tasks).

2   Influence on final products referred to the number of lines in the final text attributable to each student. The contribution had to be substantive and credit was given only to the first person who raised a particular idea included in the final text, even if other group members repeated it in subsequent utterances.

3   Rejected contributions referred to ideas that did not appear in the final text.

The subject-specific approach to measuring contributions to group productivity measures disciplinary-specific conversational turns that contribute to student learning. Discipline-based explanations are built around conventions of the disciplines for building new knowledge. Leinhardt (2001) presented a model of instructional explanations consisting of a query, the use of examples, the role of intermediate representations such as analogies and models, and devices that limit or bound explanation (errors, principles and conditions of use). In her model these elements represent the integration of goals, action and the knowledge required to meet the goal. Leinhardt illustrated the model with examples from mathematics and history, showing how each of these elements is manifest in quite different forms in the two disciplines. Although most of Leinhardt's discussion focused on teacher explanations to students, in an earlier study, Leinhardt (1993) demonstrated that the same categories could be used to categorize the quality of individual student contributions to group understanding. In addition, qualitative researchers, particularly in mathematics education, have constructed coding schemes for interpreting student conversations as they jointly solve problems, such as the examples of challenges, justifications and explanations of Cobb *et al.* (1992).

Summary

In our discussion we have focused on individual contributions to group work because researchers (and teachers) unhesitatingly aggregate individual scores when a group measure is required. The research evidence suggests that when teachers are deciding what kinds of individual contribution to measure they should focus on two distinct types and keep their assessments of these separate. The first set consists of contributions to the learning of group members – researchers have identified a core of help-seeking and help-giving behaviours that robustly predict learning across a range of samples. The second set consists of contributions to group productivity. Here there is much less consistency but researchers have identified several sets of behaviours for assessing the intellectual quality of individual contributions at the general and subject-specific levels.

How to measure

Teacher concerns

The third major category of concerns expressed by teachers and non-administrators in the GLACIE survey focused on techniques and tools of assessment. Teachers focused on the need to use a variety of assessment types and to develop assessment protocols that are challenging while at the same time relevant to students. Particular attention was given to the integration of peer, self and portfolio evaluation, along with navigating the problems associated with teaching students how to carry out these forms of assessment. GLACIE participants expressed a need to have a broader knowledge base related to the assessment of CL; that is, to have executive control of a wide repertoire of assessment tools (e.g. 'What assessment methods do we use and when do we use them?').

Research evidence

Which assessment techniques should be included in the toolkit of the assessment literate CL teacher?

Although CL researchers have demonstrated convincingly the contribution of CL to student learning, few studies have disentangled the unique contribution of student assessment to outcomes. The effects of assessment are almost invariably confounded with other CL elements.

The few exceptions to this pattern have all involved self-evaluation. Johnson *et al.* (1990) found that a treatment in which students and teacher shared responsibility for the assessment of group products and procedures made a greater contribution to group productivity than teacher- or student-led processing. Our research found that teaching self-assessment procedures to students contributed to the frequency and quality of help-giving and help-seeking (Ross 1995), and to achievement in language (Ross *et al.* 1999) and mathematics (Ross *et al.* 2002). We also found that students identified a number of positive features of self-evaluation: it gave them a sense of ownership, clarified teacher expectations, enabled them to participate in evaluation decisions with the teacher, and helped them to set self-improvement goals (Ross *et al.* 2002).

Involving students in setting the standards of assessment was a key part of the four-step procedure used in our research (the others were teaching students how to apply assessment criteria, giving them feedback on their applications and using self-assessments to set learning goals). Specific self-assessment techniques are outlined in Rolheiser (1996). Other researchers (e.g. Arter *et al.* 1994) found that providing students with rubrics and exemplars contributes to a shared understanding of assessment criteria and impacts positively on achievement. Such an understanding is essential to peer assessment, which has been found to be a reliable technique (Falchikov and Goldfinch 2000) that contributes to student achievement (Topping 1998).

Other forms of authentic assessment, such as portfolio assessment, have benefits for CL teachers. Portfolios, and especially electronic portfolios, can provide students with the means to portray many aspects of their learning. They can display evidence of academic and social growth and they can capture the process of learning. Portfolios can be powerful vehicles for sharing learning with peers, parents and teachers. With this broader resource base for students, learning is made more public and is accordingly enriched (Rolheiser and Anderson in press). The challenge for teachers includes understanding how to plan and implement the portfolio process so that it can be a useful and valuable source of both individual and collaborative assessment information (Rolheiser et al. 2000). In addition, the challenge for teachers is to ensure that qualities of good work are articulated so that students can recognize these qualities and select samples that exhibit the identified criteria.

Regardless of the assessment technique used, student processing of evaluation data is influenced by parent and peer interpretations (Ross et al. 2002). When peers or parents focused exclusively on marks, social comparisons tended to be dysfunctional, leading to negative feelings and misrepresentations of achievement. We found that older student peers focused attention, to a greater extent than did most parents, on specific aspects of student performance that could be ameliorated through self-remediation. This study provided ample evidence that student cognitions mediated between achievement and evaluation and that these cognitions were impressively influenced by peers – an important finding for CL teachers.

Conclusions

In reviewing the research on CL it becomes clearer that there is more to offer teachers than first appears. A range of research findings and practical assessment ideas have recently emerged to provide substantial direction for CL teachers. The findings reveal that teacher commitment and success with CL in the classroom is linked closely to their understanding and skill in how to fairly and accurately assess and evaluate student performance (Rolheiser and Anderson in press). A major challenge, therefore, is to ensure that knowledge-building occurs between researchers and practitioners. Learning from and with one another will increase the chances that the respective groups will be influenced and guided by the insights which emerge from both theory and practice.

In these times of greater accountability, standards and expectations, the need for assessment literacy has never been greater. For a number of school districts this need is being addressed through comprehensive large-scale reform efforts focused on the development of assessment literacy for all educators (Edge *et al.* 2002). The agenda of future research and applied work needs to focus on better understanding of how teachers are developing their collective assessment literacy, and how they are dealing with the issues and concerns they face as they disentangle individual from collective performance, report to parents and administrators, share control with students through self and peer evaluation, and fairly measure both social and cognitive growth. There can never be simple prescriptions for assessment, but our future agenda needs to be focused on developing clearer options to guide educators as they grapple with the complexities of implementing and sustaining the use of CL in classrooms and schools.

References

Arter, J., Spandel, V., Culham, R. and Pollard, J. (1994) 'The impact of training students to be self-assessors of writing', paper presented at the annual meeting of the American Educational Research Association, New Orleans, April.

Bandura, A. (1997) *Self-Efficacy: The Exercise of Control*, New York: W.H. Freeman.

Bargh, J.A. and Schul, Y. (1980) 'On the cognitive benefits of teaching', *Journal of Educational Psychology*, 72: 593–604.

Bellanca, J. and Berman, S. (1994) 'How to grade the thoughtful, cooperative classroom (if you must)', paper presented at the International Conference on Cooperative Learning, Portland, Oregon.

Bennett, B., Rolheiser-Bennett, C. and Stevahn, L. (1991) *Cooperative Learning: Where Heart Meets Mind*, Toronto: Educational Connections.

Bennett, S., Wragg, E., Carré, C. and Carter, D. (1992) 'A longitudinal study of primary teachers' perceived competence in, and concerns about, National Curriculum implementation', *Research Papers in Education*, 7(1): 53–78.

Billington, R. (1994) 'Effects of collaborative test taking on retention in eight third-grade mathematics classes', *Elementary School Journal*, 95(1): 23–31.

Briscoe, C. (1994) 'Making the grade: perspectives on a teacher's assessment practices', *Mid-Western Educational Researcher*, 7(4): 14–16, 21–5.

Cobb, P., Wood, T., Yackel, E. and McNeal, B. (1992) 'Characteristics of classroom mathematics traditions: an interactional analysis', *American Educational Research Journal*, 29: 517–44.

Cohen, E. (1994) 'Restructuring the classroom: conditions for productive small groups', *Review of Educational Research*, 64(1): 1–35.

Cohen, E. and Lotan, R. (1995) 'Producing equal-status interaction in the heterogeneous classroom', *American Educational Research Journal*, 32: 99–120.

D'Apollonia, S., Poulsen, C., Chambers, B. and Abrami, P. (1996) 'Modifiers of effectiveness of cooperative learning: reward type, ability, and grouping', paper presented at the annual meeting of the American Educational Research Association, New York, April.

Dale, H. (1993) 'Conflict and engagement: collaborative writing in one ninth-grade classroom', paper presented at the annual meeting of the American Educational Research Association, Atlanta, GA.

Deci, E.L., Ryan, R.M. and Koestner, R. (2001) 'The pervasive negative effects of rewards on intrinsic motivation: response to Cameron (2001)', *Review of Educational Research*, 71(1): 43–52.

Edge, K., Rolheiser, C. and Fullan, M. (2002) 'Case studies of assessment literacy-driven educational change', report submitted to Edmonton Catholic Schools, Edmonton, Alberta.

Falchikov, N. and Goldfinch, J. (2000) 'Student peer assessment in higher education: a meta-analysis comparing peer and teacher marks', *Review of Educational Research*, 70: 287–322.

Fall, R., Webb, N. and Chudowsky, N. (2000) 'Group discussion and large-scale language arts assessment: effects on students' comprehension', *American Educational Research Journal*, 37: 911–42.

Fredericksen, J. and Collins, A. (1989) 'A systems approach to educational testing', *Educational Researcher*, 18(9): 27–32.

Fuchs, L., Fuchs, D., Hamlett, C., Phillips, N., Karns, K. and Dutka, S. (1997) 'Enhancing students' helping behavior during peer-mediated instruction with conceptual mathematical explanations', *Elementary School Journal*, 97: 223–50.

Fuchs, L., Fuchs, D., Karns, K., Hamlett, C., Katzaroff, M. and Dutka, S. (1998) 'Comparisons among individual and cooperative performance assessments and other measures of mathematics competence', *Elementary School Journal*, 99(1): 23–52.

Gillies, R. and Ashman, A. (1996) 'Teaching collaborative skills to primary school children in classroom-based work groups', *Learning and Instruction*, 6: 187–200.

Griffin, M., Griffin, B., Warkentin, R., Quinn, G., Driscoll, M. and McCown, R. (1995) 'The effects of cooperative assessment on goals, perceived ability, self-regulation and achievement', paper presented at the annual meeting of the American Educational Research Association, San Francisco.

Hooper, S. (1992) 'Effects of peer interaction during computer-based mathematics instruction', *Journal of Educational Research*, 85: 180–9.

Hooper, S. and Hannafin, M. (1988) 'Cooperative CBI: the effects of heterogeneous versus homogeneous grouping on the learning of progressively complex concepts', *Journal of Educational Computing Research*, 4: 413–24.

Impara, J., Plake, B. and Fagar, J. (1993) 'Teachers' assessment background and attitudes toward testing', *Theory into Practice*, 32: 113–17.

Johnson, D.W. and Johnson, R. (1996) *Meaningful and Manageable Assessment Through Cooperative Learning*, Edina, MN: Interaction Book Company.

Johnson, D.W., Johnson, R., Stanne, M. and Garibaldi, A. (1990) 'Impact of group processing on achievement in cooperative groups', *Journal of Social Psychology*, 130: 507–16.

Johnson, D.W., Maruyama, G., Johnson, R., Nelson, D. and Skon, L. (1981) 'Effects of cooperative, competitive, and individualistic goal structures on achievement: a meta-analysis', *Psychological Bulletin*, 89(1): 47–62.

Joint Advisory Committee (1992) *Principles for Fair Student Assessment Practices for Education in Canada*, Edmonton, Alberta: Joint Advisory Committee.

Karau, S. and Williams, K. (1993) 'Social loafing: a meta-analytic review and theoretical integration', *Journal of Personality and Social Psychology*, 65: 681–706.

King, A. (1990) 'Enhancing peer interaction and learning in the classroom through reciprocal questioning', *American Educational Research Journal*, 27: 664–87.

King, A., Staffieri, A. and Adelgais (1998) 'Mutual peer tutoring: effects of structuring tutorial interaction to scaffold peer learning', *Journal of Educational Psychology*, 90: 134–52.

King, L. (1993) 'High and low achievers' perceptions and cooperative learning in two small groups', *Elementary School Journal*, 93: 399–416.

Leinhardt, G. (1993) 'Weaving instructional explanations in history', *British Journal of Educational Psychology*, 63: 46–74.

—— (2001) 'Instructional explanation: a commonplace for teaching and location for contrast', in V. Richardson (ed.) *Handbook of Research on Teaching* (4th edn), 333–57, Washington, DC: American Educational Research Association.

Linn, R. (1994) 'Performance assessment: policy, promises and technical measurement standards', *Educational Researcher*, 23(9): 4–14.

Markman, E. (1979) 'Realizing that you don't understand: elementary school children's awareness of inconsistencies', *Child Development*, 50: 643–55.

Matthews, M. (1992) 'Gifted students talk about cooperative learning', *Educational Leadership*, 50(2): 48–50.

Morgan, B. (1999) 'Cooperative learning in higher education: undergraduate student reflections on group examinations for group grade', paper presented at the annual meeting of the American Educational Research Association, Montreal, April.

Nelson-Le Gall, S. (1990) 'Academic achievement orientation and help-seeking behavior in early adolescent girls', *Journal of Early Adolescence*, 10: 176–90.

Robinson, A. (1990) 'Cooperation or exploitation? The argument against cooperative learning for talented students', *Journal for the Education of the Gifted*, 14(1): 9–27.

Rolheiser, C. (ed.) (1996) *Self-evaluation: Helping Kids get Better at it: A Teacher's Resource Book*, Toronto: Ontario Institute for Studies in Education, University of Toronto and the Durham Board of Education.

Rolheiser, C. and Anderson, S.E. (in press) 'Practices in teacher education and cooperative learning at the University of Toronto', in E. Cohen, M. Sapon-Shevin and C. Brody (eds) *Practices in Teacher Education and Cooperative Learning*, Albany, NY: SUNY Press.

Rolheiser, C., Bower, B. and Stevahn, L. (2000) *The Portfolio Organizer*, Alexandria, VA: Association for Supervision and Curriculum Development.

Ross, J.A. (1988) 'Improving social-environmental studies problem solving through cooperative learning', *American Educational Research Journal*, 25: 573–91.

—— (1995) 'Effects of feedback on student behavior in cooperative learning groups in a grade 7 math class', *Elementary School Journal*, 96: 125–43.

—— (1996) 'The influence of computer communication skills on participation in a computer conferencing course', *Journal of Educational Computing Research*, 15(1): 37–52.

Ross, J.A. and Cousins, J.B. (1993) 'Enhancing secondary school students' acquisition of correlational reasoning skills', *Research in Science and Technological Education*, 11: 191–206.

—— (1995a) 'Giving and receiving explanations in cooperative learning groups', *Alberta Journal of Educational Research*, 41(1): 104–22.

—— (1995b) 'Impact of explanation seeking on student achievement and attitudes', *Journal of Educational Research*, 89: 109–17.

Ross, J.A., Rolheiser, C. and Hogaboam-Gray, A. (1998) 'Student evaluation in cooperative learning: teacher cognitions', *Teachers and Teaching: Theory and Practice*, 4: 299–316.

—— (1999) 'Effects of self-evaluation training on narrative writing', *Assessing Writing*, 6(1): 107–32.

—— (2002) 'Influences on student cognitions about evaluation', *Assessment in Education*, 9(1): 81–95.

Ross, J.A., Hogaboam-Gray, A. and Rolheiser, C. (2002) 'Student self-evaluation in grade 5–6 mathematics: effects on problem solving achievement', *Educational Assessment*, 8(1): 43–59.

Sharan, S. and Shachar, H. (1988) *Language and Learning in the Cooperative Classroom*, New York: Springer-Verlag.

Slavin, R. (1977) 'Classroom reward structure: an analytic review', *Review of Educational Research*, 47: 633–50.

—— (1980) 'Cooperative learning', *Review of Educational Research*, 50: 315–42.

—— (1986) 'Best-evidence synthesis: an alternative to meta-analytic and traditional reviews', *Educational Researcher*, 15(9): 5–11.

—— (1995) *Cooperative Learning: Theory, Research, and Practice* (2nd edn), Boston, MA: Allyn & Bacon.

Stuart, M. (1994) 'Effects of group grading on cooperation and achievement in two fourth-grade math classes', *Elementary School Journal*, 95(1): 11–21.

Topping, K. (1998) 'Peer assessment between students in colleges and universities', *Review of Educational Research*, 68: 249–76.

Webb, N. (1989) 'Peer interaction and learning in small groups', *International Journal of Educational Research*, 13(1): 21–39.

Webb, N., Nemer, K. and Chizhik, A. (1995) 'Using group collaboration as a window into students' cognitive processes', paper presented at the annual meeting of American Educational Research Association, San Francisco, April.

Webb, N., Nemer, K.M., Chizhik, A.W. and Sugrue, B. (1998) 'Equity issues in collaborative group assessment: group composition and performance', *American Educational Research Journal*, 35: 607–51.

Wiggins, G. (1998) *Educative Assessment: Designing Assessments to Inform and Improve Student Performance*, San Francisco, CA: Jossey-Bass.

Wilkinson, L.C. and Spinelli, F. (1983) 'Using requests effectively in peer-directed instructional groups', *American Educational Research Journal*, 20: 479–501.

Wilson, R.J. (1996) *Assessing Students in Classrooms and Schools*, Scarborough: Allyn & Bacon.

Woodruff, E. (1995) 'Investigating collaborative maieutics: an examination of the effects of face-to-face and computer networked communication mediums on peer-assisted knowledge-building', unpublished doctoral dissertation, University of Toronto, Toronto.

Yackel, E., Cobb, P. and Wood, T. (1991) 'Small-group interactions as a source of learning opportunities in second-grade mathematics', *Journal for Research in Mathematics Education*, 22: 390–408.

Chapter 9

Student motivation in co-operative groups

Social interdependence theory

David W. Johnson and Roger T. Johnson

Motivation

In August 1942 US troops landed on Guadalcanal (an island covered by dense, malaria-ridden jungle) and the battle for the Pacific islands began in earnest. Hundreds of thousands of men were killed (24,000 died in the taking of Iwo Jima alone including the reporter, Ernie Pyle) before in June 1945 the Allies took Okinawa, an island within striking distance of the mainland of Japan.

The beautiful island of Okinawa lies equidistant from Manila and Tokyo and was of strategic importance because its fall would leave Formosa (Taiwan) isolated. The first American landings began on 7 April when the Machinato Line was hit; it took six days of fighting to get past it. Massive suicide attacks of Japanese kamikaze pilots on the surrounding American fleet caused the death of 5,000 American sailors. On Okinawa the marines hit the Shuri Line and then faced the final efforts of the Japanese at the edge of the island. When the Japanese defence crumbled, many Japanese soldiers leapt off cliffs to their death rather than surrender. Americans suffered 50,000 casualties while 110,000 Japanese soldiers died (another 7,000 were wounded).

Author William Manchester wrote several years ago in *Life Magazine* about revisiting Sugar Loaf Hill in Okinawa, where thirty-four years before he had fought as a Marine. He describes how he had been wounded, sent to a hospital and, in violation of orders, escaped from the hospital to rejoin his army unit at the front. Doing so meant almost certain death. *'Why did I do it?'* he wondered. In revisiting Sugar Loaf Hill in Okinawa William Manchester gained an important insight:

> I understand at last, why I jumped hospital that long-ago Sunday and, in violation of orders, returned to the front and almost certain death. It was an act of love. Those men on the line were my family, my home. They were closer to me than I can say, closer than any friends had been or ever would be. They were comrades; three of them had saved

my life. They had never let me down, and I couldn't do it to them. I had to be with them, rather than let them die and me live with the knowledge that I might have saved them. Men, I now knew, do not fight for flag or country, for the Marine Corps or glory or any other abstraction. They fight for their friends.

There are individuals who engage in acts of heroism and bravery. There are scientists who work seven days a week, fifteen hours a day for years to discover a cure for a disease or to solve an important problem. What creates such extraordinary motivation? For that matter, what creates motivation to do anything? The Latin root of the word 'motivation' means 'to move'. Hence the study of motivation is the study of action. Motivation may be defined as the degree to which individuals commit effort to achieve goals that they perceive as being meaningful and worthwhile. Motivation is the driving force, the energy that moves people towards their desired outcomes.

Understanding motives is the key to understanding both oneself and others. When confronted with a crime, police ask questions about motive, seeking to discover 'why' the perpetrator may have engaged in the criminal behaviour. The search for motives is often pursued as aggressively as is the search for the criminal. In our interactions with other people, we ask questions about motivation in order to understand their behaviour. Searching for motives may be inherent to human nature. As young as six months of age, infants appear to understand that people do things for a reason (Woodward 1998).

To understand motivation, it is necessary to take into account four propositions:

1   Motivation is aimed at achieving goals.
2   Motivation is powered by emotions.
3   Motivation has interpersonal and social origins.
4   Social interdependence provides the context in which motivation takes place.

Goals and motivation

Motivation is inherently aimed at achieving goals. Motivation and goals are two sides of the same coin. Committing oneself to achieve a goal creates motivation and motivation is aimed at achieving goals. Goals are desired future state of affairs or outcomes. Kurt Lewin (1935) proposed that all motivation was aimed at achieving goals, although individuals may vary in the degree to which they are explicitly aware of their goals. When a goal is formed, a tension system is created in the person that motivates the person's actions until the goal is achieved or abandoned. If there are no goals, there can be no motivation. All actions are given meaning, direction and purpose by the goals that individuals seek, and the quality and intensity of motivation will change as goals change.

In the literature on achievement goals, two different forms of goals are usually specified. While there are some differences in terminology – Dweck (1991) contrasts learning goals with performance goals, Ames (1984) and Butler (1992) differentiate mastery goals from ability goals, and Nicholls (1989), Ryan (1982) and Koestner *et al.* (1987) compare task involvement with ego involvement – the formulations share enough similarities to justify the differentiation between mastery goals (learning goals, mastery goals and task involvement) and performance goals (performance goals, ability goals and ego involvement) (Ames and Archer 1987). Mastery goals focus on developing competence and mastering tasks. Performance goals focus on demonstrating competence relative to others. Mastery goals may be structured either individualistically or co-operatively and performance goals are clearly competitive.

Goals may be structured so that they are independent or interdependent with the goals of others in the same situation (Deutsch 1949a; Johnson and Johnson 1989). A goal structure specifies the ways in which individuals' goals are interdependent, and therefore how they must interact to achieve their goals. The goals that motivate people are rarely independent from the goals of other participants in the situation. The relationship between one's goals and the goals of others largely determines the impact of goals on motivation. Individuals' goals in any given situation may be positively correlated (i.e. co-operation) or negatively correlated (i.e. competition). Motivation is qualitatively and quantitatively different depending on whether individuals' goal attainments are positively or negatively correlated in the situation.

The literature on motivation has focused largely on achievement goals. There are also numerous social goals, such as building caring and committed relationships and belonging to a group, there are prosocial goals such as contributing to the well-being of others and the common good, there are societal goals such as becoming a responsible and contributing citizen of a community and nation, and there are personal goals such as coping with stress and adversity in more constructive ways. All of these goals are important, and the principles addressed in this chapter apply to all goal accomplishment, not just to academic achievement.

It should be noted that in most organizations, including schools, many goals are imposed on members. Thus the school will usually insist that a student learn to read and master simple mathematics whether the student wants to or not. The imposed goals are somewhat problematic for discussions of motivation, since there is considerable research indicating that motivation to achieve a goal is related directly to the sense of ownership a person has for the goal (Johnson and Johnson 2003). Ownership is typically induced by involving the person in setting the goal. Involvement leads to ownership which leads to motivation and commitment. Perhaps one of the most basic axioms of motivation is, 'while indifferent to other's goals, individuals seek out opportunities to achieve their own goals and commit considerable energy to doing so' (Johnson and Johnson, 2003). Thus in psychology, considerable attention is paid to how to induce commitment to imposed goals.

Emotions and motivation

Motivation is inherently emotional. Emotions may (1) create motivation (i.e. desire, hope, anticipation); (2) accompany motivated actions (i.e. determination, stubbornness, excitement, joy, anxiety); and (3) follow the success or failure of the motivated actions (i.e. pride, satisfaction, celebration).

At each of these stages, emotions may (1) exist within a single person or (2) be shared by all who engage in a co-operative effort. Pride may be for one's own success or it may be a joint pride in the success of a team. The origin of emotions may be from the person's own motivation or it may be from the reactions of others to the person's attempts to achieve the goal. The reactions of others may be (1) how they perceive the person or (2) the feelings the person elicits from others while striving to achieve goals. For example, other people may perceive the person in positive or negative ways (thus creating emotions in the person) or the person achieving a difficult goal may win others' praise, envy or admiration, whereas failing to achieve an easy goal may elicit ridicule, contempt or pity. Most emotions experienced in striving to achieve a goal are of a social nature; that is, the emotions include considerations of other people and social norms (e.g. Fischer and Tangney 1995). Pride, shame and guilt are based on considerations of social standards, the reactions and evaluations of others, or both (Fischer and Tangney 1995; Ortony et al. 1988), and as such may also be regarded as social emotions.

Emotions are contagious; that is, they are transferred in a seemingly automatic way from one person to another. Neumann and Strack (2000), for example, found that when individuals listen to another person read a speech, the tone of the person's voice (happy, neutral or sad) can influence the listeners' moods even though they are concentrating on the content of the speech and not on the reader's emotional state. This contagion creates an emotional interdependence among the emotions of individuals in the same situation; that is, emotions tend to be correlated positively within most situations. Le Bon (1960) argued that not only are emotions contagious, but that in groups they become amplified so that the level of the emotion is intensified. Shared feelings tend to be more powerful and meaningful than feelings experienced in isolation. In most situations, therefore, it is difficult to conceive of a person's emotions as independent from the emotions of the other participants. Emotions are social in that typically they are influenced by the actions and emotions of the people with whom a person is interacting.

Finally, Sheldon and Houser-Marko (2001) demonstrated that the relations are bi-directional from (1) personal commitment to achieving a goal to (2) progress in achieving the goal to (3) feelings of well-being. Using a two-cycle prospective design, they found that not only does goal progress result in greater feelings of well-being, but the enhanced well-being increases personal commitment to goals, which in turn fosters further successful efforts to achieve the goals, which results in further enhancement of feelings of well-being.

Social determination of motivation

Motivation is inherently social. It occurs within a network of interpersonal relationships. Motivated behaviour, goals, their outcomes, and the evaluations of success and failure do not occur in a social vacuum, but rather within a social setting (e.g. Johnson 2003; Johnson and Johnson 2003; Johnson and Johnson 1974; Osterman 2000). The social origins of motivation may include past relationships that have been internalized through processes such as identification, past and current social roles, and the interaction among the individuals involved in the current situation (Johnson and Johnson 2003). The latter is reflected in (1) the positive interdependence between one's goals and the goals of others (i.e. when one person takes action to achieve his or her goals, the likelihood of other people in the situation achieving their goals is affected); (2) other individuals observing and reacting to a person's attempt to achieve goals; and (3) the person being cognizant of other people's actual and potential reactions to his or her immediate and long-term attempts to achieve goals. These interpersonal influences have far-reaching consequences. Acceptance and rejection, feedback and other aspects of social life have great impact on motivation and striving to achieve goals (Butler 1994; Juvonen and Wentzel 1996; Osterman 2000; Patrick *et al.* 1999). Osterman (2000) stressed that belonging had a variety of significant effects on various aspects of motivation and achievement (such as persistence and performance). Success or failure in achieving a goal has social implications and at times the reactions of others may even override the significance of the achievement itself in determining future behaviour. Of the interpersonal relationships in task situations, peers may be the most influential on motivation (Johnson 1980).

Lewin and Deutsch assumed that all motivation is aimed at achieving goals, although individuals vary in the degree to which they are explicitly aware of their goals. It is a rare situation, however, when individuals' goals are independent of each other and each person may pursue his or her goals independently from others. In most cases, a person's goals are related, either positively or negatively, to the goals of others. For most significant and long-term goals (such as curing cancer, starting a new business, or being elected to political office), the efforts of many people working together to achieve their common goal are needed. For many short-term goals, individuals may work against each other for personal advantage or gain. Rarely, however, can an individual work to achieve a significant goal whose accomplishment does not enhance or obstruct the goal achievement of others.

In addition, group membership powerfully influences the adoption of goals and commitment to achieve them. Solomon Asch (1952) was concerned with how new needs or goals came into existence and became part of the person. He posited that new goals became internalized through social processes such as membership of a group. He believed that subordinating one's own interests to the interests of the group or community was as intrinsic to humans and as powerful as acting on self-interests. He stated that selfishness (i.e. the total focus on self-benefit while ignoring the well-being of others) has a low survival value because in a society each individual is dependent on others for the most basic things, such as food, water, shelter, clothes, transportation and communication (not to mention love and caring). To meet his or her own needs each individual must co-operate with others and form a community. To promote one's own well-being, the individual needs to be a member of the group, to be valued by other group members, to engage in joint enterprises with others, to count in their lives, and to be an object of significance for others. A person's happiness and well-being thus become intertwined with the happiness and well-being of others, and one's self-interests thereby include the interests of others (such as spouse and children) and the community as a whole. Thus, the striving for co-operation and community are among the most powerful motives in humans and result in the emergence of new social needs and goals that include the well-being of others and the common good.

Social interdependence as context

Given that (1) motivation is aimed at achieving goals that are interdependent on the goals of other participants in the situation, (2) motivation is fuelled by emotions which are interdependent with the emotions of other participants in the situation, and (3) motivation has social origins and does not occur in a social vacuum, but rather in a social setting within a network of interpersonal relationships, then it may be concluded that motivation may be conceived of as occurring within the context of social interdependence.

Social interdependence theory, therefore, may provide the framework from which to discuss motivation. Much of the existing research on motivation has isolated the achiever from the relevant social context that surrounds him or her. Yet the role of interpersonal context is of considerable importance to motivation theories (e.g. Eccles and Midgley 1989; Turner and Meyer 1999; Urdan 1999) and the nature of the context greatly influences motivation and achievement (Eccles *et al.* 1998; Stipek 1998; Stipek and Seal 2001). It may be impossible to understand individuals' motivation without also understanding the social context in which it occurs.

From social interdependence theory it is clear that motivation will be markedly different in co-operative, competitive and individualistic contexts. In this chapter, therefore, social interdependence theory is reviewed (see Table 9.1). Then the impact of social interdependence theory is examined on (1) the value or benefit of the goal (i.e. mutual benefit, differential benefit or self-benefit); (2) the perceived ability to achieve the goal (i.e. joint, differential, self-efficacy); (3) intrinsic and extrinsic motivation; (4) epistemic curiosity and continuing motivation; and (5) commitment to succeed. The practical application of co-operative learning to increase students' motivation is then presented.

Social interdependence and motivation

> Achievement is a we thing, not a me thing, always the product of many heads and hands.
>
> (Atkinson 1964)

In the 1930s and 1940s Kurt Lewin (1935, 1948) proposed that a person's behaviour is motivated by states of tension that arise as desired goals are perceived and that it is this tension which motivates actions aimed at achieving the desired goals. This premise inspired a number of studies concerned with the recall and resumption of interrupted activities (Hornstein *et al.* 1980; Lewis 1944; Ovsiankina 1928). The results of these studies suggest that (1) the tendency to recall uncompleted tasks is greater than

Table 9.1 Social interdependence and motivation

Co-operation	Competition	Individualistic
Mutual benefit	Differential benefit	Self-benefit
Joint efficacy	Differential efficacy	Self-efficacy
Intrinsic motivation	Extrinsic motivation	Extrinsic motivation
Epistemic curiosity aroused by opposing views	Defensive adherence aroused by opposing views	No intellectual challenge
High commitment	Low commitment	Low commitment

the tendency to recall completed tasks, (2) the tendency to resume interrupted tasks is greater than the tendency to resume completed tasks, (3) the tendency to recall interrupted tasks is greater when the task is interrupted near its end, (4) the tendency to recall interrupted tasks is less when the tasks are completed by a co-operating partner than when the task is completed by a non-co-operative person, and (5) a partner's interrupted tasks were recalled significantly more frequently than his or her completed ones in a co-operative rather than a competitive or individualistic context. Together with his colleagues, Lewin also studied individuals' level of aspiration, the predecessor to achievement motivation (Lewin *et al.* 1944). This view of conscious goals that create internal tension systems which motivate actions towards goal achievement was largely ignored in the 1950s and 1960s, as the field of motivation became dominated by behaviourists (who argued that motivation lies outside the person in the form of reinforcers and punishers) and Freudians (who asserted that motivation was subconscious). One of Lewin's students, Morton Deutsch (1949a), developed the theory of social interdependence as an extension of Lewin's field theory.

Social interdependence exists when the accomplishment of each individual's goals is affected by the actions of others (Deutsch 1949a; Johnson and Johnson 1989). There are two types of social interdependence: positive (co-operative) and negative (competitive). Positive interdependence exists when individuals perceive that they can reach their goals if and only if the other individuals with whom they are co-operatively linked also reach their goals, and therefore they promote each other's efforts to achieve the goals. Negative interdependence exists when individuals perceive that they can obtain their goals if and only if the other individuals with whom they are competitively linked fail to obtain their goals, and therefore obstruct each other's efforts to achieve those goals. No interdependence results in a situation in which individuals perceive that they can reach their goal regardless of whether or not other individuals in the situation attain their goals.

The basic premise of social interdependence theory is that the way in which interdependence is structured determines how individuals interact, and the interaction pattern determines the outcomes of the situation (Deutsch 1949a; Johnson and Johnson 1974, 1989) (see Figure 9.1). Positive interdependence results in promotive interaction (such as mutual help and assistance and trust), negative interdependence results in oppositional or contrient interaction (such as obstruction of each other's goal achievement efforts and distrust), and no interdependence results in the absence of interaction.

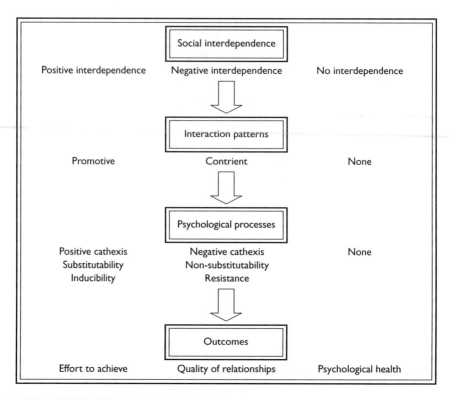

Figure 9.1 Overview of social interdependence theory

Psychological processes

The psychological processes created by positive interdependence and the resulting promotive interaction includes substitutability (i.e. the degree to which actions of one person substitute for the actions of another person), inducibility (i.e. openness to being influenced and to influencing others), and positive cathexis (i.e. investment of psychological energy in objects outside of oneself) (Deutsch 1949a). These processes explain how self-interest is expanded to joint interest and how new goals and motives are created in co-operative and competitive situations. Self-interest becomes expanded to mutual interest through other people's actions substituting for one's own, through an emotional investment in achieving goals that benefit others as well as oneself and generalizes to caring and committed relationships which are working for the same purposes and goals, and through an openness to being influenced so that joint efforts are more effective. Demonstrating the transition from self-interest to mutual interest is perhaps one of the most important aspects of social interdependence theory.

Basic elements

Operationalizing co-operation involves more than positive interdependence and promotive interaction (Johnson and Johnson 1989). In addition to these basic elements, it is necessary to structure individual accountability (i.e. assessing the quality and quantity of each member's contributions and giving the results to the group and the individual), the appropriate use of social skills (i.e. leadership, decision-making, trust-building, communication and conflict-management skills), and group processing (i.e. discussing how well they are achieving their goals and maintaining effective working relationships among members). These five basic elements may be used to create effective co-operation in almost any social system.

Individual accountability affects motivation. Motivation decreases when group members see their efforts as non-essential for group success. Members will reduce their contributions to goal achievement (that is, engage in social loafing) when their contributions cannot be identified, their efforts are redundant, they dislike the group and the other members, and they are not held responsible for the final outcome (Johnson and Johnson 1989). Generally, social loafing increases as the size of the group increases, since members are less likely to see their own personal contribution to the group as being important to the group's chances of success. As group size increases, individual team members tend to communicate less frequently (which may reduce the amount of information called upon in arriving at a decision) and individuals may be more likely to alter their statements to conform to the perceived beliefs of the overall majority. Morgan et al. (1970) found that team performance actually improved when one team member was missing from five-person teams, perhaps because members believed that their contributions were more necessary. Increasing individual accountability tends to increase perceived positive interdependence among group members (Archer-Kath et al. 1994).

Research findings

There is considerable research on social interdependence (Johnson and Johnson 1989). In the past hundred years or more, over 800 research studies have been conducted on a wide variety of dependent variables. Those variables may be subsumed into three categories. Overall, the evidence indicates that co-operation (compared with competitive and individualistic efforts) tends to result in:

1   Greater effort exerted to achieve (e.g. higher achievement and greater productivity, more frequent use of higher level reasoning, more frequent generation of new ideas and solutions, greater intrinsic and

achievement motivation, greater long-term retention, more on-task behaviour, and greater transfer of what is learned within one situation to another).

2   Higher quality of relationships among participants (e.g. greater interpersonal attraction, liking, cohesion and *esprit de corps*, valuing of heterogeneity, and greater task-oriented and personal support).

3   Greater psychological adjustment (e.g. greater psychological health, greater social competencies, higher self-esteem, a shared identity, and greater ability to cope with stress and adversity).

While it is clear that motivation takes place within a social context, the exact nature of that context has never been clearly specified. Social interdependence theory provides a framework from which to understand the social context of motivation. Social interdependence has powerful effects on the perceived values of goals (i.e. whether they involve mutual, differential or self-benefit), the perceived ability to achieve goals (i.e. joint, differential or self-efficacy), the intrinsic or extrinsic nature of motivation, epistemic curiosity and continuing motivation, and commitment to achieve goals. Each of these topics will be discussed below.

Co-operation derived from self-interest

One of the issues within the field of motivation is how new goals and motives are created. Of most interest may be how a person moves from goals and motives based on self-interest to goals and motives based on concern for others and for the community as a whole (Asch 1952). This issue is especially puzzling, since both behavioural and Freudian theories posit that individuals are egocentrically motivated only by personal pleasure and pain. In a critique of the Freudian and behavioural position, Asch (1952) observed that if individuals acted only selfishly, no society would be possible. He stated that a person needs to be a member of the group, to work with others and to be of significance in their lives. He concluded that subordinating one's own interests to those of the community is as intrinsic and powerful a motive as acting on self-interests. Social interdependence theory provides an answer for how new goals based on concern for others and the common good are developed. The movement from self-interests to mutual interests begins with perceiving that there are common goals and a mutual fate. As positive interdependence is perceived among goals, then the internal tension system that results is focused on mutual as well as individual goals (Deutsch 1949a). The actions of collaborators substitute for one's own, creating a positive cathexis for their actions that generalizes to a liking for them as people. Each individual is open to being influenced by collaborators as they co-ordinate their actions towards effectively achieving the goal. Through this process of perceived positive interdependence and substitutability, positive cathexis and inducibility, self-interests become redefined to include the interests of others.

Value of goal accomplishment

Motivation is influenced by the value of the goal (Atkinson 1964). Value refers to meaningfulness, incentives or reasons for accomplishing the goal. Social interdependence theory posits that the value of a goal is determined largely by whether individuals are working for mutual, differential or self-benefit. Positive, negative and no interdependence create three different orientations towards goal accomplishment. The motivating qualities of a goal change as it is structured co-operatively, competitively or individualistically.

Mutual benefit

Positive interdependence promotes working together to maximize the mutual benefit or joint outcome of all members. By definition, when one member achieves the goal, all others with whom the person is co-operatively linked achieve their goals too (Deutsch 1949a). Thus group members share a common fate where they all gain or lose on the basis of the overall performance of group members. Actions that help achieve the goals (1) benefit oneself, (2) benefit other collaborators, and (3) contribute to the common good. There are at least five reasons why working as part of a co-operative effort increases a person's motivation.

Empowering an individual to achieve difficult goals

Motivation in co-operative efforts increases because co-operation empowers an individual to achieve goals that he or she could not achieve alone. Goals that would be hopeless for an individual (such as putting a man on the moon, curing AIDS, creating a successful business) become quite possible when a co-operative system is established bringing together all the necessary expertise and resources. With other people on one's side, one can accomplish task that one would never dream of tackling on one's own. The American Civil Rights movement in the late 1950s and early 1960s is an example. Martin Luther King Jr. achieved goals as head of the movement that he could have never achieved alone. Conversely, with others against one, the simplest task can become impossible. Achieving the most meaningful and significant goals typically requires the resources of numerous people and can be achieved only through co-operative efforts. Quite often, 'I can't' is transformed into 'We can!'

Peer pressure to achieve

While striving to achieve for mutual benefit there is considerable peer pressure to achieve and to engage in on-task behaviour. Encouraging collaborators to work hard has an impact on those receiving the encouragement and those giving the encouragement. There are dozens of studies indicating considerably more peer support and encouragement for as well as actual facilitation of achievement and on-task behaviour in co-operative than in competitive or individualistic situations (Johnson and Johnson, 1989). Actively engaging in encouraging and facilitative behaviour is a public commitment to group productivity. Such public commitment makes students less open to attempts at persuading them to lower their efforts to achieve and more open to attempts at persuading them to increase their efforts to achieve. In addition, actively encouraging others to achieve and actively facilitating their success makes the importance of contributing to the group's success more salient and less easily denied or forgotten in subsequent situations (Wicklund and Brehm 1976). Taking a public stand for group productivity will clearly increase the achievement-oriented behaviour of students (Pallak *et al.* 1980).

Benefiting others and the common good

Working to benefit others and the common good results in the goals being perceived as more meaningful, worthwhile and significant. Meaning increases as goals go beyond self-interest and involve a higher purpose. Helping another student to achieve a high grade on an algebra test, contributing to a winning effort as part of a football team, gaining a crucial contract that will keep your company in business and ensure all other employees will be paid, telling a joke that makes others laugh, and many other such activities give your life meaning and a sense of accomplishing something worthwhile that does not exist in competitive or individualistic situations. The pursuit of prosocial goals is clearly related to students being liked and respected by their peers (Wentzel 1994).

Goals become even more meaningful when they benefit not only oneself and others, but the common good as a whole. Finding a cure for breast cancer, for example, may benefit millions of people all over the world. Succeeding in accomplishing such a goal may result in feelings of pride, satisfaction and accomplishment that cannot be achieved in any other way. The more goals benefit others and the common good (i.e. the organization, community, society or world) as well as oneself, the more meaningful and significant they are perceived to be.

Creating interdependence with significant others

Motivation increases when one's goals are interdependent with those of significant others. When a person joins a co-operative effort in which people they admire and respect and wish to be with are participating, the significance of the goal increases. Because people who are significant to a person value the goal, the goal becomes more meaningful for the person. In addition, there is a shared identity based on group membership that binds members together emotionally. Besides being a separate individual, one is a member of a team that includes significant others. Finally, there is an expectation for a joint celebration based on mutual respect and appreciation among group members.

Linking personal to group aspirations

In addition, the more the goals reflect group aspirations as well as personal aspirations, the more significant the goals will be and the more committed individuals will be to achieving them. The desire for individuals to achieve for the sake of the group is a well-known phenomenon (Hertz-Lazarowitz *et al.* 1992). There are dozens of studies, furthermore, indicating that individuals perceive much more peer support and encouragement for achievement and on-task behaviour in co-operative than in competitive or individualistic situations (Johnson and Johnson 1989).

Accomplishing both achievement and social goals simultaneously

Motivation increases in co-operative efforts because they allow for the simultaneous accomplishment of multiple goals. Social goals, for example, may be accomplished simultaneously with achievement goals. There are a wide variety of social goals that may be achieved simultaneously as part of a co-operative effort.

First, working as part of a co-operative effort enables an individual to make friends and avoid isolation. A central purpose of social behaviour is to form and maintain friendly associations with other people (Baumeister and Leary 1995; Johnson 2003; Taylor *et al.* 2000). The goal of establishing social relationships reveals itself in such motives as the desire to be seen as likeable, to fit in, to conform to the preferences of others, and to gain other people's approval (Johnson and Johnson 2003). Social goals such as making friends and being responsible to others are given high priority by children of virtually all ages (Ford 1992), often even higher than the pursuit of academic goals (Wentzel 1991, 1992). In a meta-analysis of the research, Johnson and Johnson (1989) found that more positive relationships result from co-operative than from competitive (effect size = 0.67) or individualistic (effect size = 0.60) efforts. Co-operative efforts commonly result in higher levels of group cohesion, *esprit de corps* and sense of belonging than do competitive or individualistic experiences (Johnson and Johnson 2003; Johnson and Johnson 1989). Alternatively, social isolation can become a noxious state that creates considerable unhappiness. William James noted that social isolation was the cruelest of tortures, stating, 'To one long pent up on a desert island, the sight of a human footprint or a human form in the distance would be the most tumultuously exciting of experiences' (1890: 430). Thus working co-operatively with others is a very powerful procedure for creating positive relationships and building friendships and reducing social isolation.

Second, social goals can increase motivation to achieve. Although they are valued in their own right, the pursuit of social goals can help organize, direct and empower individuals to achieve more fully (Farmer *et al.* 1991; Schneider *et al.* 1996).

Third, being part of a group generates a motive to maintain membership. Group cohesion may be defined as the mutual attraction among members of a group and the resulting desire to remain in the group. Highly cohesive groups, where members like each other, are characterized by greater ease in setting goals, greater likelihood in achieving those goals, and greater susceptibility to influence by group mates (Johnson and Johnson 2003). As cohesiveness increases, absenteeism and turnover of membership decrease, member commitment to group goals increases, feelings of personal responsibility to the group increase, willingness to take on difficult tasks increases, motivation and persistence in working towards goal achievement increase, satisfaction and morale increase, willingness to endure pain and frustration on behalf of the group increases, willingness to defend the group against external criticism or attack increases, willingness to listen to and be influenced by colleagues increases, commitment to each other's professional growth and success increases, and productivity increases (Johnson and Johnson 1989). Fourth, being part of a co-operative effort provides allies and comrades who may help protect a person from being bullied or scapegoated, and who may provide support and assistance during times of adversity and stress (Johnson and Johnson 1989).

Finally, social and academic goals seem to be intimately linked. Co-operative behaviour (such as being willing to share and promote others' success) is associated positively with academic success. Wentzel (1996), for example, in a study of seventh grade English classes, found that the amount of time students spent on their homework depended on the degree to which they endorsed socially responsible goals, such as helping peers understand their assignments. Increases in effort levels from the sixth to the eighth grade depended on the combined pursuit of social and academic goals (as opposed to pursuing academic goals only).

Teachers may be the key to linking social and academic goals. Willingness of students to form a consensus around the goals of doing well academically and helping peers do well academically depends on their perceptions that teachers care about them both as persons and students (Harter 1996). On the other hand, when students perceive teachers as having failed to provide support, they feel no obligation to behave in socially responsible ways, nor do they particularly enjoy school (Dray *et al.* 1999). Furthermore, teachers who are well liked by students model social motivation, as they are rated as willing to treat children's ideas with respect, give of their time and resources unstintingly, and providing positive encouragement and feedback (Wentzel 1996).

Creating personal benefits as side effects

There are a number of side effects of working co-operatively with others that enhance motivation. One is the impact of co-operative efforts on the self-esteem of participants. The results of the meta-analyses indicated that co-operation promoted higher self-esteem than did competitive (effect size = 0.58) or individualistic (effect size = 0.44) experiences (Johnson and Johnson 1989). Co-operative experiences, furthermore, tended to be related to basic self-acceptance, reflected self-esteem, comparative self-evaluation and competence self-esteem. Competitive experiences tended to be related to conditional self-esteem. Individualistic experiences tended to be related to basic self-rejection. It seems that one's self-view is changed by contributing to the well-being of others and to society at large. Leary *et al.* (1995), furthermore, argue that social relationships are necessary to maintain self-esteem. When individuals are excluded from a group, or when they merely think about doing something that is likely to lead to social rejection (such as causing an accident or cheating on a test), they report feelings of lowered self-esteem. Leary and his colleagues have conducted five experiments supporting their hypothesis that self-esteem is a sociometer – an index of whether individuals feel included or excluded by other people (Leary and Baumeister 2000).

There is some evidence to indicate that engaging in co-operative efforts will improve general psychological health. Five studies have measured directly the relationship between social interdependence and psychological health (see Johnson and Johnson 1989). The samples studied included suburban high school seniors, juvenile and adult prisoners, step-couples, Olympic hockey-players and individuals in the military. The results indicate that co-operative attitudes are correlated highly with a wide variety of indices of psychological health, competitiveness was in some cases positively and in some cases negatively related to psychological health, and individualistic attitudes were related negatively to a wide variety of indices of psychological health.

Finally, the social goals promoted by co-operative experiences include the development of civic values and social responsibility (Johnson *et al.* 2002). Some of the values inherently taught by co-operative efforts are working towards others' success (and the common good), as well as one's own success, facilitating and promoting the well-being of others, taking pride and pleasure in others' success and happiness, viewing other people as potential contributors to one's success, being intrinsically motivated to achieve goals, and viewing one's own and other people's worth as being unconditional.

Creating unique emotions

Motivation increases as emotions are harnessed to support the effort. In co-operative efforts there are emotions possible that cannot be achieved any other way. Group celebrations are qualitatively different from individual celebrations. Belonging, being part of a group effort, sharing important experiences, for example, result in emotions that are unique to group situations. In co-operative situations, feelings of success are shared and pride is taken in other members' accomplishments as well as one's own. There is a mutual investment in each other. These emotions, and the promise of such emotions, help motivate efforts within co-operation.

Cathexis

Motivation increases as positive cathexis is created from working together for mutual benefit. Cathexis is an investment of psychological energy in objects outside of oneself, such as friends, family and work (Deutsch 1949a). Cathexis may be positive or negative. Deutsch posits that in co-operative situations, effective actions are cathected positively while within competitive situations actions are cathected negatively. People do react positively when they make progress towards goals and negatively when they fail to reach their goals (Diener *et al.* 1999). Koestner *et al.* (2002) reviewed nine studies and found an overall effect size of 0.61, indicating that individuals report significantly more positive affect and less negative affect over time as they make progress in achieving their goals. They also conducted two experiments that found a significant relationship between progress in achieving goals and positive affect over time; progress in achieving goals was related negatively to negative affect. Since more progress tends to be made in co-operative than in competitive or individualistic situations, there tend to be more positive emotions by more individuals in co-operative situations (Johnson and Johnson 1989). There is also considerable evidence that the positive emotions generated when individuals work co-operatively for mutual benefit generalize into increased liking for each other.

Inducing commitment to imposed goals

There is reason to believe that it is easier to increase motivation within a group than in an individual setting. Members of groups that are evaluated as a unit become more highly motivated than do groups in which individuals are evaluated as individuals. The classic studies by Kurt Lewin and his associates (Johnson and Johnson 2003) indicate that discussions in co-operative groups that resulted in public commitment to the groups' goals resulted in greater goal achievement than did individualistic interventions.

Increasing perceived probability of success

Within co-operative efforts individuals' expectations for success typically go up. The substitutability inherent in co-operative situations means that individuals may specialize according to their expertise and each completes his or her part of the task, thereby increasing the likelihood of success. In doing so, individuals must trust each other to complete their part of the task and responsibly complete their share of the task. The overall result is to perceive considerably more resources being available to achieve the goal. The inducibility, furthermore, ensures that collaborators are quite open to being influenced so they can co-ordinate their efforts effectively. Finally, the positive cathexis results in collaborators liking each other and committing themselves to each other's well-being and success. The combination of these psychological processes results in the expected probability of success being higher in co-operative than in competitive or individualistic situations.

Differential benefit

Negative interdependence promotes working against other individuals to create a differential benefit where, when one person wins, the others lose. By definition, when one person achieves his or her goal, all others with whom the person is competitively linked fail to achieve their goals (Deutsch 1949a). Thus individuals have a negatively linked fate where they win or lose depending on how their performance compares to the performances of the other participants. Actions which increase the likelihood that a person will win decrease the likelihood of winning for all other participants. Competition may affect participants' motivation in a number of ways.

First, competition focuses individuals on winning rather than on the intrinsic qualities of the task. Since winning is external to the task, motivation tends to be extrinsic. Second, competition is motivating only if a person believes he or she has a chance to win. When the person believes there is little or no chance to win, the goal is devalued and motivation is non-existent. Third, in competitive situations social and academic motives tend to be contradictory and operate against each other. The desire to be accepted by and friends with one's peers is directly opposed to consistent winning or losing. Wentzel (1996) found that the pursuit of social goals was unrelated to performance goals, and Covington (1992) concluded that performance goals are inherently contrary to positive social goals, as competition involves sabotage, deception and a reluctance to co-operate. The contradictory pressures by various motives will tend to reduce the actual achievement-oriented behaviour of individuals in competitive situations. Fourth, in competition the need to maintain one's self-esteem enhances the motivation to win. Because competition is based on contingent self-esteem where if you win you are worthwhile and if you lose you are worthless, individuals can become highly motivated to win in order to maintain their sense of self-worth. Thus one's identity is based on one's relative performance ranking.

Finally, whenever students engage in competitive efforts, for example, they learn the values of being extrinsically motivated to win (not mastery or excellence), succeeding at other people's expense, opposing and obstructing the success of others, feeling joy and pride in one's wins and others' losses, and viewing one's work as conditional and contingent on whether one won or lost.

Self-benefit

No interdependence promotes working alone for self-benefit only. By definition, when one person achieves his or her goal, the goal achievement of all others in the situation is unaffected. Thus individuals recognize they have an individual fate unrelated to the fates of others where the achievement of one's goals depends solely on one's performance. An individualistic goal structure affects participants' motivations in a number of ways.

First, individualistic learning is often powered by extrinsic rewards (Skinner 1968). In addition, the value of an individual goal may include attainment value (i.e. the personal importance of doing well on the task), intrinsic value (i.e. the enjoyment the person receives from engaging in the activity or the person's subjective interest in the subject), utility value (i.e. the ways a task relates to current and future goals) and cost (i.e. the negative aspects of engaging in the task, such as performance anxiety, fear of both failure and success, amount of effort needed, the lost opportunities resulting from engaging in the activities and so on). Second, individualistic goals are motivating only if they are achievable with one's own resources. If the goals seem too difficult, motivation decreases.

Third, in individualistic situations social and academic motives tend to be contradictory and to operate against each other. The desire to be accepted by, and friends with, one's peers is directly opposed to working alone. Affiliation needs and the desire to be involved in interaction and relationships with others may operate directly against achievement in individualistic situations, as loneliness often accompanies long-term individualistic efforts. The contradictory pressures by various motives will tend to reduce the actual achievement-oriented behaviour of individuals in individualistic situations.

Finally, the values taught inherently by individualistic experiences include focusing on one's self-interest, viewing success as gaining extrinsic awards depending on one's own efforts, taking personal pride and pleasure in succeeding, viewing other people as irrelevant, and viewing one's work as being based on the characteristics that help the person succeed.

Efficacy

In addition to the value of the goals, motivation is influenced by the determination of whether the goal can be achieved using current resources. That is, whether the ability and effort that is available is sufficient to organize and execute a given course of action to solve a problem or accomplish a task. Efficacy is determined largely by the attributions individuals make to explain their actions. In making attributions individuals focus typically on the ability and effort available to contribute towards goal achievement and by past history of success on similar tasks.

Depending on the type of interdependence, a different form of efficacy is created (see Tables 9.2 and 9.3). Co-operation tends to result in joint

Table 9.2 Efficacy and motivation

Co-operative	Competitive	Individualistic
Advantages of joint efficacy	Problems with differential efficacy	Advantages of self-efficacy
Ability	Ability	Ability
Resource management	Contingent self-esteem	
	Defensive avoidance	
Effort	Effort	Effort
		Transformation into competition

Table 9.3 Expectations for successful achievement

	Co-operative	Competitive	Individualistic
Own abilities	+	+	+
Other's abilities	+	−	0
Own efforts	+	+	+
Other's efforts	+	−	0
Previous history	+ or −	+ or −	+ or −
	Joint efficacy	Differential efficacy	Self-efficacy

efficacy, competition tends to result in differential efficacy, and individual-istic efforts tend to result in self-efficacy. Assessments of one's own and others' abilities may be monopolistic (i.e. single-dimensional focus) or multi-dimensional (i.e. focus on many relevant and related abilities). The salient information for determining efficacy in co-operative situations is how much effort oneself and the other group members are willing to commit and how able members are to complete the task and work together effectively (effort focus, self-group comparison). In competition the salient information is how much effort one is willing to commit and how one's ability compares with the ability of the other individuals involved (ability focus, self–other comparison). In individualistic situations the salient information is how much effort one is willing to commit and whether one has the ability to improve on past performances (effort focus, comparison with own past performances).

Co-operation

Joint efficacy

Co-operation results in joint (and self-) efficacy. Since the desired goal is achievable only through co-operative efforts, individuals have to work together to secure what they cannot accomplish on their own. Joint effi-cacy may be defined as collaborators' shared beliefs in their collective power to solve a problem or accomplish a task. Perceived joint efficacy influences the nature of the goals the group strives to achieve, how well group members use their resources, how much effort they put into their group endeavour, their persistence when confronted with difficulties and forcible opposition, and their potential discouragement resulting from taking on difficult tasks (Bandura 2000). In addition, the greater the per-ceived collective efficacy, the higher the groups' motivational investment in their undertakings, the stronger their staying power in the face of impediments and setbacks, and the greater their success in achieving their mutual goals (Mullen and Cooper 1994).

Based on perceptions of previous performances in similar situations, in co-operative situations joint efficacy depends on an assessment of (1) one's own abilities, (2) the abilities of collaborators, (3) one's own effort, and (4) the efforts of collaborators. The greater one's own and collaborators' abili-ties and the more effort oneself and collaborators are willing to exert, the higher the joint efficacy and expectations for success.

Multi-dimensional perceptions of ability

The abilities available to contribute to goal achievement directly affect joint efficacy and the expectations of success. In co-operative situations, success is attributed partially to the combined abilities of all group members. Not only do members of co-operative groups attribute performance to ability, they attribute as high and even higher abilities to their collaborators as they do to themselves. Joint abilities tend to be more than the sum of individual collaborators' abilities due to their complementarity, substitutability and synergistic qualities.

Assessments of ability are based on perceptions of two types of ability: (1) those directly relevant to achieving the goal, and (2) those connected abilities that may be tangentially related to goal accomplishment or required for co-ordination of efforts and organization of the joint work. In co-operative situations, therefore, collaborators tend to have a multi-dimensional view of their own and each other's competencies. One group member may have directly relevant abilities but no related abilities, while another member may have few relevant abilities but many related abilities. Individuals who are low in relevant abilities can promote the productivity of more able collaborators and contribute to the effectiveness of the group. Thus, even when their task performances are markedly discrepant, members tend to view themselves and their collaborators as being similar in overall ability and deservingness of reward (Ames and Felker 1979; Ames and McKelvie 1982). Co-operation seems to create a climate for perceived similarity where peers (and superiors) are less likely to translate performance differences into ability differences and all group members may feel equally satisfied with their level of performance (Ames 1981).

RESOURCE MANAGEMENT

The complexity of co-operative efforts directly affects the perceived efficacy and expectations of success. Because of the number of people involved, co-operative situations have a complexity and richness that is absent in competitive and individualistic efforts. Each group member has different levels of directly relevant abilities. In a maths class, for example, some members may find maths easy while other members may find it difficult. It takes more than a conceptual understanding of maths, a good memory and calculating ability, however, to complete maths assignments co-operatively. The efforts of group members have to be organized and co-ordinated, relationships among members have to be effectively managed, and conflicts have to be resolved. Resource management becomes a concern and members must consider how to pool their resources, allocate responsibilities, and use external resources for the purpose of accomplishing the task (cf. Johnson and Johnson 2003).

Joint efforts

The effort available to contribute to goal achievement directly affects joint efficacy and the expectations of success. In co-operative situations the effort available includes one's own and the effort of one's collaborators. The joint efforts of collaborators tend to be more than the sum of the individual efforts due to the complementarity, substitutability and synergistic qualities of their efforts. The knowledge that there is a team effort in achieving the goal provides added confidence that the group will be successful.

Members of co-operative groups tend to view the group's success as the result of their own and their collaborators' efforts (e.g. Garibaldi 1979). The more co-operative individuals' attitudes, the more they believe that effort (rather than luck) determines their success (Johnson et al. 1978). Thus within co-operative situations individuals tend to attribute success to personal, recurring and controllable causes.

Members of unsuccessful co-operative groups tend to attribute failure to task difficulty and bad luck (e.g. Bukowski and Moore 1980) and to a lack of effort by group members (e.g. Gill 1980). Because insufficient effort is perceived to be a controllable cause, it is an adaptive attribution in the face of failure and leads to greater future persistence and performance on the task. Individuals who attribute failure to insufficient effort on the part of one's collaborators, furthermore, can be optimistic about future success since collaborators can be induced to try harder (Deutsch 1949b). There is also evidence that co-operators tend to feel less responsible for their outcome when the group fails, thus decreasing the possibility of demoralization.

One reflection of the effort exerted to achieve a goal is time on-task. Individuals working co-operatively tend to spend more time on-task than do individuals working competitively (ES = 0.76) or individualistically (ES = 1.17) (Johnson and Johnson 1989).

Finally, Johnson et al. (1985) found that co-operative experiences, compared with individualistic ones, promoted greater self-efficacy. Bandura (1977) defined self-efficacy as individuals' confidence in their ability to organize and execute a given course of action to solve a problem or accomplish a task. Self-efficacy is important for several reasons. When goals are self-set, people with high self-efficacy set higher goals than do people with lower self-efficacy, are more committed to goal achievement, and are more optimistic about achieving the goals. They are also more committed to assigned goals, find and use more effective and more strategic task strategies to attain the goals, engage in more constructive actions, persevere, respond with resilience, engage in more helping and sharing actions, and respond more positively to negative feedback than do people with low self-efficacy (Locke and Latham 1990).

Competitive goal structure

Differential efficacy

The salient information for determining differential efficacy and subjective probability of success in competition is how one's abilities and efforts compare with the abilities and efforts of the other individuals involved. Differential efficacy may be defined as individuals' confidence that, compared to their competitors, they are more able to organize and execute a given course of action to achieve a goal and are willing to commit more effort in doing so. The current assessment is perceived within the context of previous performance in similar situations. When one perceives that he or she has higher ability and is exerting more effort than others, and the greater one's past success in similar situations, the greater the differential efficacy and the expectations for success.

Competition has a number of important characteristics that may influence efficacy in achievement situations. First, social comparison is required whether all competitors wish it or not. Without social comparison, there can be no competition. Thus there are no fixed standards for achievement, only relative ones dependent on the performances of others. Second, rewards are restricted and given to only one or a few winners. An Olympic gold medal is prized because only one person in the world can win it. All others lose. While there are numerous merit scholars, they represent only a very small percentage of the overall student population. Without restriction of rewards there would be no competition. Third, the probability of success is uncertain because what is needed for a win depends on the performance of the other competitors. Sometimes one can win a marathon with a time of 2:12; at other times a person must run a 2:09 to win. It depends on who else is in the race and whether or not they are having a good day. Fourth, competition may result in *schadenfreude*, where the suffering and misfortunes of others creates feelings of pleasure. *Schadenfreude* literally denotes joy with the shame of another (Ben-Zev 1992; Smith *et al.* 1999). This means that competitors will take joy in defeating one, and one is expected to feel shame if one loses. Fifth, there is evidence that when someone fails in a competition, observers may feel contempt. Contempt tends to be elicited in situations where one needs to feel stronger, more intelligent, more civilized, or in some way better than another. The result of these factors may be the awareness that on any day one can be defeated, which will result in being devalued by others and personal feelings of shame. The feelings of vulnerability and anxiety interfere with achieving the desired goals.

Differential ability focus

In competitions individuals work against each other, and therefore perception of efficacy and the probability of success of one individual is reduced by the presence of capable others. Generally, it is assumed that when individuals perceive their task-related ability to be greater than their competitors, they will have a high sense of efficacy and subjective probability of success, and when individuals perceive their task-related ability to be less than their competitors, they will have low efficacy and a subjective probability of success.

There is a marked difference in the attributions concerning ability made by winners and losers. On one hand, winners tend to attribute their success to superior ability (Ames 1984) and to attribute the failure of others to lack of ability. Losers, on the other hand, tend to attribute failure to external factors such as luck. If failure cannot reasonably be attributed to external factors, however, competitors tend to view their failure as being caused by lack of ability (Ames 1984). The success of the winners, furthermore, is often attributed to situational factors. Competitive attitudes tend to be significantly related to believing that luck and other external factors (rather than one's own efforts) determine success (Johnson *et al.* 1978), probably because in most competitions there are many more losers than winners. This attribution pattern tends to result in over-confidence and lack of motivation on the part of habitual winners, and under-confidence and lack of motivation on the part of habitual losers.

The perception of ability in competition is affected by three basic dynamics. First, there is constant social comparison (whether or not competitors want it) aimed at ensuring competitors evaluate their ability relative to the ability of others (Ames and Ames 1984; Nicholls 1989). Thus competition tends to increase individuals' tendencies to assess their ability, and when children were asked what they were thinking after a performance, those who were competing displayed a stronger ability focus than children performing alone (Ames 1984). Competition tends to make differential achievement salient, and thereby contribute to an ability focus and fixed perceptions of one's own and others' abilities.

Second, competition tends to result in a monopolistic focus on task-related ability on which to base expectations for success. On a maths test, for example, expectations for success tend to be based on a comparison of one's own and others' maths ability – no other abilities tend to be relevant or related. Third, in competition perceived distribution of one's own and others' abilities becomes polarized and dichotomized. The ability of high and low performers is perceived to be significantly different. You are a winner or a loser, but not in between. Both experimental and field studies have shown that individuals' perceptions of their own and others' ability become dichotomized (i.e. high vs. low) when social comparison is emphasized. Perceptions of ability become highly differentiated by superiors as well as peers.

The focus on differential abilities in competitive situations tends to result in contingent self-esteem and defensive avoidance of future competitions.

CONTINGENT SELF-ESTEEM

The monopolistic focus on ability and the forced social comparison inherent within competitive situations result in individuals making self-ascriptions of high versus low ability contingent on their success or failure. Self-ascriptions of ability have been found to co-vary with success (winning) and failure (losing) (Ames 1981; Halperin and Abrams 1978). Success (relative to others) leads to inferences of high ability and failure (relative to others) to inferences of low ability.

In addition, competition tends to result in self-aggrandizement and self-disparagement. A number of studies have found evidence of self-aggrandizement as competitive winners consistently give themselves higher rewards than they give to losers or other winners (Ames 1992). College-age males have been found to over-emphasize the contribution of ability to their own successful outcome in a competitive game situation.

There is also evidence of self-disparagement in competition, as the self-evaluations of losers become increasingly negative (Ames 1992). For example, losers' allocation of reward to themselves versus to winners tends to be more discrepant in competitive than in non-competitive settings and individuals give themselves substantially less reward when they are the losers than they give to others who are losers. Losing seems to have a very personal impact on self-worth that results in self-devaluation and self-disparagement. These effects appear to be unique to competitive situations. When failure accompanies losing to another, self-disparagement seems to follow.

DEFENSIVE AVOIDANCE

Since only one or a few individuals can win in a competition, the monopolistic focus on task-related ability tends to demoralize most people. The more able one's competitors are perceived to be, the more discouraged and hopeless one tends to feel. The discouragement and hopelessness result in a low expectation for success. Low expectations for success, in turn, lead to ego-defensive avoidance of competition. If individuals lose in competitive situations, they tend to repress thoughts about the task and avoid engaging in the task in the future in order not to reawaken the embarrassment and failure experienced. As failure becomes repetitive and as the rewards for success increase, achievement motivation decreases.

If one does not believe one can win, the only option is to avoid the embarrassment and humiliation of losing. This can be done by selecting unrealistic difficult tasks, not trying ('failure with honour') and procrastination. If competition cannot be avoided, considerable anxiety may occur. Individuals will focus on their perceived incompetence, producing negative affect and interference with their capacity to employ adaptive learning or problem-solving strategies (Diener and Dweck 1978).

Effort expended to win

No matter how hard one tries in a competition, if one does not have more knowledge or skill than the other participants, one will usually lose. In competitive situations effort, therefore, becomes of secondary importance in estimating differential efficacy and expectations for success. Once a hierarchy of ability is established, however, the effort exerted within competitive situations is affected. Habitual winners, who believe that winning is almost certain, may exert only enough effort to win and no more. Habitual losers, who believe they cannot win no matter how hard they try, may exert minimal or no effort. Lepley (1937), for example, placed two rats in a runway and rewarded the faster runner. He found that the slower runner quickly quit running at all, whereas the faster runner maintained the speed that led to success, with little evidence of enhancement of speed. Thus when the same individuals compete against each other again and again, stable patterns of winning and losing may develop and the level of individuals' performance may be reduced. The winners may exert only enough effort to win and the losers will stop trying. Thus the performance of both the winners and losers may decrease.

Individualistic goal structure

Advantages of self-efficacy

Individualistic situations are assumed to promote self-efficacy. Self-efficacy may be defined as individuals' confidence in their ability to organize and execute a given course of action to achieve a goal. In an individualistic situation the probability of success of an individual is neither diminished nor enhanced by the presence of capable or incapable others. Success or failure is perceived to depend on one's own task-related abilities and efforts. If one has the relevant abilities and tries hard enough, he or she will succeed. In a review of literature, Bandura (2000) concludes that perceived self-efficacy results in more strategic (vs. erratic) thinking, optimism (vs. pessimism), constructive courses of action chosen to pursue, challenging goals, greater commitment, more effort, greater expectations for success, perseverance in the face of obstacles, resilience to adversity, lower levels of stress and depression in coping with taxing environmental demands, and greater goal accomplishment. In addition, self-efficacy tends to promote a prosocial orientation characterized by co-operativeness, helpfulness and sharing.

Ability attributions

Individuals often select tasks they believe match their ability. A high level of self-efficacy and a high subjective probability of success result. When required to achieve a goal that is beyond their ability to do so, individuals may make only token efforts to succeed.

Effort attributions

When the goal is to improve on one's previous performance, effort becomes the dominant influence on efficacy and expectations for success (Covington 1992). A self–self temporal comparison (i.e. comparing present with past performance) determines the perceived difficulty of the task and a focus on effort rather than ability. Ames (1984) found that children performing in an individualistic structure reported significantly more effort-related cognitions than did children in competitive situations. Moreover, these children reported significantly more self-instructional and self-monitoring types of thoughts (e.g. 'I will work carefully ... I will take my time ... I will make a plan ...'). Although the children were focused on their efforts, their reports also reflected an active search for ways to maintain or improve their performance through self-planning. When the goal involves a self-challenge (e.g. 'Try to do your best, try to solve as many problems as you can') or provides an opportunity for self-improvement (e.g. 'Can you set a new personal best?'), success and failure outcomes tend to elicit effort attributions.

Transformation into competition

In our culture, individualistic situations can be quickly transformed into competitive ones. In many cases, individuals begin making self–other comparisons rather than self–self comparisons. Consequently, individualistic structures often result in patterns of attribution (Nicholls 1989), affect and attitudes that are similar to competition.

Intrinsic and extrinsic motivation

Positive, negative and no interdependence result in different levels of intrinsic and extrinsic motivation. Intrinsic motivation may be defined as motivation that is inherent in the activity and its perceived meaning. It is interest in and enjoyment of an activity for its own sake (Deci and Ryan 1985). Learning for the joy of it, to benefit others, and as the result of meaningful feedback is intrinsic to learning activities. Extrinsic motivation may be defined as motivation for outcomes separate from and following the activity. Individuals engage in activities for instrumental or other reasons, such as receiving a reward. Winning (beating other individuals or teams) and performing up to external criteria are extrinsic to learning activities.

Demonstrating the impact of social interdependence on individuals' intrinsic enjoyment of achievement-related activities has both theoretical and practical significance. Theoretically, it would create a conceptual link between the two literatures. Practically, it has direct implications for educational, occupational and sport settings.

Co-operation

Co-operation tends to promote intrinsic motivation. Co-operative experiences, compared with individualistic ones, tends to result in (1) more motivation to do work because it is interesting, fun and enjoyable (Garibaldi 1979; Johnson et al. 1976), and (2) greater internal pressure to succeed. The more co-operative individuals' attitudes, the more they see themselves as being intrinsically motivated, persevering in pursuit of goals, believing that their own efforts determine their success, wanting to be high achievers, and believing that learning new ideas is important and enjoyable.

Co-operation involves striving to reach mastery goals. There is evidence that mastery goals promote challenge appraisals, encourage task absorption, and support self-determination and feelings of autonomy (factors facilitative of intrinsic interest and enjoyment) (Butler 1987; Dweck 1991). Rawsthorne and Elliot (1999) found in a meta-analysis of intrinsic motivation studies that the pursuit of mastery goals produced significantly more free-choice persistence at the task (ES = 0.17) and self-report interest and enjoyment (ES = 0.36) than did the pursuit of performance goals. In other words, co-operation produces more intrinsic motivation than does competition.

It is the nature of co-operation that group members strive to achieve for (1) own well-being, (2) the well-being of others, and (3) the common good. Intrinsic motivation tends to result when individuals see their own achievement as of possible service to others. Weiseltier (cited by Kruglanski 1978) found more intrinsic motivation among medical individuals who wished to help cure cancer patients than among medical individuals who wanted a high income. The study of medicine seemed inherently worthwhile to the former but not to the latter.

In co-operative situations, meaningful feedback is supplied by both collaborators and superiors (Johnson and Johnson 1989). Meaningful feedback signifies the extent to which individuals are performing competently the behaviours required by the current task. Such feedback tends to increase intrinsic motivation. Individuals may need to be able to assess how well they are performing to remain intrinsically interested in an activity.

Finally, working co-operatively with others tends to amplify the emotions experienced while working on a task. Group enjoyment of an activity, for example, is more powerful than individual enjoyment (otherwise we would always play tennis alone).

Competition

The oppositional interaction resulting from a competitive goal structure tends to result in extrinsic motivation based on winning and benefiting at the expense of others. There is evidence that the more competitive individuals' attitudes are, the more they see themselves as being extrinsically motivated (Johnson and Johnson 1983). In competition, individuals place more value on winning than on performing a task well (Ames 1984; Johnson and Johnson 1999), and individuals' attention is focused on their own ability to perform or win rather than on 'how' to do the task (Nicholls 1989). Pritchard et al. (1977) found that competition decreased intrinsic motivation. Face-to-face competition has been found to decrease subjects' intrinsic motivation and increase their extrinsic motivation even when there were no rewards involved. There is evidence, furthermore, that competition is a negative incentive, not unlike electric shock, so that individuals may learn to escape from or terminate competition through instrumental responses.

Motivation may be oriented towards the attainment of success or the avoidance of failure. Competition is based on performance goals, where each participant strives to outperform all other participants, participants are ranked from highest to lowest, and a normative evaluation system is used. In competition, however, there are winners and losers. Some participants enter the competition with the expectation of winning; others may enter the competition afraid they will lose. The research on performance goals, therefore, has differentiated between performance-approach situations in which the goal is focused on the attainment of favourable judgements of normative competence (i.e. potential positive outcomes), and performance-avoidance situations in which the goal is focused on avoiding unfavourable judgements of normative competence (i.e. potential negative outcomes) (Elliot 1997). Elliot and his associates argue that viewing the task as a challenge elicits feelings of excitement, and encourages cognitive and affective immersion in the activity. On the other hand, performance-avoidance goals may produce threat appraisals and anxiety.

Performance-avoidance goals are therefore expected to produce lower intrinsic motivation.

There is evidence that performance goals tend to promote evaluative pressures and anxiety (factors opposed to intrinsic motivation) (Ryan and Stiller 1991). Rawsthorne and Elliot (1999) conducted a meta-analysis of twenty-three studies on intrinsic motivation and found that performance-avoidance goals (compared to mastery goals) had a significant undermining effect on free-choice persistence (ES = −0.46) and self-reports of interest and enjoyment (ES = −0.29). There were no significant differences between mastery goals and performance-approach goals for either the free-choice persistence or self-report measures (ES = −0.04 for both). Performance goals, therefore, tend to produce a larger undermining effect when experimental procedures focus participants' attention on the possibility of a negative performance outcome, thereby inducing a performance-avoiding orientation.

Rawsthorne and Elliot (1999) also found that when participants were provided with positive, competence-confirming feedback, performance goals undermined free-choice persistence on a task (ES = −0.26) but did not have a significant effect on feelings of interest and enjoyment (ES = −0.13). They concluded that, compared to individuals with mastery goals, people pursuing performance goals were likely to persist at the task out of a sense of pressure and urgency rather than continued interest and enjoyment and likely experienced this state as psychologically aversive.

Individualistic efforts

Individualistic efforts may result in either intrinsic or extrinsic motivation. Like co-operation, individualistic efforts may be based on mastery goals, which tend to promote intrinsic motivation. Most often in educational and career settings, however, individuals engage in individualistic activities for instrumental or other reasons, such as receiving a reward. Individualistic efforts are promoted by external reward systems, such as programmed instruction and behaviour modification. When external rewards are present, motivation is extrinsic. The absence of the interpersonal influences found in co-operation, furthermore, tends to increase the likelihood that motivation will be extrinsic. In order to earn a reward, individuals strive to meet a standard of performance set by their superiors, such as a sales quota or requirements for A level work.

Epistemic curiosity and continuing motivation

Epistemic curiosity and continuing motivation are related in that the arousal of the former leads to the latter. Epistemic curiosity is motivation to search actively for more information concerning the topic being studied or discussed. The major cause of epistemic curiosity is academic disagreement and conflict among individuals (Johnson and Johnson 1989). The research indicates that within a co-operative situation, disagreement over information, conclusions, theories and opinions tends to lead to uncertainty, epistemic curiosity and a re-evaluation of one's conclusions. Within a competitive situation, such academic conflicts tend to result in uncertainty, a closed-minded justification of one's own conclusions, and a derogation of opposing points of view. Within an individualistic situation there is no opportunity for disagreement, and therefore initial conclusions are not challenged and fixation on initial impressions is common.

Continuing motivation is motivation to seek further information about the topic being studied in the future. Thomas Allen (1979) in his dissertation monitored three fifth and three sixth grade science classes in an attempt to identify variables that affect students' willingness to pursue classroom material on their own time (i.e. continuing motivation). The 168 students were both observed during class and completed a series of questionnaires. Three analyses were performed on the data. The first analysis found no strong mediating effects of attributions. The second analysis found no significant influence of achievement orientation on continuing motivation. The third analysis found that the science students who worked in co-operative learning groups demonstrated more continuing motivation than did students who were taught with a lecture-competition format. Similarly, Gunderson and Johnson (1980) found co-operative learning experiences to be related to increases in continuing motivation.

While co-operation may result in increased continuing motivation, the combination of co-operation and intellectual conflict has very powerful effects on epistemic curiosity and many other positive outcomes (Johnson and Johnson, 1979, 1989, 1995).

Commitment to goal achievement

> The reason we were so good, and continued to be so good, was because he (Coach Joe Paterno) forces you to develop an inner love among the players. It is much harder to give up on your buddy, than it is to give up on your coach. I really believe that over the years the teams I played on were almost unbeatable in tight situations. When we needed to get that six inches we got it because of our love for each other.
>
> (Dr Dave Joyner describing his experiences playing football for Penn State University)

Commitment to accomplishing goals is necessary to sustain motivation over a period of weeks, months, perhaps years. Individuals need to be committed to the short-term and long-term goals of the organizations to which they belong. Commitment to goal achievement is reflected in a cluster of variables including willingness to exert effort to achieve the goal (already discussed), belief in the value of the goal (already discussed), liking for the task, liking for the experience of working on the task, involvement in the task, believing success is important, spending time on the task, and persisting in trying to achieve the goal.

Co-operative, compared with competitive and individualistic experiences, have been found to promote more positive attitudes towards the task being worked on and the experience of doing so (effect sizes = 0.57 and 0.42 respectively) (Johnson and Johnson 1989). A number of studies, furthermore, found that most individuals prefer co-operative over competitive and individualistic experiences. Individuals, in co-operative compared with competitive and individualistic situations, were typically more involved in activities and tasks, attached greater importance to success and engaged in more on-task behaviour and less apathetic, off-task, disruptive behaviours (Johnson and Johnson 1989). Attitudes towards co-operation have been found to be related positively to liking to persevere in achieving goals. Overall, these results indicate that individuals tend to be more committed to goals when they work co-operatively than when they work competitively or individualistically.

Enhancing motivation through co-operative learning

Students' motivation to enquire, reason, learn and apply is increased when educators ensure that classrooms and schools are dominated by co-operative rather than competitive or individualistic learning. Co-operative learning is the instructional use of small groups so that students work together to maximize their own and each other's learning (Johnson *et al.* 2002). Any assignment in any curriculum for any age student can be done co-operatively. There are three types of co-operative learning: formal, informal and co-operative base groups.

Formal co-operative learning consists of students working together, for one class period to several weeks, to achieve shared learning goals and complete jointly specific tasks and assignments (Johnson *et al.* 2002). In formal co-operative learning groups teachers:

1   Make a number of pre-instructional decisions. Teachers specify the objectives for the lesson (both academic and social skills) and decide on the size of groups, the method of assigning students to groups, the roles students will be assigned, the materials needed to conduct the lesson, and the way the room will be arranged.

2   Explain the task and the positive interdependence. A teacher clearly

defines the assignment, teaches the required concepts and strategies, specifies the positive interdependence and individual accountability, gives the criteria for success, and explains the expected social skills to be used.

3   Monitor students' learning and intervene within the groups to provide task assistance or to increase students' interpersonal and group skills.

4   Assess students' learning and helping students process how well their groups functioned. Students' learning is carefully assessed. Members of the learning groups then discuss how effectively they worked together and how they can improve in the future.

Informal co-operative learning consists of students working together to achieve a joint learning goal in temporary, *ad hoc* groups that last from a few minutes to one class period (Johnson *et al.* 2002). During a lecture, demonstration or film, informal co-operative learning can be used to focus student attention on the material to be learned, set a mood conducive to learning, help set expectations as to what will be covered in a class session, ensure that students cognitively process and rehearse the material being taught, summarize what was learned and pre-cue the next session, and provide closure to an instructional session. The procedure for using informal co-operative learning during a lecture entails having three- to five-minute focused discussions before and after the lecture (i.e. bookends) and two- to three-minute interspersing pair discussions throughout the lecture.

Co-operative base groups are long-term, heterogeneous co-operative learning groups with stable membership whose primary responsibilities are to provide support, encouragement and assistance to make academic progress and develop cognitively and socially in healthy ways as well as holding each other accountable for striving to learn (Johnson *et al.* 2002). Typically, co-operative base groups (1) are heterogeneous in membership, (2) meet regularly (e.g. daily or biweekly), and (3) last for the duration of the semester, year, or until all members have graduated. When students know that the base group will stay together for some time, they become committed to find ways to motivate and encourage their group mates and solve any problems in working together. The procedure for using base groups is to assign students to base groups of three to four members, for them to meet at the beginning and end of each class session (or week) to complete academic tasks such as checking each members' homework, routine tasks such as taking attendance, and personal support tasks such as listening sympathetically to personal problems or providing guidance for writing a paper.

These three types of co-operative learning may be used together. A typical class session may begin with a base group meeting, followed by a short lecture in which informal co-operative learning is used. The lecture is followed by a formal co-operative learning lesson. Near the end of the class session another short lecture may be delivered with the use of informal co-operative learning. The class ends with a base group meeting.

Conclusions and summary

On 15 July 1982, Don Bennett, a Seattle businessman, was the first amputee ever to climb Mount Rainier (reported in Kouzes and Posner 1987). He climbed 14,410 feet on one leg and two crutches. It took him five days. When asked to state the most important lesson he learned from doing so, without hesitation he said, *'You can't do it alone.'* When asked to clarify he replied that during one very difficult trek across an ice field in Don Bennett's hop to the top of Mount Rainer, his daughter stayed by his side for four hours and with each new hop told him, *'You can do it, Dad. You're the best dad in the world. You can do it, Dad.'* He climbed Mount Rainier on the strength and support of the people who cared about him.

Motivation is reflected in the effort individuals commit purposely to strive to achieve goals they perceive as being meaningful and worthwhile. Motivation is aimed at achieving goals, it is fuelled by emotions, and it has social origins. Motivation, therefore, may be seen as occurring within the context of social interdependence. Social interdependence theory posits that individuals' goals may be positively interdependent, negatively interdependent, or independent. The interdependence among goals determines the interaction pattern among the individuals involved, and the interaction patterns in turn determine the outcomes of the situation; that is, the degree to which the goals are achieved.

The motivational system promoted within co-operative situations includes the value and meaning of the goals being promoted through striving for mutual benefit, seeing the ability to achieve the goal being based on joint efficacy, intrinsic motivation, high epistemic curiosity and continuing interest in achievement, high commitment to achieve, and high persistence. The motivational system promoted within competitive situations includes the value of the goal being determined by differential benefit, seeing the ability to achieve the goal based on differential efficacy, extrinsic motivation to win, low epistemic curiosity and a lack of continuing interest to achieve, a relative lack of commitment to achieving, and relatively low task persistence by most individuals. The motivational system promoted within individualistic situations includes the value of the goal being determined by self-benefit, seeing the ability to achieve the goal based on self-efficacy, extrinsic motivation to meet pre-set criteria of excellence, low epistemic curiosity and continuing interest to achieve, relatively low commitment to achieving, and relatively low task persistence by most individuals.

Co-operation may be implemented in classrooms and schools through co-operative learning. There are three types of co-operative learning: formal co-operative learning, informal co-operative learning, and co-operative base groups. Together they provide a system for instructional organization and design and classroom management that ensures a high level of positive motivation by most students most of the time.

References

Allen, T. (1979) 'Students' predisposition toward achievement, their causal attributions of success and failure, and classroom structural variables as predictors of continuing motivation', unpublished doctoral dissertation, University of Minnesota, Minneapolis.

Ames, C. (1981) 'Competitive versus cooperative reward structures: the influence of individual and group performance factors on achievement attributions and affect', *American Educational Research Journal*, 18: 273–87.

—— (1984) 'Competitive, cooperative, and individualistic goal structures: a cognitive-motivational analysis', in R. Ames and C. Ames (eds) *Research on Motivation in Education*, Vol. 1 (177–208), New York: Academic Press.

—— (1992) 'Achievement goals and the classroom motivational climate', in D. Schunk and J. Meece (eds) *Student Perceptions in the Classroom* (327–48), Hillsdale, NJ: Lawrence Erlbaum.

Ames, C. and Ames, R. (1984) 'Systems of student and teacher motivation: toward a qualitative definition', *Journal of Educational Psychology*, 76: 535–56.

Ames, C. and Archer, J. (1987) 'Mothers' belief about the role of ability and effort in school learning', *Journal of Educational Psychology*, 79: 409–14.

Ames, C. and Felker, D. (1979) 'An examination of children's attributions and achievement-related evaluations in competitive, cooperative, and individualistic reward structures', *Journal of Educational Psychology*, 71: 413–20.

Ames, C. and McKelvie, S. (1982, April) 'Evaluation of students' achievement behavior within cooperative and competitive reward structures', paper presented at the annual meeting of the American Educational Research Association, New York.

Archer-Kath, J., Johnson, D.W. and Johnson, R. (1994) 'Individual versus group feedback in cooperative groups', *Journal of Social Psychology*, 134: 681–94.

Asch, S. (1952) *Social Psychology*, Englewood Cliffs, NJ: Prentice-Hall.

Atkinson, J.W. (1964) *An Introduction to Achievement Motivation*, New York: Van Nostrand.

Bandura, A. (1977) 'Self-efficacy: toward a unifying theory of behavioral change', *Psychological Review*, 84: 191–215.

—— (2000) 'Exercise of human agency through collective efficacy', *Current Directions in Psychological Science*, 9(3): 75–8.

Baumeister, R. and Leary, M. (1995) 'The need to belong: desire for interpersonal attachments as a fundamental human motivation', *Psychological Bulletin*, 117: 497–529.

Ben-Zev, A. (1992) 'Pleasure in another's misfortune', *Iyyun: The Jerusalem Philosophical Quarterly*, 41: 41–61.

Bukowski, W. and Moore, D. (1980) 'Winners' and losers' attributions for success and failure in a series of athletic events', *Journal of Sport Psychology*, 2: 195–210.

Butler, R. (1987) 'Task-involving and ego-involving properties of evaluation: effects of different feedback conditions on motivational perceptions, interest and performance', *Journal of Educational Psychology*, 79: 474–82.

—— (1992) 'What young people want to know when: effects of mastery and ability goals on interest in different kinds of social comparisons', *Journal of Personality and Social Psychology*, 62: 934–43.

—— (1994) 'Teacher communication and student interpretations: effects of teacher responses to failing students on attributional inferences in two age groups', *British Journal of Educational Psychology*, 64: 277–94.

Covington, M. (1992) *Making the Grade: A Self-worth Perspective on Motivation and School Reform*, New York: Cambridge University Press.

Covington, M. and Beery, R. (1976) *Self-worth and School Learning*, New York: Holt, Rinehart & Winston.

Deci, E. (1971) 'Effects of externally mediated rewards on intrinsic motivation', *Journal of Personality and Social Psychology*, 18: 105–15.

Deci, E. and Ryan, R. (1985) *Intrinsic Motivation and Self-determination in Human Behavior*, New York: Plenum.

Deutsch, M. (1949a) 'A theory of cooperation and competition', *Human Relations*, 2: 129–52.

—— (1949b) 'An experimental study of the effects of cooperation and competition upon group processes', *Human Relations*, 2: 199–232.

Diener, C. and Dweck, C. (1978) 'An analysis of learned helplessness: continuous changes in performance, strategy and achievement cognitions following failure', *Journal of Personality and Social Psychology*, 36: 451–62.

Diener, C., Suh, E., Lucas, R. and Smith, H. (1999) 'Subjective well-being: three decades of progress', *Psychological Bulletin*, 125: 276–302.

Dray, L., Beltranena, R. and Covington, M. (1999) 'Nurturing intrinsic motivation in schools: a developmental analysis', paper presented at annual meetings of the American Educational, Research, Association, Montreal, April.

Dweck, C. (1991) 'Self-theories and goals: their role in motivation, personality, and development', in R. Dienstbier (ed.) *Nebraska Symposium on Motivation*, Vol. 38 (199–255), Lincoln, NE: University of Nebraska Press.

Eccles, J. and Midgley, C. (1989) 'Stage/environment fit: developmentally appropriate classrooms for early adolescents', in R. Ames and C. Ames (eds) *Research on Motivation in Education*, Vol. 3 (139–81), New York: Academic Press.

Eccles, J., Wigfield, A. and Schiefele, U. (1998) 'Motivation', in N. Eisenberg (ed.) *Handbook of Child Psychology*, Vol. 3 (5th edn) (1017–95), New York: Wiley.

Elliot, A. (1997) 'Integrating the "classic" and "contemporary" approaches to achievement motivation: a hierarchical model of approach and avoidance achievement motivation', in M. Maehr and P. Pintrich (eds) *Advances in Motivation and Achievement*, Vol. 10 (143–79), Greenwich, CT: JAI Press.

Farmer, H., Vispoel, W. and Maehr, M. (1991) 'Achievement contexts: effect on achievement values and causal attributions', *Journal of Educational Research*, 85: 26–38.

Fischer, K. and Tangney, J. (1995) 'Self-conscious emotions and the affect revolution: framework and overview', in J. Tangney and K. Fischer (eds) *Self-*

conscious Emotions: The Psychology of Shame, Guilt, Embarrassment, and Pride (3–22), New York: Guilford Press.

Ford, M. (1992) *Motivating Humans: Goals, Emotions, and Personal Agency Beliefs*, Newbury Park, CA: Sage.

Garibaldi, A. (1979) 'Affective contributions on cooperative and group goal structures', *Journal of Educational Psychology*, 71: 788–94.

Gill, D. (1980) 'Success–failure attributions in competitive groups: an exception to egocentrism', *Journal of Sport Psychology*, 2: 106–14.

Gunderson, B. and Johnson, D.W. (1980) 'Building positive attitudes by using cooperative learning groups', *Foreign Language Annals*, 13: 39–46.

Halperin, M. and Abrams, D. (1978) 'Sex differences in predicting final examination grades: the influence of past performance, attributions and achievement motivation', *Journal of Educational Psychology*, 70: 763–71.

Harter, S. (1996) 'Teacher and classmate influences on scholastic motivation, self-esteem, and level of voice in adolescents', in J. Juvonen and K. Wentzel (eds) *Social Motivation: Understanding Children's School Adjustment* (11–42), New York: Cambridge University Press.

Hertz-Lazarowitz, R., Kirdus, V. and Miller, N. (1992) 'Implications of current research on cooperative interaction for classroom application', in R. Hertz-Lazarowtz and N. Miller (eds) *Interaction in Cooperative Groups: The Theoretical Anatomy of Group Learning* (253–80), New York: Cambridge University Press.

Hornstein, H.A., Marton, J., Rupp, A.H., Sole, K. and Tartell, R. (1980) 'The propensity to recall another's completed and uncompleted tasks as a consequence of varying social relationships', *Journal of Experimental Social Psychology*, 16: 362–75.

James, W. (1890) *Principles of Psychology*, New York: Henry Holt.

Johnson, D.W. (1980) 'Constructive peer relationships, social development, and cooperative learning experiences: implications for the prevention of drug abuse', *Journal of Drug Education*, 10: 7–24.

—— (2003) *Reaching Out: Interpersonal Effectiveness and Self-actualization* (8th edn), Boston, MA: Allyn & Bacon.

Johnson, D.W. and Johnson, F. (2003) *Joining Together: Group Theory and Research* (8th edn), Boston, MA: Allyn & Bacon.

Johnson, D.W. and Johnson, R. (1974) 'Instructional goal structure: cooperative, competitive, or individualistic', *Review of Educational Research*, 44: 213–40.

—— (1979) 'Conflict in the classroom: controversy and learning', *Review of Educational Research*, 49: 51–70.

—— (1983) 'The socialization and achievement crisis: are cooperative learning experiences the solution?', in L. Bickman (ed.) *Applied Social Psychology Annual 4* (119–64), Beverly Hills, CA: Sage.

—— (1989) *Cooperation and Competition: Theory and Research*, Edina, MN: Interaction Book Company.

—— (1995). *Creative Controversy: Academic Conflict in the Classroom*, Edina, MN: Interaction Book Company.

—— (1999) *Learning Together and Alone: Cooperative, Competitive, and Individualistic Learning* (6th edn), Boston, MA: Allyn & Bacon.

Johnson, D.W., Johnson, R. and Anderson, D. (1978) 'Student cooperative, competitive, and individualistic attitudes and attitudes toward schooling', *Journal of Psychology*, 100: 183–99.

Johnson, D.W., Johnson, R. and Holubec, E. (2002) *Circles of Learning*, Edina, MN: Interaction Book Company.

Johnson, D.W., Johnson, R., Johnson, J. and Anderson, D. (1976) 'Effects of cooperative versus individualized instruction on student prosocial behavior, attitudes toward learning, and achievement', *Journal of Educational Psychology*, 68: 446–52.

Johnson, D.W., Johnson, R., Pierson, W. and Lyons, V. (1985) 'Controversy vs. concurrence seeking in multi-grade and single-grade learning groups', *Journal of Research in Science Teaching*, 22: 835–48.

Juvonen, J. and Wentzel, K. (eds) (1996) *Social Motivation: Understanding Children's School Adjustment*, New York: Cambridge University Press.

Koestner, R., Zuckerman, M. and Koestner, J. (1987) 'Praise, involvement, and intrinsic motivation, *Journal of Personality and Social Psychology*, 53: 383–90.

Koestner, R., Lekes, N., Powers, T. and Chicoine, E. (2002) 'Attaining personal goals: self-concordance plus implementation intentions equals success', *Journal of Personality and Social Psychology*, 83: 231–44.

Kouzes, J. and Posner, B. (1987) *The Leadership Challenge,* San Francisco, CA: Jossey-Bass.

Kruglanski, A. (1978) 'Endogenous attribution and intrinsic motivation', in M. Lepper and D. Green (eds) *The Hidden Costs of Reward: New Perspectives on the Psychology of Human Motivation*, Hillsdale, NJ: Erlbaum.

Leary, M. and Baumeister, R. (2000) 'The nature and function of self-esteem: sociometer theory', *Advances in Experimental Social Psychology*, 32: 1–62.

Leary, M., Tambor, E., Terdal, E. and Downs, D. (1995) 'Self-esteem as an interpersonal monitor: the sociometer hypothesis', *Journal of Personality and Social Psychology*, 68: 518–30.

Le Bon, G. (1960) *The Crowd*, New York: The Viking Press. (Original work published in 1895.)

Lepley, W. (1937) 'Competitive behavior in the albino rat', *Journal of Experimental Psychology*, 21: 194–201.

Lewin, K. (1935) *A Dynamic Theory of Personality*, New York: McGraw-Hill.

—— (1948) *Resolving Social Conflicts*, New York: Harper.

Lewin, K., Dembo, T., Festinger, L. and Sears, P. (1944) 'Level of aspiration', in J. Hunt (ed.) *Personality and the Behavior Disorders* (333–78), New York: Ronald Press.

Lewis, H. (1944) 'An experimental study of the role of the ego in work: I. The role of the ego in cooperative work', *Journal of Experimental Psychology*, 34: 113–26.

Locke, E. and Latham, G. (1990) *A Theory of Goal Setting and Task Performance*, Englewood Cliffs, NJ: Prentice-Hall.

Morgan, B., Coates, G. and Rebbin, T. (1970) *The Effects of Phlebotomus Fever on Sustained Performance and Muscular Output (Tech. Rep. No. ITR-70-14)*, Louisville, KY: University of Louisville, Performance Research Laboratory.

Mullen, B. and Cooper, C. (1994) 'The relation between group cohesiveness and performance: an integration', *Psychological Bulletin*, 115: 210–27.

Neumann, R. and Strack, F. (2000) '"Mood contagion": the automatic transfer of mood between persons', *Journal of Personality and Social Psychology*, 79: 211–23.

Nicholls, J. (1989) *The Competitive Ethos and Democratic Education*, Cambridge, MA: Harvard University Press.

Ortony, A., Clore, G. and Collins, A. (1988) *The Cognitive Structure of Emotions*, Cambridge: Cambridge University Press.

Osterman, K. (2000) 'Students' need for belonging in the school community', *Review of Educational Research*, 70: 323–67.

Ovsiankina, M. (1928) 'Investigations on the psychology of action and affection: VI. The resumption of interrupted acts', *Psychologische Forschung*, 11: 302–89.

Pallak, M., Cook, D. and Sullivan, J. (1980) 'Commitment and energy conservation', in L. Bickman (ed.) *Applied Social Psychology Annual 1*, Beverly Hills, CA: Sage.

Patrick, H., Ryan, A., Alfeld-Liro, C., Fredricks, J., Hruda, L. and Eccles, J. (1999) 'Adolescents' commitment to developing talent: the role of peers in continuing motivation for sports and the arts', *Journal of Youth and Adolescence*, 28: 741–63.

Pritchard, R., Campbell, K. and Campbell, D. (1977) 'Effects of extrinsic financial rewards on intrinsic motivation', *Journal of Applied Psychology*, 62: 9–15.

Rawsthorne, L. and Elliot, A. (1999) 'Achievement goals and intrinsic motivation: a meta-analytic review', *Personality and Social Psychology Review*, 4: 326–44.

Ryan, R. (1982) 'Control and information in the intrapersonal sphere: an extension of cognitive evaluation theory', *Journal of Personality and Social Psychology*, 43: 450–61.

Ryan, R. and Stiller, J. (1991) 'The social context of internalization: parent and teacher influences on autonomy, motivation, and learning', in M. Maehr and P. Pintrich (eds) *Advances in Motivation and Achievement*, Vol. 7 (115–49), Greenwich, CT: JAI Press.

Schneider, R., Ackerman, P. and Kanfer, R. (1996) 'To "act wisely in human relations": exploring the dimensions of social competence', *Personality and Individual Differences*, 21: 469–81.

Sheldon, K. and Houser-Marko, L. (2001) 'Self-concordance, goal attainment, and the pursuit of happiness: can there be an upward spiral?', *Journal of Personality and Social Psychology*, 80: 152–65.

Skinner, B. (1968) *The Technology of Teaching*, New York: Appleton-Century-Crofts.

Smith, R., Parrott, W., Dierner, E., Hoyle, R. and Kim, S. (1999) 'Dispositional envy', *Personality and Social Psychology Bulletin*, 25: 1007–20.

Stipek, D. (1998) *Motivation to Learn: From Theory to Practice*, Boston, MA: Allyn & Bacon.

Stipek, D. and Seal, K. (2001) *Motivated Minds: Raising Children to Love Learning*, New York: Holt & Company.

Taylor, S., Kemeny, M., Reed, G., Bower, J. and Gruenwald, T. (2000) 'Psychological resources, positive illusion, and health', *American Psychologist*, 55: 99–109.

Turner, J. and Meyer, D. (1999) 'Integrating classroom context into motivation theory and research: rationale, methods, and implications', in T. Urdan (ed.) *The Role of Context: Advances in Motivation and Achievement*, Vol. 11 (87–122), Stamford, CT: JAI Press.

Urdan, T. (ed.) (1999) *The Role of Context: Advances in Motivation and Achievement*, Vol. 11, Stamford, CT: JAI Press.

Wentzel, K. (1991) 'Relations between social competence and academic achievement in early adolescence', *Child Development*, 61: 1066–78.

—— (1992) 'Motivation and achievement in adolescence: a multiple goals perspective', in D. Schunk and J. Meece (eds) *Student Perceptions in the Classroom: Causes and Consequences* (287–306), Hillsdale, NJ: Lawrence Erlbaum.

—— (1994) 'Relations of social goal pursuit to social acceptance, classroom behavior, and perceived social support', *Journal of Educational Psychology*, 86: 173–82.

—— (1996) 'Social and academic motivation in middle school: concurrent and long-term relations to academic effort', *Journal of Early Adolescence*, 16: 390–406.

Wicklund, R. and Brehm, J. (1976) *Perspectives on Cognitive Dissonance*, Hillsdale, NJ: Lawrence Erlbaum.

Woodward, A. (1998) 'Infants selectively encode the goal object of an actor's reach', *Cognition*, 69: 1–34.

Chapter 10

Computer support for collaborative learning of child pedestrian skills

Hugh Foot, Andrew Tolmie, James Thomson, Kirstie Whelan, Sheila Morrison and Pepi Sarvary

Introduction

Collaborative learning has been deployed in an increasing variety of learning contexts in recent years. Not surprisingly, much of the existing research has focused upon curriculum-based school subjects, such as science, mathematics and literacy, because of the understandable concern about improving the effectiveness of formal educational systems (Tolmie *et al.* 2000). However, most learning occurs in informal settings as a natural outcome of the repeated exposure of children to everyday events in their lives, and much of this is taken for granted.

Pedestrian behaviour is an excellent example of everyday activity in which children learn to participate and for which relatively little formal instruction is given. None the less, to survive in the traffic environment children must acquire what Whitebread and Neilson (1998) call 'real world practical intelligence'. With little explicit guidance they are expected to pick up 'road sense', largely through experience and modelling of others' behaviour. It goes almost without saying that parents and adults are often lamentable pedestrian models whose own road-crossing behaviours display, from the child's point of view, both undesirable and unsafe characteristics. As models, adults typically compound their felony by failing to give any proper instruction or explanation of what safe behaviour they should have displayed in that situation. With respect to formal educational instruction, as recent cases of child abductions in the UK have testified, schools are much more likely to spend curriculum time teaching children how to resist the overtures of strangers than teaching them about road safety. Yet thousands more children are killed or injured on our roads than are ever harmed by abductors.

In this chapter we shall first address the assumption implicit in the title that pedestrian skills can be trained, and then consider the evidence based upon our own research about how such training can best be promoted by computer-assisted collaborative learning.

The training of pedestrian skills

To interact safely with their traffic environment children need a range of fundamental skills together with the ability to deploy these skills strategically across different road-crossing situations (Thomson *et al.* 1996). Among the most salient of these skills are detecting the presence of traffic, making visual timing judgements, co-ordinating information from different directions and integrating perception and action (cf. Avery 1974; Older and Grayson 1974; van der Molen 1981; Vinji 1981). In functionally more precise terms, this means that before children can know that it is safe to cross the road at a particular time, there are a number of features they need to assess. They need to recognize whether it is a potentially safe place to cross (i.e. no obstruction or sharp bend which obscures visibility of the road), they need to search selectively for approaching vehicles or hazards, to judge vehicle speeds and gaps in oncoming traffic, and then make an appropriate crossing decision in the light of all this information and bearing in mind the time it takes to cross the road.

The developmental evidence is strong that, as children grow older, they become more competent in these kinds of skills: they become more efficient at picking up on relevant information, making decisions on the basis of it and organizing appropriate behavioural responses (Thomson *et al.* 1996). In acquiring road-crossing competencies, therefore, children must learn to deploy their skills more strategically.

On the strength of these age-related changes it could, of course, be argued that children's competencies are only the manifestation of natural maturational advances and that they are constrained in what they can learn until the next appropriate stage of psychological development has been reached. This view, based on a common interpretation of Piaget's stage theory of development (e.g. Piaget 1955a), was strongly espoused by Sandels (1975) whose pioneering work on child pedestrian behaviour in Sweden led her to conclude that young children of about 10 years old cannot be adapted to the traffic environment and that our efforts should therefore be directed to segregating children from traffic altogether. However, developmentalists are now considerably less convinced about the inflexibility of the Piagetian stages and suggest that there is a large amount of research over the past ten to fifteen years which 'has comprehensively demonstrated that children can frequently learn to solve problems ahead of the supposedly "correct" developmental stage and sometimes far in advance of it' (Thomson *et al.* 1996).

While maturational changes may occur which are progressively refining the road-safety competency of children, this does not mean to say that training programmes designed to improve pedestrian skills are doomed to failure. Research and evaluation studies strongly suggest that practical roadside training, tailored to the age of the children being trained, can and does improve their levels of skill. For example, Thomson and Whelan (1997) showed that, under adult supervision and guidance, children of 5 to 6 years of age could be trained to recognize hazardous features which would make certain crossing routes unsafe. Four to six thirty-minute training sessions involving dialogue with the children aimed at helping them identify unsafe routes resulted in a threefold improvement in subsequent unsupervised performance. Using the same method of training, Thomson *et al.* (1992) showed that identification by children of safe crossing places could equally be improved using a table-top model of a road layout as well as at the roadside. Other improvements through training have been shown, also with children as young as 5 years old, in relation to visual timing skills (Demetre *et al.* 1993) and vulnerability to distraction (Limbourg and Gerber 1978).

Computer support for learning

Computer support for learning was designed originally for individual children or students interacting with computers one-to-one (e.g. Sewell 1990). The flexibility of modern software systems enables children working with computers to proceed at their own individual pace, with the content and level of materials tailored to their own needs and developmental stage, and to deliver individualized feedback (Self 1988; Sleeman and Brown 1982). More recently, however, the effective use of computers for group work has been recognized (Anderson *et al.* 2000; Crook 1994; O'Malley 1995) and, in practice, the shortage of resources has meant that computers were very often used in small groups. Computer support may take the form of facilitating communication across a network (e.g. chat lines, buddy clubs) in which interactants are working individually at their computers. Alternatively, it may take the form of the interactants being physically clustered around one (or more) computer(s) working interactively with information provided by the computer. This latter structure, in particular, offers the potential for integrating computer support with collaborative learning. There are various ways in which this comes about, but principally the computer software can be developed to support collaborative learning by structuring the discussion that occurs to encourage the kinds of interaction which tend to produce successful outcomes and deter unproductive discussion. Working with pairs of undergraduate students, for example, Howe *et al.* (1992) developed software to support their interaction on problems in kinematics. It achieved this by instructing the participants, *inter alia*, to compare their previous individually generated answers and agree a joint solution, and then gave feedback on the correctness of their proposed solution.

From this brief description it is clear that computers may have much to offer in representing the skills required for becoming a safe road user.

They provide structured problem-solving together with simulations of traffic scenarios designed to test and train pedestrian skills. Computers can create as rich a road environment as the real world in both static features (e.g. road layout and street furniture) and in dynamic features (e.g. traffic movement and density). Varying the combinations of these features means that it is possible to simulate simple and complex traffic environments and control precisely the elements of traffic and pedestrian movements and the interactions between them. This control affords substantial advantages over real road situations where exposure to an adequate range of traffic events and interactions may be considerably restricted and becomes a matter of chance or luck rather than anything else. Such haphazard exposure is not conducive to systematic training.

Apart from the obvious point that simulations offer a safe environment, there are therefore at least two main advantages of using simulation for training support. The first is that simulations permit the repeated and systematic exposure of children to many kinds of traffic event, some of which they may encounter only occasionally in everyday use of the roads. Children can be trained to consider first simple and then more complex traffic environments in a way that enables them to build up their knowledge and their conceptual understanding systematically. The second advantage of computer simulations is that they allow trainers to overcome some of the practical disadvantages of roadside training. It takes time and resources for trainers to take children on to the streets, especially in winter when children have to wrap up to brave the elements. Simulations can be set up very quickly at home, at school, at children's clubs or anywhere where the software is available. Similarly, bad weather may militate against roadside training. Finally, as already implied, finding suitable locations in streets nearby for training different kinds of skill may prove very difficult, if not impossible, without at least moving from one street site to another over what may be a considerable distance.

There are nevertheless some important caveats to the use of computer simulations for training purposes. The first is that simulations should never be seen as a substitute for roadside training. Roadside training is still essential when conditions allow, and training programmes such as 'Kerbcraft', which is a community-centred practical roadside training scheme, are still among the most effective methods of improving young children's behaviour in traffic (Thomson 1997; Thomson and Whelan 1997). In any case it is inevitable that, while children are receiving simulation training, they will also be experiencing traffic at first hand even if not explicitly being trained at the roadside. This parallel experience of simulation and roadside crossings is actually desirable because both experiences feed into each other and enable comparisons to be drawn and lessons to be (doubly) learned. For example, children may carry back problems witnessed at the roadside for discussion during simulation training.

Coupled to the last point made about the linkage between simulation and roadside experiences it almost goes without saying that the simulation training is only as useful as it transfers real benefit to the roadside. For this reason evaluation of the simulation programmes needs to show improvements in both procedural knowledge and the conceptual understanding that will support transfer. This last point is important because we would argue strongly that training should not be thought of as simply developing children's knowledge of a set of specific procedures. For training to be successful in the longer term, children's procedural knowledge needs to be placed in a broader conceptual understanding of the dynamics of the traffic environment and their relationship to it. Any training programme needs to address this issue by ensuring that children are encouraged to take a deep learning approach (Marton et al. 1984) in which they play a more active role in their knowledge management.

Another point is our emphasis on the use of systematic exposure of children from simple to more complex road and traffic configurations. This assumes that there is a hierarchy of skills and that some skills (e.g. safe place finding) are inherently easier for children to pick up at a younger age than other skills (e.g. gap timing or drivers' intentions). We shall address this point again below. Suffice it to say that, the younger the children receiving the training, the more important it is that they receive that training according to a structured sequence from simpler to more complex skills. To some extent, older children can dip into the training at any point without necessarily having undertaken initial training in the more elementary skills.

The final and perhaps most important caveat of all is that simulation training programmes, even those shown to have good transfer to the roadside, should never be seen as programmes that can take young novice pedestrians and turn them into expert, independent road users. Training programmes are designed to help prepare children for the time when they do become more independent but they are essentially aimed at raising awareness and alerting children to the many factors they need to take into account when deciding whether they can make a safe crossing.

Research rationale

It will be clear by now that the direction of our thinking about pedestrian training is towards bringing together the use of computer simulations and collaborative learning methods. Before embarking on our research paradigm in detail we need to focus upon some of the relevant theoretical aspects of collaborative learning which have not yet been addressed.

Given the thrust of other chapters in this volume we do not deem it necessary to make out a detailed case for collaborative learning *per se*. Developmental theory and research have presented a cogent story about the manner in which social interaction shapes and promotes cognitive development. Through Piaget and research that followed his ideas the most important element that emerged was the creation of conflict between ideas and experience (Doise and Mugny 1979, 1984; Piaget 1955b). To make sense of the world such conflicts have to be addressed, requiring cognitive effort, self-examination and a reappraisal of one's ideas. In practice, of course, most conflicts occur in our social encounters with others when, through dialogue, we discover that other people's experiences and ideas are not the same as our own and we need to resolve the conflict and achieve reconciliation or co-ordination. It is the processes involved in resolving the conflict that promote cognitive change, some of which is brought about by internally motivated reappraisal, scrutiny and reflection, and some of which is produced by explicit interaction with others, involving debate, argument, disagreement and justification. There is little doubt that externally induced conflict is a catalyst for subsequent internal reflection (Howe *et al.* 1992; Reid *et al.* 1989; Tolmie *et al.* 1993).

There is also wider evidence that other aspects of interaction, such as agreements, prompts, questions, examination and reference back to previous examples have a positive impact upon cognitive change. These are not conflictual behaviours but they do provoke further cognitive reaction and understanding. Howe *et al.* (1995), for example, showed how agreements and explanations are characteristics of productive exchanges.

This line of discussion may seem far removed from the (superficially viewed) straightforward and uncontentious task of crossing the road. However, as we have already seen, crossing is not just a set of procedures to be deployed in any given situation. Each and every crossing represents a problem and a challenge, especially to young children. For this reason there is no better way of promoting conceptual understanding than by confronting children with firsthand experience that the views which they hold about making a safe decision in a particular crossing situation may not be shared by their peers. Through collaboration at the roadside it is apparent that children do not necessarily share the same level of confidence about a safe crossing decision and they may not hold the same perspective about roadside locations where it is or is not safe to cross (Thomson and Whelan 1997). Therefore, the process of collaboration encourages debate, allows disagreements between views to surface, and gives children an opportunity to reason and justify their own perceptions about their judgements. It brings into play all the interactive processes which facilitate the co-ordination of children's perspectives and enables them to reach a wiser and more mature decision (Doise and Mugny 1984).

Theoretically, this reasoning sounds very plausible and a firm basis for empirical verification. In practice our research lends considerable support to the value of peer collaboration for learning pedestrian skills, but the picture is not quite as straightforward as suggested by the above analysis, as will be explained below.

Research on the collaborative learning of pedestrian skills

Stage 1: Individual performance

The starting point for our research was a series of studies focusing entirely on individual performance and designed to investigate how attuned children between 5 and 11 years of age are to traffic-relevant information when presented with an array of traffic situations (Tolmie *et al.* 1998). At the outset we started developing simple computer simulations of traffic environments in order to be able to control and structure the informational complexity of the scenes to which children were to respond. These scenes were constructed on a Macintosh Performa 630 using Hypercard and AddMotion software. In addition to controlling complexity, simulations also enabled the control of the time to which children were exposed to the traffic scenes and the presence or absence of distractions: events or stimuli which were likely to be appealing to young children and which might be expected to draw their attention away from potential hazards on the road.

We also used carefully edited video scenes of real traffic sequences which were constructed to match the computer animations. These scenes, developed for comparison purposes, afforded similar control of traffic complexity, distractions and scene length. For validation purposes performance at the roadside was also measured but without the systematic control which the other two forms of presentation offered.

The tasks were not constructed to test children's road-crossing skills directly. Indeed, children were not even asked to indicate whether or when they thought it was safe to cross the road in the scenes depicted in the computer animations, video sequences and roadside situations. Instead, the studies were designed to assess:

1 what aspects of the traffic environment children of different ages perceive as salient and what objects or events they spontaneously focus on when viewing traffic scenarios;
2 whether children give more priority to traffic-relevant information when explicitly asked what to 'look and listen out for' if they had wanted to cross the road;
3 whether the priority they give to different kinds of events or features changes as the complexity of the scenarios increases and as the exposure time of the scenes increases;

4   how susceptible they are to the effects of visual and auditory distractions, some of which are relevant cues (e.g. ambulance siren) and some of which are irrelevant (e.g. dog walking on the pavement and barking).

Without going into detail, the results showed consistent and significant differences suggesting clear age trends. Broadly, when given a road-crossing set, older children gave greater priority to traffic-relevant features and less priority to irrelevant information. Younger children were much less able to do this. All children were affected by increasing complexity, number of distractions and by decreasing viewing time. What was particularly important was that children's attentional strategies on the simulations (and to a lesser extent using the video) were barely distinguishable from those generated at the roadside, which provided firm evidence of correspondence and of their potential usefulness as suitable contexts for training.

Stage 2: Adult-led vs. peer collaboration

Interesting though these results are, they offer little insight into the processes mediating increased attention to traffic-relevant features. While children responded moderately well to questioning about the features they noticed in the traffic scenes, it was not clear developmentally why they shifted from more random and undifferentiated responses to giving more priority to salient traffic features. To gain a fuller picture of children's cognitive processes, a window on to their cognitions was needed. To achieve this, some kind of social input was essential that required children to articulate explicitly their ideas and opinions and to evaluate these against the ideas of others. We initially adopted two interactive learning approaches because it was not obvious which forms of social input would be most effective either in terms of educational outcomes for the children, or for furthering our own understanding of the developmental processes involved.

The first method was adult-led, guided participation in which an adult trainer works through a series of traffic problems with a child, using scaffolding and structured guidance to direct the child's attention towards those features of the situation which are relevant and away from those which are not. Based upon Vygotsky's (1978) notions of expert-led tutoring, there is considerable research evidence that structured guidance of the performance of an activity is a natural and effective means of promoting skill acquisition in children (Damon and Phelps 1989; Rogoff 1986). The second method was peer collaboration involving children being confronted collectively with a series of traffic problems and having to discuss and work out for themselves the solutions to the problems. As we have seen, such collaborations have been demonstrated to be effective in promoting more explicit and more accurate conceptualizations about the world (Tolmie *et al.* 1993).

These two methods were selected as the most appropriate forms of social input because deployment of attention at the roadside requires both perceptual-motor skill and conceptualization of the traffic environment. Guided participation is known to facilitate the development of perceptual-motor skill and peer discussion to promote better understanding.

A study was designed to compare these two kinds of social input and broadened to include a roadside crossing decision task as well as attention to relevant and irrelevant features of the traffic environment (Tolmie *et al.* 1998). The study also involved a training element to allow direct comparison of the impact of these two types of interactive learning approach.

Forty-nine children aged 6 to 8 years were pre-tested on their ability to detect relevant and ignore irrelevant features of a series of traffic scenes presented by computer and at the roadside. As before, scenes varied in complexity and the presence of distractors. The children also participated in making actual road-crossing judgements by standing at the roadside and, over a series of trials, shouting out when they thought it was safe to cross the road.

After pre-testing, a subsample of the children took part in a series of four computer-based training sessions, working either in one-to-one adult–child pairs (adult guidance, $n = 18$) or in groups of three (peer collaboration, $n = 18$). Children working in the adult–child dyads progressed through a series of animations of traffic scenes, identifying if and when it would be safe for an animated character to cross a road, and, in the light of the feedback on their decisions, either move on to the next scenario or attempt the problem again. Adult volunteers were briefed merely to help the children with no other instruction about how to interact with them. Those working in the peer collaboration condition worked through the same traffic scenes, discussing their decisions with each other and with no adult assistance. The remaining children formed the control group who received neither version of the training task. A week or two after training, children were post-tested on the same tasks as a pre-test, yielding measures of change in the extent to which children (1) attended more to relevant than irrelevant features – at the roadside and in the simulations; (2) were aware of why these features are important; (3) made correct crossing decisions; and (4) became more sensitive to road-crossing opportunities in their crossing decisions as measured by 'size of accepted gap' and starting delays (Demetre *et al.* 1993). Video-recordings of the training sessions also enabled a detailed analysis of the dialogue that occurred within the adult–child and peer collaboration conditions.

The performance results that emerged from this study strongly favoured the adult-led condition. Children in this condition improved significantly in their attentional shift towards relevant road-crossing features (22 per cent shift from pre- to post-test) and in their 'elaboration' score, which is an index of their conceptual understanding of why these features are important. They also improved in accepted gap size and starting delays which provide a measure of their sharper judgement and ability to anticipate the presence of a gap. Most importantly, they increased the number of correct decisions they made on the crossing task. Associations between pre- to post-test performance shifts on the computer and roadside tasks were also stronger in the adult-guidance condition. There were systematic relationships between the reporting of relevant features and elaborations on computer and roadside tasks. Increases in reporting relevant features on the computer simulations were correlated with reductions in starting delays and smaller accepted gap sizes.

In contrast, children in the peer collaboration condition, along with the control group, showed no such improvements as a result of training on any of the performance measures and, indeed, a slight regression in the identification of relevant traffic features. At first sight this appeared very disappointing and could not be explained from the performance data. It was conjectured that the nature of the interactions might throw some light on the results. To this end, the videos of the dialogue that occurred in the adult-led and peer collaboration training conditions were scrutinized.

This analysis provided substantial evidence that the performance differences between conditions were a function of differences in the patterns of interaction during training. Profiling first the interactions of the adult-led dyads, various types of scaffolding were evident, despite the adult trainers not having been groomed to interact with the children in any particular way. Thus, for example, adults typically developed styles of dialogue dominated largely by suggestions, questions, prompts and agreements which they used to draw children's attention to relevant features of the environment but without providing the answers or being too directive. They also provided some degree of explanation to help the children understand why certain features may be important but progressively encouraged children to provide their own explanations as training proceeded. Instances of adult chairing or controlling the dialogue also diminished as training proceeded, allowing the child to take more responsibility for the progress of the task and simply interceding with prompts, questions and suggestions when the child perhaps appeared to be moving in the wrong direction or hesitated for too long.

The profile of dialogue in the peer collaboration condition was very different and symptomatic of unproductive interaction. The children made a promising start with disagreements (cognitive conflicts) which were handled through explanations and suggestions, and considerable subsequent agreements. However, this level of productive exchange deteriorated over time (beyond the first session) as did the number of correct decisions reached. The children showed decreasing attention to the content of the task, and more interest in task procedures, such as turn-taking and suggestions for action. Their exchanges became somewhat chaotic, especially as training progressed and some of the problems became more difficult (Tolmie *et al.* 1998). It is, of course, possible that children in this condition were just too young to co-ordinate their activity on their own, but since they managed some level of co-ordination in the first session there is no reason in principle why this should not have continued. A more likely explanation for the unproductive nature of the peer discussion is that the children had enough knowledge to cope when the problems remained relatively simple and straightforward but, as the problems became conceptually harder, they did not have sufficient knowledge to suggest solutions. Consequently, discussion did not help and they merely went through the motions of performing the task.

Stage 3: Adult guidance and peer collaboration

If this explanation of the failure of peer collaboration is plausible, then the results of this study should not be interpreted as an indictment of the use of peer collaboration in this context. Far from it, in fact. Since we know a considerable amount about the ingredients that are necessary for a successful and productive dialogue which is likely to lead to performance gains, the focus should be upon structuring the training in such a way as to maximize these desirable types of dialogue and minimize the undesirable types. This feature was missing from the last study.

With this purpose in mind the next stage of our research programme was to devise a training programme that would, on the one hand, structure the dialogue in ways that are consistent with productive exchanges and, on the other, ensure that the information to be learned is tailored to the level of knowledge of the child and presented in such a way as to sustain children's continuing engagement in the task, and help surmount any problems experienced. In principle, this recipe could be achieved by combining adult guidance with peer collaboration to gain the advantages that accrue from both expert guidance and peer discussion. In addition, because the road-crossing task draws upon both procedural and conceptual understanding, this training approach should reap the best of both worlds in the sense that expert guidance is most suited to procedural learning (Vygotsky 1978), and peer collaboration is most conducive to conceptual understanding (Howe *et al.* 1995; Tolmie *et al.* 1993). It is, of course, true that collaborative and guidance approaches are based on different theoretical models of learning and have traditionally been used separately and often in opposition to each other. However, assuming that they are handled appropriately (e.g. with learners of approximately the same developmental level), there is no reason to presume that they are incompatible if integrated within a single intervention strategy.

Given, however, that the efficacy of adult guidance in one-to-one adult–child dyads has been demonstrated already, it also needs to be shown that the combination of adult guidance and peer collaboration actually offers extra value. It is plausible that the effect of adult guidance swamps any additional benefit from peer collaboration or even that, in combination, the effects pull in opposite directions and cancel each other out.

The next study, therefore, provided a direct test of this by comparing adult guidance in one-to-one adult–child training with adult guidance in tandem with peer collaboration. More detail of this study is provided in Tolmie *et al.* (2000). The experimental design followed the same paradigm as in the last study, but used the simulated traffic scenes above and no roadside testing. Children were pre-tested on traffic scenes varying in complexity, traffic movement and number of distractors. They were then trained to make safe crossing decisions on another series of animated traffic scenes of increasing difficulty and post-tested on the priority they gave to traffic-relevant features. There were three training conditions: adult–child ($n = 24$), adult–group ($n = 24$) and control group ($n = 15$) who received no training between pre- and post-tests. Peer groups were of three children. Unlike the study reported in Stage 2 where adult volunteer trainers received no instruction concerning their interactions with the children, in this study trainers were briefed in advance on the interactional role they should adopt. This briefing of the trainers involved guidance on using the computer software, watching an experienced trainer working with children, and an opportunity to work with children themselves. The session focused on the appropriate language to use with the children, techniques of questioning and prompting to elicit discussion among the children. Essentially it addressed how to handle what children might say, how to encourage them to take the lead and to explain the conceptual basis for their judgements.

Results produced clear benefits of training. Whereas the controls showed no pre- to post-test changes, both of the training conditions showed considerable shifts in pre- to post-test scores in reporting more relevant and fewer irrelevant traffic features. What is more, the adult–group condition displayed an even greater shift (in the order of 30 per cent) than the adult–child condition (22 per cent) and a commensurate increase in elaborations (conceptual understanding).

The conclusion is compelling. This study confirms what had been demonstrated already in our previous study, namely that adult guidance has a clear impact on children's attention to traffic-relevant features of the road environment. Beyond this, however, it also demonstrates the additional benefits, particularly conceptual benefits, when that guidance is supported by peer discussion. The adult–group condition offers a blend of guidance and collaboration which focuses children's attention on appropriate elements necessary for sound decision-making, and also affords them a better understanding of why those elements are important.

These differences in performance and conceptual outcomes in the adult–group and adult–child conditions are also matched by qualitative differences in the interactions during training. In both conditions trainers used non-directive scaffolding methods to steer children's responses to the road-crossing problems in the right direction, by drawing their attention, as necessary, to features of the traffic scenes that they needed to take into consideration. However, in the adult–group situation, trainers tended to restrain themselves from providing explanations of why certain features mattered, using prompts and questions to encourage the children to provide their own explanations to support suggestions they made. Consistent with conflict models of peer collaboration this led to more disputes, and it appeared to be disagreements that fuelled conceptual change. Adult trainers increasingly took a back seat, but when they did intervene to steer discussion with occasional disagreements and explanations, this usually had a beneficial effect.

Adult guidance in the absence of opportunity for peer discussion also involved some conceptual input. However, explanations came more from the trainers themselves as a commentary on what the child was doing. Hence, their explanations were more likely to arise from their own suggestions and not as part of a discussion about alternative solutions. Adult explanations, therefore, affected performance more than conceptual understanding inasmuch as they served to help focus children's attention on relevant features. However, because they did not provide a basis for evaluating alternative solutions, they were less effective than explanations arising from peer discussion for providing a conceptual underpinning of performance.

Implications for educational practice

Results from this research point to the main conclusion that the training of pedestrian skills in young children is accomplished most effectively using a combination of adult (expert) guidance and collaboration. They also highlight the importance of structured dialogue capturing elements of discussion which contribute to both procedural and conceptual understanding.

It is in relation to the provision of structure that the computer simulations play such a crucial role. Discussion takes place around the activities produced on-screen by the computer and, as we have seen, these activities may be shaped to reflect a wide range of traffic scenes and different kinds of crossing situations. Essentially, the activities on-screen can be designed to mirror the kinds of practical dilemmas with which children are faced at the roadside and to encourage constructive discussion targeted at identifying factors which affect crossing decisions. The simulated actions of traffic provide the hooks on which discussion hangs, supported by adult guidance and the opportunity for peer collaboration.

The development of these somewhat simplistic and representational computer graphics in our earlier work has given way to much more sophisticated software in our more recent studies, using Macromedia Director 6.0 on the PC platform. This has enabled us to create a realistic 3D traffic environment featuring high-quality animation sequences of vehicle movements and manoeuvres. It has also permitted us to produce run-time versions of the software that can operate satisfactorily on low-end computers, typical of those in many schools and homes. (More recently still we have replaced animated traffic scenes with real photographic images of street scenes and superimposed animated but realistic figures and vehicles on to these scenes, using Director 6.0 in combination with Adobe Photoshop.)

The new software has also enabled us to introduce interactivity between operator and traffic scenes. A series of child characters, varying in gender and ethnicity, have been created to negotiate the traffic environment in a simulated small town with houses, shops, school, swimming pool and park. The streets in this town offer a variety of configurations and roadside obstacles including junctions, blind bends, hump bridges and parked vehicles. The task of children operating the software is to control the actions and movements of those characters as they navigate different routes through this environment; for example, from home to school or from school to swimming pool.

The software has been developed as a training program designed for use with children between the ages of 5 and 11. It focuses on four related areas of pedestrian skills which, together, encompass the essential competencies that children need for safe pedestrian behaviour:

1 *Safe place finding* – perceiving hazards posed by aspects of road layouts and, if necessary, adjusting crossing routes to minimize those hazards.
2 *Roadside search strategies* – awareness of actual and potential vehicle movements in the vicinity of the crossing site.
3 *Gap timing* – co-ordinating road crossing with oncoming vehicle movements.
4 *Perceptions of drivers' intentions* – awareness of cues to drivers' future actions and the need to adjust road-crossing decisions.

These skills form a natural progression from more simple to more complex and need ideally to be taught in sequence because each builds on its predecessor. Safe place finding and roadside search strategies are the first skills to be learned focusing upon children's ability to recognize hazards associated with road layout and traffic movement. Gap timing and perception of drivers' intentions are higher order skills which depend upon children's ability to integrate vehicle movements with their own potential actions, and to anticipate drivers' intended manoeuvres and how to respond to them.

The advantages of this interactive engagement of the child with the on-screen traffic environments are several. First, the task has real motivational appeal with a defined social objective of navigating the on-screen character safely from one destination to another. This stands in contrast to some 'disembodied' road safety exercises in which the task of crossing the road is not linked to any specific purpose. Second, the interactive nature of the task focuses children's attention on actions and decisions governing the movement of the on-screen character, and not only on traffic movements and road configurations. Children will quickly learn, for example, that they cannot 'walk' the character across the road until they have made the character look in both/all directions to check that the road is clear. Thus the integration between the road conditions and pedestrian actions is much more focal. Third, the software can provide feedback on the adequacy of the decision by allowing the character to proceed across the road (if the crossing is safe) and to continue his or her journey to the next crossing point. Alternatively, if an oncoming vehicle is too close, the children may witness the unfortunate consequences of their unsafe decision by seeing the character step into the road and evaporate into a ghost, thus forcing them back to reconsider the crossing and try again.

These elaborations and refinements to the software, enabling a considerable degree of control on the part of the children, bring into sharp relief the respective roles of adult trainers and peer collaborators. Initially, the adult's role is relatively proactive, encouraging children to take control of the actions of the on-screen character (via the mouse), making suggestions, asking questions, prompting, reminding the children of earlier (other) events and steering discussion if it flags or wanders off-task. At the same time the trainer is encouraging children to discuss the challenges presented by the software for themselves: how to make the character cross the road, whether he or she is in the best position to cross; what alternative manoeuvres are possible for approaching vehicles. As time progresses the trainer would aim to retreat into the background, leaving the children to take over the role of chairing, questioning, arguing, offering explanations, and merely intervening if control needs to be exercised. The essential point is that the computer simulations are ideally suited to this dual form of social input. The structure of the software and the children's interactions with that software are conducive to types of peer discussion which are both constructive and self-sustaining.

Practical applications

The training program has been subjected to a large-scale evaluation. This involved children aged 5 to 6, 7 to 8, and 9 to 10 attending schools in two areas of Glasgow with differing accident rates and socio-economic status. Over two school years approximately 150 children worked through each of the four training modules in turn under the supervision of adult trainers drawn from among the parents of the participating schools. Each skill itself comprised four training sessions taken by the children at approximately weekly intervals. Prior to training, children took a pre-test to establish their baseline performance on that skill, and were post-tested after training. They were further post-tested, some up to eight months later, to gauge the longer term effects of the training. Testing was conducted at the roadside to gauge the effect of training on actual behaviour. Measures of conceptual understanding were also included. Control children of the same ages were tested at the same time points but received no training.

A detailed analysis of the results is given in Tolmie et al. (2002). In brief, the results of the evaluation study were almost entirely positive. Improvements occurred between pre- and post-test in each of the four skills and, in some skills (e.g. safe place findings), these improvements were substantial. Generally the benefit of training on all skills was spread across children of all ages but there was one exception to this: safe places training had little impact on 6-year-olds although this training did seem to enhance their subsequent performance on roadside search. Our overall impression from the pattern of results from 6-year-olds was that they may need more initial training on safe places to grasp the connection between the computer simulations and the roadside. However, for all ages and for all skills conceptual improvements following training were mostly substantial when compared with controls.

The outcomes of the evaluation show, therefore, that the training resource was substantially successful, leading to improvements both in roadside behaviour and children's understanding in all four skills under scrutiny. The study also demonstrated the effectiveness of the training materials for children over the age of 6. However, given that the skills themselves involve progressively more difficult and complex perceptual and cognitive processes, there is substantial merit in presenting the skills for training in the same sequence in which they were tested in the evaluation study. This is supported further by the fact that results showed some cumulative benefits in the sense that training in one skill impacted positively upon the performance of the next.

In conclusion, the results of this research tell a very promising story about the ways in which different types of social input can be integrated into a coherent learning model. The research has demonstrated emphatically how processes of learning associated with adult (expert) guidance can be combined with processes of learning associated with peer collaboration to produce a training resource that is more effective than through using either type of social input on its own.

At the same time we must guard against over-rating the value of the training resource. We still believe that practical roadside training is the most effective type of training for children, especially younger children, and we see the computer resource as a supplement, not as a substitute, to such training. Its great advantage, as has been mentioned, lies in its potential to expose children to traffic situations that they might not ordinarily experience during roadside training, except by chance. It also provides the opportunity for systematic discussion and consideration of scenarios in a way that might be more difficult to achieve at the roadside. In other words, the training software provides an opportunity to develop conceptual frameworks that will help children make more sense of their roadside experience. However, it must be repeated that the resource is *not* intended to transform children into mature, independent pedestrians. Children, after training, cannot be expected to reach adult levels of pedestrian skill. The resource should be envisaged as a means whereby children can become more effective learners, but still need parental supervision when crossing roads.

Author note

This research has been supported by a series of grants from the (UK) Department of Transport and by the ESRC: Department of Transport: DUP 9/31/11; Department of the Environment, Transport and the Regions: DPU 9/31/41; and Economic and Social Research Council Grant: R000222468.

References

Anderson, A., Cheyne, W., Foot, H., Howe, C., Low, J. and Tolmie, A. (2000) 'Computer support for peer-based methodology tutorials', *Journal of Computer Assisted Learning*, 16: 41–53.

Avery, G.C. (1974) *The Capacity of Young Children to Cope with the Traffic System: A Review*, Sydney: New South Wales Department of Motor Transport, Traffic Accident Research Unit.

Crook, C. (1994) *Computers and the Collaborative Experience of Learning*, London: Routledge.

Damon, W. and Phelps, E. (1989) 'Critical distinctions among three approaches to peer education', *International Journal of Educational Research*, 13: 9–19.

Demetre, J.D., Lee, D.N., Grieve, R., Pitcairn, T.K., Ampofo-Boateng, K. and Thomson, J.A. (1993) 'Young children's learning on road-crossing simulations', *British Journal of Educational Psychology*, 63: 348–58.

Doise, W. and Mugny, G. (1979) 'Individual and collective conflicts of centrations in cognitive development', *European Journal of Psychology*, 9: 105–8.

Doise, W. and Mugny, G. (1984) *The Social Development of the Intellect*, Oxford: Pergamon.

Howe, C.J., Tolmie, A. and Rogers, C. (1992) 'The acquisition of conceptual knowledge in science by primary school children: group interaction and the understanding of motion down an incline', *British Journal of Developmental Psychology*, 10: 113–30.

Howe, C.J., Tolmie, A., Anderson, A. and MacKenzie, M. (1992) 'Conceptual knowledge in physics: the role of group interaction in computer-supported teaching', *Learning and Instruction*, 2: 161–83.

Howe, C.J., Tolmie, A., Greer, K. and MacKenzie, M. (1995) 'Peer collaboration and conceptual growth in physics: task influences in children's understanding of heating and cooling', *Cognition and Instruction*, 13: 483–503.

Limbourg, M. and Gerber, D. (1978) 'A parent training program for the road safety education of preschool children', *Accident Analysis and Prevention*, 13: 255–67.

Marton, E., Hounsell, D. and Entwhistle, N. (1984) *The Experience of Learning*, Edinburgh: Scottish Academic Press.

Older, S.J. and Grayson, T.G.B. (1974) *Perception and Decision in the Pedestrian Task, Department of the Environment Report 49UC*, Crowthorne: Transport and Road Research Laboratory.

O'Malley, C. (ed.) (1995) *Computer Supported Collaborative Learning*, Berlin: Springer-Verlag.

Piaget, J. (1955a) 'Les stades du dévelopement intellectual de l'enfant et de l'adolescent', in P. Osterreith (ed.) *Le Probléme des Stades en Psychologie de L'Enfant*, Paris: Presses Universitaires de France.

—— (1955b) *The Language and Thought of the Child*, New York: Meridian Press.

Reid, J., Forrestal, P. and Cook, J. (1989) *Small Group Learning in the Classroom*, Portsmouth, NH: Heinemann.

Rogoff, B. (1986) 'Adult assistance of children's learning', in T.E. Raphael (ed.) *The Contexts of School-based Literacy*, New York: Random House.

Sandels, S. (1975) *Children in Traffic*, London: Elek.

Self, J. (1988) 'A perspective on intelligent computer-assisted learning', *Journal of Computer-Assisted Learning*, 1: 159–66.

Sewell, D.F. (1990) *New Tools for New Minds: A Cognitive Perspective on the Use of Computers with Young Children*, New York: Harvester Wheatsheaf.

Sleeman, D. and Brown, J. (1982) *Intelligent Tutoring Systems*, New York: Academic Press.

Thomson, J.A. (1997) *Kerbcraft: A Handbook for Road Safety Professionals*, London: Department of the Environment, Transport and the Regions.

Thomson, J.A. and Whelan, K.M. (1997) *A Community Approach to Road Safety Education Using Practical Training Methods: The Drumchapel Report, Department of Transport Road Safety, Research Report No. 2*, London: HMSO.

Thomson, J.A., Tolmie, A., Foot, H.C. and McLaren, B. (1996) *Child Development and the Aims of Road Safety Education: A Review and Analysis, Department of Transport Road Safety Research Report No. 1*, London: HMSO.

Thomson, J.A., Ampofo-Boateng, K., Pitcairn, T., Grieve, R., Lee, D.N. and

Demetre, J.D. (1992) 'Behavioural group training of children to find safe routes to cross the road', *British Journal of Educational Psychology*, 62: 173–83.

Tolmie, A., Thomson, J. and Foot, H. (2000) 'The role of adult guidance and peer collaboration in child pedestrian training', in R. Joiner, K. Littleton, D. Faulkner and D. Miell (eds) *Rethinking Collaborative Learning* (101–18), London: Free Association Books.

Tolmie, A., Howe, C., MacKenzie, M. and Greer, K. (1993) 'Task design as an influence on dialogue and learning: primary school group work with object flotation', *Social Development*, 2: 183–201.

Tolmie, A., Thomson, J.A., Foot, H.C., McLaren, B. and Whelan, K.M. (1998) *Problems of Attention and Visual Search in the Context of Child Pedestrian Behaviour*, London: Department of Transport, the Environment and the Regions, Road Safety Division.

Tolmie, A., Thomson, J., Foot, H., Whelan, K., Sarvary, P. and Morrison, S. (2002) *Development and Evaluation of a Computer-based Pedestrian Training Resource for Children Aged 5–11 Years, Road Safety Research Report No. 27*, London: Department for Transport, Local Government and the Regions.

van der Molen, H.H. (1981) 'Blueprint of an analysis of the pedestrian task – 1: Method of analysis', *Accident Analysis and Prevention*, 13: 175–91.

Vinji, M.P. (1981) 'Children as pedestrians: abilities and limitations', *Accident Analysis and Prevention*, 13: 225–40.

Vygotsky, L.S. (1978) *Mind in Society: The Development of Higher Psychological Processes*, ed. and trans. M. Cole, V. John-Steiner, S. Scribner and E. Souberman, Cambridge, MA: Harvard University Press.

Whitebread, D. and Neilson, K. (1998) *Cognitive and Metacognitive Processes Underlying the Development of Children's Pedestrian Skills, Road Safety Research Report No. 6*, London: Department of the Environment, Transport and the Regions.

Young, D.S. and Lee, D.N. (1987) 'Training children in road crossing skills using a roadside simulation', *Accident Analysis and Prevention*, 19: 327–41.

Chapter 11

Peer support networks in school and community settings

Adrian F. Ashman and Robyn M. Gillies

Learning can be a solitary experience but, generally, it revolves around partnerships between the learner and another, or a number of others. Those involved might be children, parents, teachers, tertiary instructors, a training officer at work, supervisor or the boss. Proxy teaching–learning partners may also be involved such as the author of a textbook, the creator of a website or instructional compact disc, or the director of a film or video.

In this chapter, we explore some of the domains in which learning occurs and where peers might have a significant effect on one another. First, we describe briefly the early influences on learning and then look at issues associated with culture and the importance of mediated learning experiences. Finally, we consider learning that occurs in a diversity of natural environments and compare these to learning in formal educational settings, such as the school classroom.

Learning during the early years of life

Teaching and learning occurs in almost every situation and, arguably, even from the time the foetus is developing in its mother's womb (see e.g. Hertzig and Farber 1997; Joseph 2000; Karmiloff and Karmiloff-Smith 2001; Savage-Rambaugh *et al.* 2001). In the early years, the setting is primarily the home and experiences there are hugely influential on the young person. Family characteristics and the attitudes and beliefs of parents influence the way in which the child will react and respond to educational opportunities later in life.

During the first five years, the child gains much through the bonding process with parents, and this facilitates language development and cognitive and emotional growth. Routines of the household may demonstrate regularity and purpose, planning and problem-solving. At the same time, sensible and reasoned discipline establishes boundaries, positions and responsibilities in relationships, a sense of what is right and wrong, and the rudiments of identity that allow children to position themselves in relation to others. Interactions with siblings and peers also facilitate positive and negative attitudes towards social interactions, learning, problem-solving and discovery.

In time, the teaching-learning ecology expands to include the school, community and, indeed, the rest of the world through television and the World Wide Web. Closer to home, the neighbourhood becomes an increasingly significant contributor to the child's education. Social contacts expand and access to resources such as libraries, museums, art galleries, shopping centres, parks, and recreation and leisure facilities further enhance educational opportunities. Conversely, if the child lives in a situation where there are few opportunities to learn about the world and interact with it successfully, or is not exposed to positive models of learning, then the childhood and adolescent years may be characterized by intellectual, social or emotional isolation, confusion or conflict (see e.g. Brooks-Gunn *et al.* 1995).

Throughout life, some tensions and challenges are important to stimulate motivation and enhance performance. Modest levels of challenge can have positive outcomes by exposing young people to situations that involve competition and co-operation. Even rebellion has a place in the process of learning. For example, children intermittently treat with contempt some limitations and rules imposed by parents, schools and society. They may, for example, play with matches, skip school, mix with undesirable companions and take items that are not theirs. While these activities may be exasperating for parents and authority figures, valuable life experiences are acquired, usually without detrimental physical or emotional effects or involvement with law enforcement agencies. Of course, some young people do find themselves standing before a magistrate, but even those who engage in delinquent behaviour generally survive the experience. Carroll (1995), for example, reported that 85 per cent of youths admit to engaging in some law-breaking activity but only 1 to 2 per cent actually appear in court and, of these, only 3 per cent are repeat offenders.

While challenges to law and order are not to be ignored, experiences which enable children and youth to test their independence and the consequences of their actions alone and with others are essential prerequisites of functional learning and problem-solving skills. These various life events are also crucial for the development of initiative-taking and self-determination, and for establishing values, attitudes and beliefs about one's own culture and other cultures that will endure across the course of their lives.

Culture, society and learning

Learning is a culturally mediated experience (Salili *et al.* 2001). In the pursuit of learning, students are assisted or hindered by a constellation of characteristics, circumstances and events. Each student is affected differently by motivation, attitudes, personality, gender, ethnic or racial background, and family circumstances. Residential location can be a significant element in the learning and problem-solving equation if few facilities are available and input from support personnel and significant others is limited. Such a situation might occur if one lives in a home environment that is not conducive to exploration or resourcefulness or in a remote community where there are few facilities. In many countries that are large in area but sparse in population, such as Canada and Australia, there are substantial disparities in educational opportunities between metropolitan centres and isolated rural communities that may be 500 or 600 kilometres from the nearest city or regional town. In developing countries access to resources may be limited, even in large metropolitan areas.

While we might expect that schooling should compensate for differences in community and family circumstances, school can have both positive and negative effects on students that can make equality of opportunity a hit-or-miss encounter. There is some justification for holding the education system responsible for a student's failure and, in some countries, schools are held accountable for not overcoming the pre-existing differences between students, and teachers – either individually or collectively – are held accountable for students' failure to meet minimum attainment standards. Mortimore claimed that the school is one of the few social mechanisms available to students that can redress disadvantaged circumstances and provide a compensating boost. The more effective the school, the higher will be the proportion of students who 'will get to the starting line in the competition for favourable life-chances. How well such students will perform in the subsequent race will depend on their talents, motivation, and luck; but at least they will have a chance to compete' (Mortimore 1997: 483). Such are the ideals enshrined in the mission statement and goals of most school systems but, as we know, the rhetoric does not always reflect reality.

School should be a place where equality is paramount, where difference is minimized, and diversity and variation accepted as a fundamental aspect of the learning community, but not all appear to fulfil this expectation. Some writers (e.g. Preston and Symes 1992) have suggested that school actually promotes social stratification and inequality, and that the needs of the least advantaged are infrequently educational priorities. The funding mechanisms operating in school systems do not always adequately take into consideration the huge differences that occur across communities. In some locations, for example, a computer in the home, a cell phone in one's pocket and a television in the bedroom is considered to be the minimum standard. It is interesting to note that the American Academy of Pediatrics (2001) reported that 32 per cent of 2- to 7-year-olds and 65 per cent of 8- to 18-year-olds have television sets in their bedrooms and, in an Australian

Bureau of Statistics (2001) report, it was noted that one-third of Australian households had Internet access in 2000, a 49 per cent increase over 1999. In some places, however, making a telephone call might require a fifteen-minute walk to where the pay phone may or may not work, depending upon the level of vandalism that week.

In most education systems these days, there is an imperative to recognize social and cultural influences, and to provide experiences that reduce inequity and promote difference and diversity while still acculturating young members of society in the values and standards of the dominant group. There is also a growing recognition that school cannot be all things to everyone and that the family and friendship networks still play a significant part in achieving educational objectives, often by mediating learning experiences.

Mediation and identity

The term 'mediated learning' is drawn from the work of Vygotsky, who emphasized the role of social interaction in which an expert guides a novice through a task to ensure that the learner acquires higher level skills. Vygotsky's writings (e.g. 1962, 1978) have had a substantial impact upon the theory and practice of cognitive psychology and its application to education. One of his primary contentions was that education should be designed to accelerate children's cognitive development, rather than provide experiences at the individual's current level of cognitive maturity.

Vygotsky argued that meaning is socially constructed; hence learning and cognitive development can be affected by the interactions an individual has with another who is more skilled or knowledgeable. Two concepts were used to explain the manner in which an individual gains knowledge through interaction with others: mediation and internalization.

Mediation refers to the need for someone other than the learner to translate knowledge about the society and culture so that it can be internalized by the learner. Internalization refers to the individual's ownership of concepts or meaning that have been provided through instruction. In the present context, children must comprehend meaning and integrate the knowledge into their own thinking. They transform external stimuli to internal codes that are consistent with their own knowledge by changing and modifying the original ideas and applying their unique cognitive character to them.

How one learns about the world, therefore, is influenced by one's readiness to learn and how one is taught. Hence a teacher's role becomes one of facilitating the learner's thinking and learning skills through questioning, stimulation, modelling and supporting the use of appropriate strategies.

Other children or youths are often more successful in mediating learning for their peers than adults. One important reason is their use of a common language that expresses commonly held values, attitudes, beliefs and current life experiences. To some extent, young people employ a form of apprenticeship with each other that involves coaching, modelling and vicarious learning. Unlike apprenticeships that occur during vocational training, peer mediation among children and adolescents typically operates within a social interaction and allows for observation, practice and reflection. Rojewski and Schell (1994) described similar processes in formal education settings where apprenticeships operate to assist students to develop specific cognitive skills.

Lee (1995) provided an example of an apprenticeship model for teaching literacy interpretation skills to African-American high school students. Two learning environments were created. One involved small work groups, scaffolded learning experiences based on the students' own social discourse, African-American literature and the use of students' social knowledge. The other had a traditional white middle-class orientation typical of high school teaching methods. Not surprisingly, students in the first setting made significant improvements in their independent mastery of problem-solving strategies while those in the traditional setting did not.

The notion of an apprenticeship and mediation of learning draws attention to the importance of establishing an identity as a learner and connects learning to the culture in which one lives. The development of a social identity is an issue of some concern during the adolescent years in particular (see e.g. Cheshire 2000; Tarrant et al. 2001), but the issue of who we are, as learners and teachers, is also of great importance.

Identity

Identity is established within one's milieu, and involves a series of transitions and transformations that occur across time and within and between the various levels of social interaction with others. At a basic level, identity can involve adopting dress conventions and behaving in ways that emulate the conduct standards that prevail in the subgroup or circle of friends with whom one seeks affiliation. Presented in another way, seeking identity involves consciously employing strategies that enhance personal and social power (see e.g. Unger 2000).

At a more theoretical level, the transitions and transformations become important because they create tensions between perceptions of self-sufficiency and independence and the social connection and support that we gain from others over time. Furman and Simon (1998) suggested that family members are the most important in the development of identity during early childhood and early adulthood especially in terms of sources of support. Adults move on to gain greater support outside of their biological family. Adult males, for example, rated romantic relationships as the most supportive, as did females, although they also included the affiliation with their mothers, friends and siblings as valuable sources of support.

Some authors, such as Newman and Newman (2001), have argued that there has been an over-emphasis on individual identity, self-reliance and autonomy. They claimed that more important considerations are the developmental trajectory of adolescents and the blurring of the positive, normative pressures that encourage young people to achieve a sense of belonging and connection with their own peer group. These connections often develop most effectively through social interactions, peer support systems and informal learning on the periphery of the academic agenda.

Identity has become a more complex concept in the past decade since the expansion of telecommunication networks, the ease of international travel, and the worldwide economic and financial interdependence that has promoted the notion of a global community, or globalization. Where once youths developed a perception of self in relation to their neighbourhood, state and country, they are now exposed to ideas and values that are multicultural and multinational in nature. In this regard, Arnett (2000, 2002) suggested that most people now have a bi-cultural identity, part of which is linked to their local culture and part to the international community. Arnett suggested that this creates identity confusion, especially among youths living in non-Western cultures when they find themselves torn between their own culture and that of the apparently more wealthy global community.

Peer support systems

There have been attempts in some education jurisdictions to introduce and maintain peer support systems to enhance both social learning and academic outcomes, especially for disadvantaged or marginalized groups. In some schools and tertiary institutions (and in recreation and leisure programmes) peers may play an active role in the induction of new members into a community and sometimes in their selection into that community. In the professional literature there have been accounts of peer-support programmes that complement the work of pastoral care staff. Whether these operate at the formal or informal level, they rely on the training of supporters in communicator skills and problem resolution. The most common forms of peer support include befriending, mediation or conflict resolution, mentoring and, in some situations, counselling under professional supervision.

As with most educational practices, peer support programmes have limitations. Cowie and Olafsson (2000) reported that in some schools they fail because staff are reluctant to share the pastoral care responsibility with young people or because the school environment is hostile to the extent that peer support is undermined. Cowie and Olafsson (2000) and

Cowie *et al.* (2002) noted that boys are less likely to maintain their involvement in sanctioned school-based peer support programmes because of the hegemonic values that prevail predominantly among boys in school. The most significant obstacles seem to be fear of retaliation, peer hostility or indifference to a student being unable to cope without peer support.

Notwithstanding these limitations, Cowie *et al.* (2002) provided an analysis of the advantages of peer support systems within the context of their commentary on a programme that operated in a UK school over a two-year period. Those included identified opportunities for students to address real problems in their school community and increases in participants' self-confidence and communication skills.

Of note over time was the change in operation from the formal support mechanisms put in place at the commencement of the UK school programme to more informal, befriending strategies. Those who sought support reported that the primary benefit to them was having the chance to talk about issues of concern with a peer. Those who provided peer support also developed their ability to hold alternative points of view, in particular, during conflict resolution. Cowie *et al.* (2002) reported that the peer support programme also had a positive institutional impact by reducing victimization in school and developing an ethos of care.

Concerns about bullying and victimization are not unfamiliar in schools today, and some concern has been expressed that interventions designed to reduce vilification and prejudice directed at differences based upon gender, ethnic and religious background, and sexual identity have not been as successful as one might hope. In terms of our present discussion about peer support, the situation affecting same-sex attracted youth (SSAY) is an alarming example.

SSAY are especially disadvantaged as they share many experiences with other minority groups (e.g. the sense of being different, challenges to self-perception, discrimination) but, unlike others who may be visibly different, many SSAY hide their sexual identity and their fears. Regardless of how successfully they deal with their dilemma, society's intrinsic endorsement of opposite-sex attraction creates additional problems through the denigration of the same-sex attracted minority, the most powerful and insidious problem being expressions of homophobia through verbal abuse and violence. Unlike other minority groups that generally have parental support and sanctuary within the family, SSAY rarely share their minority status with their parents who are usually heterosexual. They almost never tell their parents first, and many feel anxious within their own homes and constantly under pressure from those outside the family (see e.g. Martino 2000).

Researchers in several Western countries (e.g. Hillier *et al.* 1999; Kosciw and Cullen 2001) have documented SSAY's experiences of abuse and prejudice, painting a picture of systemic vilification in the culture of many schools with one-third indicating that they had been subjected to discrimination and almost 50 per cent reporting serious verbal abuse. The acceptability of homophobic behaviour among youth and young adults is reflected in the results of an Australian study in which more than 25 per cent of male respondents aged 10 to 21 expressed the view that it was 'always', 'mostly' or 'occasionally' acceptable to assault homosexuals physically (Colman 2001). Such a finding lends credibility to researchers who have found that over 50 per cent of perpetrators of anti-gay attacks are 21 years of age or younger and 87 per cent are teenagers or in their twenties (Berrill 1992).

In the USA, peer networks have been established in many schools to support SSAY. They operate in much the same way as described by Cowie *et al.* (2002) with similar positive outcomes (see e.g. Lee 2002). In addition, Hillier *et al.* (2001) reported on the value of cyberspace chat room interactions between actual and virtual friends who can provide personal support and information. Merchant (2001) reported similar peer support benefits of Internet connections for other (not SSAY) isolated teenagers.

Informal peer networks are also of great importance in some racial groups. Townsend (1998), for example, reported significant differences in academic and social style and preferences between black and white American youth that create difficulties when teaching methods are designed primarily for the dominant culture and middle-class learners. Despite demographic changes over the years, traditional teaching approaches continue to be the standard in most schools, thus disadvantaging students whose preferred learning style is at odds with the teacher's instructional approach. Townsend suggested that one significant difference between black and white Americans is the strong need among the former to work co-operatively. Even when these students are working on tasks independently, many want to be in the company of others and are inclined to move back and forth between socially co-operative and competitive situations. Moreover, when a teacher might structure competitive learning activities, students circumvent the competition. For example, when separated on different sporting teams, friends discreetly help each other. Conversely, when a teacher might structure a learning situation to promote co-operation, black students compete.

Establishing peer groups in which black Americans have opportunities to affirm their racial identities is important, especially in settings that are not necessarily supportive of black youth. Datnow and Cooper (1997) presented an example of the success of peer support in a study of black American students who attended academically oriented private schools. These youths used access to a variety of black student clubs and social groups to enable them to negotiate their perceived outsider status within the school, and to affirm their scholastic achievements and social standing among the wider student body and with the teaching staff.

Our discussion up to this point has drawn attention to the importance of social interactions and learning experiences outside of the school classroom that are mediated by peers. There is some value, now, in drawing attention to the difference that exists between formal and informal learning environments.

Learning inside and outside of the classroom

Guided, or mediated, experiences attempt to ensure that students acquire important learning and analytical skills. Notwithstanding this, the most common tradition of education places emphasis on learning in formal instructional settings, generally the school classroom. There has been an implicit conviction that learning which takes place in the classroom or from prescribed textbooks is the quintessence of education. Certainly, there are times when a didactic form of instruction may be an efficient way of transmitting specialist knowledge (e.g. learning equations and principles), but there are also many blockages to learning that are elicited or prompted by traditional approaches to learning.

When we consider, for example, that young people spend up to thirty hours in class at school each week but about eighty wakeful hours outside school engaged in a variety of recreation and leisure pursuits, it is incongruous to think that those eighty hours are spent without any learning taking place at all. Indeed, these informal situations present many opportunities to learn though interactions with peer and adults.

Many researchers and writers have explored the nature and quality of learning outside of school; that is, in naturalistic setting. Lave and Wenger (1991), for example, referred to the notion of situated learning and documented educational opportunities available to young Africans. More recently, Ashman (1997) drew attention to the similarities and differences that existed when one compares the characteristics of learning which occurs in formal and informal settings. Here, the notion of informal learning is not as one finds it in the literature, where it typically relates to educational experiences in contexts such as art galleries and museums where there is a concerted effort to inform young visitors about the world in which they live and its cultural heritages (see e.g. Leinhardt *et al.* 2002; Paris 2002). Our notion of informal learning is that which occurs in the course of living one's life, during recreation and leisure activities, or even doing chores in the home, where there may be no explicit agenda about learning or problem-solving.

Kamps *et al.* (2002) emphasized the importance of peer mediation across the broadest range of recreation and leisure activities, especially for the development of language and social skills. They suggested that peer mediation is similar to adult-mediated instruction in that communication partners serve as models and teachers of social-communicative skills. The intensity of the learning experiences, however, varies according to the form of interaction encouraged. They argued that these types of interaction are of special assistance to students with severe disabilities and valuable learning can occur via peer-mediation programmes designed for times when programming is unusual (e.g. during mealtimes when these students learned about meal preparation and appropriate social interactions). Of note have been the positive outcomes in terms of generalization from these learning environments as applied to other natural contexts for both mediator and learner. Furthermore, such interventions have produced greater acceptance and more positive attitudes towards students with disabilities among teachers and peers.

In certain situations, learning in some formal education settings are positively disadvantageous and can lead to extreme learner resistance. Some young (and older) people, for example, react negatively to formal learning experiences by actively refusing to engage in the process. They choose to resist their learning and restrict their educational experiences. Kohl (1994) used the term 'non-learners' to distinguish those who aggressively refuse to pay attention, act dim-witted, scramble their thoughts, and override curiosity from others who do not learn because of specific intellectual limitations. Kohl's notion of non-learning was generated within the domain of cultural and social oppression, his examples being largely taken from black American and other underprivileged communities in New York. He argued that non-learning occurred when disadvantaged young people had to deal with unavoidable challenges to their integrity, cultural loyalties or their identity when there is no middle ground to which they can retreat. Their choice is either to agree to learn from a stranger who does not respect them, thereby causing a major loss of identity, or reject the stranger's advance and refuse instruction.

The reactions of non-learners in culturally disadvantaged circumstances are similar to the experiences of many other young people who engage in battles of will or authority with teachers who are intent on coercing or seducing them to learn. While young people's motives may be different, their behaviour has much in common. In many cases, active non-learners do not believe that they are failures or inferior to others who are succeeding at school. Their intent is distinctly different from other students who want to learn but cannot.

Non-learners in the schoolroom setting dismiss the importance that educators place on teaching and learning which occurs within formal education settings. They draw their knowledge and personal identity from the interactions and the considerable amount of learning (and learning about learning and problem-solving) that occur outside of the school campus. There is a sense of belonging that comes from affiliation with those in their neighbourhood or friendship groups so that the individual has a feeling of being connected. The loyalty and importance given by young people to such a connection has been found in studies of homeless young people who initially move away from their childhood neighbourhood only to return at a later time to settle in close proximity to their original home.

A sense of interpersonal connectedness is perhaps one of the most important characteristics of learning with and from peers and learning when no instruction is prescribed or intended. Another is the sense of being in control of the situation. These features distinguish the two lists given below that are drawn from Ashman (1997).

In formal teaching-learning settings:

- students participate because of curriculum and instructional requirements;
- teachers initiate learning and monitor progress;
- students are most often involved in independent learning or competitive situations;
- the student is expected to persist regardless of motivation, attitude, physical circumstances, or interest in the task;
- learning time is constrained by a timetable;
- the learning challenge is often linked to conceptual and/or book-based learning;
- the learning outcome is formally assessed and affects the students' school progress;
- learning products are often emphasized and linked to assessment;
- learning may occur through didactic teaching and books with minimal peer interaction;
- the language of instruction is often adult and middle class.

In informal settings:

- learners are involved because of personal interest;
- learners self-initiate and self-monitor progress;
- learners are involved in activities that are collaborative or competitive, personal or group based;
- when the learner gets tired or bored, the activity stops;
- there is generally time to explore and discover;
- there are usually personal challenges, repetition to consolidate skills and problem-solving in practical situations;
- learning outcomes are not tested or assessed formally but sometimes displayed;
- the process is generally more important than the product;
- learning may occur by interacting with or watching more competent others;
- there is generally mediation by peers who use the same language and who often have similar attitudes and beliefs.

As noted earlier, documentation of the differences between formal and informal learning situations is not a new idea. In comparing informal with formal learning, we are not advocating the elimination of formal instruction, but consideration of the characteristics of informal learning that might easily be incorporated with advantage into the school classroom. Others have presented similar views when advocating changes in education systems or when promoting an intervention that encourages teachers to use collaborative and peer tutoring methods in their classroom, become more democratic, more student-oriented, adopt new educational technologies, or allow for discovery and exploration. Sometimes these exhortations to teachers to develop alternative teaching practices are dismissed because of the belief that the workload would increase if changes were made to current practices.

It is our view that much has been, and will continue to be, achieved in using the resources of every participant in learning and problem-solving situations. The key to overcoming the resistance of truculent or disadvantaged groups to learning may be the translation of key features of informal learning into classroom practice.

References

American Academy of Pediatrics (2001) 'Children, adolescents, and television', *Pediatrics*, 107: 423–6.

Arnett, J.J. (2000) 'Emerging adulthood: a theory of development from the late teens through the twenties', *American Psychologist*, 55: 469–80.

Arnett, J.J. (2002) 'The psychology of globalization', *American Psychologist*, 57: 774–83.

Ashman, A.F. (1997) 'A learning experience', *Journal of Cognitive Education*, 6: 75–9.

Australian Bureau of Statistics (2001) *Communication and Information Technology: Household Use of Information Technology, Report No. 4901.0*, Canberra: Author.

Berrill, K.T. (1992) 'Anti-gay violence and victimization in the United States: an overview', in G.M. Herek and K.T. Berrill (eds) *Hate Crimes: Confronting Violence Against Lesbians and Gay Men* (19–45), Newbury Park, CA: Sage.

Brooks-Gunn, J., Denner, J. and Klebanov, P. (1995) 'Families and neighborhoods as contexts for education', in E. Flaxman and A.H. Passow (eds) *Changing Populations, Changing Schools* (233–52), Chicago, IL: NSSE distributed by the University of Chicago Press.

Carroll, A. (1995) 'The development of delinquency: integrating reputation enhancement theory and goal-setting theory', unpublished doctoral dissertation, University of Western Australia, Nedlands, Western Australia.

Cheshire, J. (2000) 'The telling or the tale? Narratives and gender in adolescent friendship networks', *Journal of Sociolinguistics*, 4: 234–62.

Colman, A. (2001) 'A national roundup of recent press reports on youth issues', *Youth Studies Australia*, 20(1): 3–10.

Cowie, H. and Olafsson, R. (2000) 'The role of peer support in helping the victims of bullying in a school with high levels of aggression', *School Psychology International*, 21: 79–95.

Cowie, H., Naylor, P., Chauhan, L.T.P. and Smith, P.K. (2002) 'Knowledge, use of and attitude towards peer support: a 2-year follow-up to the Prince's Trust survey', *Journal of Adolescence*, 25: 453–67.

Datnow, A. and Cooper, R. (1997) 'Peer networks of African American students in independent schools: affirming academic success and racial identity', *Journal of Negro Education*, 66: 56–72.

Furman, W. and Simon, V.A. (1998) 'Advice from youth: some lessons from the study of adolescent relationships', *Journal of Social and Personal Relationships*, 15: 723–39.

Hertzig, M.E and Farber, E.A. (eds) (1997) *Annual Progress in Child Psychiatry and Child Development, 1996*, Philadelphia, PA: Brunner/Mazel.

Hillier, L., Harrison, L. and Dempsey, D. (1999) 'Whatever happened to duty of care? Same-sex attracted youth people's stories of schooling and violence', *Melbourne Studies in Education*, 40: 59–74.

Hillier, L., Kurdas, C. and Horsley, P. (2001) ' "It's just easier": the Internet as a safety-net for same sex attracted young people', Melbourne: La Trobe University, Australian Research Centre in Sex, Health and Society.

Joseph, R. (2000) 'Fetal brain behavior and cognitive development', *Developmental Review*, 20: 81–98.

Kamps, D.M., Kravits, T. and Ross, M. (2002) 'Social-communicative strategies for school-aged children', in H. Goldstein, L.A. Kaczmarek and K.M. English (eds) *Promoting Social Communication: Children with Developmental Disabilities from Birth to Adolescence* (239–77), Baltimore, MD: Paul H. Brookes.

Karmiloff, K. and Karmiloff-Smith, A. (2001) *Pathways to Language: From Fetus to Adolescent*, Cambridge, MA: Harvard University Press.

Kohl, H. (1994) *'I Won't Learn From You': And Other Thoughts on Creative Maladjustment*, New York: The New Press.

Kosciw, J.G. and Cullen, M.K. (2001) *The GLSEN 2001 National School Climate Survey: The School-related Experiences of Our Nation's Lesbian, Gay, Bisexual and Transgender Youth*, New York: Office for Public Policy of the Gay, Lesbian and Straight Education Network.

Lave J. and Wenger, E. (1991) *Situated Learning: Legitimate Peripheral Participation*, New York: Cambridge University Press.

Lee, C.D. (1995) 'A culturally based cognitive apprenticeship: teaching African American high school students skills in literary interpretation', *Reading Research Quarterly*, 30: 608–30.

—— (2002) 'The impact of belonging to a high school gay/straight alliance', *High School Journal*, 85: 13–26.

Leinhardt, G., Crowley, K. and Knutson, K. (eds) (2002) *Learning Conversations in Museums*, Mahwah, NJ: Lawrence Erlbaum.

Martino, W. (2000) 'Policing masculinities: investigating the role of homophobia and heteronormativity in the lives of adolescent school boys', *Journal of Men's Studies*, 8: 213–36.

Merchant, G. (2001) 'Teenagers in cyberspace: an investigation of language use and language change in internet chatrooms', *Journal of Research in Reading*, 24: 293–306.

Mortimore, P. (1997) 'Can effective school compensate for society?', in A.H. Halsey (ed.) *Education, Culture, Economy, and Society* (476–87), Oxford: Oxford University Press.

Newman, B.M. and Newman, P.R. (2001) 'Group identity and alienation: giving the we its due', *Journal of Youth and Adolescence*, 30: 515–38.

Paris, S.G. (ed.) (2002) *Perspectives on Object-Centered Learning in Museums*, Mahwah, NJ: Lawrence Erlbaum.

Preston, N. and Symes, C. (1992) *Schools and Classrooms: A Cultural Studies Analysis of Education*, Melbourne: Longman Cheshire.

Rojewski, J.W. and Schell, J.W. (1994) 'Cognitive apprenticeship for learners with special needs: an alternative framework for teaching and learning', *Remedial and Special Education*, 15: 234–43.

Salili, F., Chiu, C.-Y. and Hong, Y-y. (2001) 'The culture and context of learning', in F. Salili, C-Y. Chiu and Y-y. Hong (eds) *Student Motivation: The Culture and Context of Learning* (1–14), New York: Plenum Press.

Savage-Rumbaugh, S., Fields, W.M. and Taglialatila, J.P. (2001) 'Language, speech, tools and writing: a cultural imperative', in E. Thompson (ed.) *Between Ourselves: Second-Person Issues in the Study of Consciousness* (273–92), Thorverton: Imprint Academic.

Tarrant, M., North, A.C., Edridge, M.D., Kirk, L.E., Smith, E.A. and Turner, R.E. (2001) 'Social identity in adolescence', *Journal of Adolescence*, 24: 597–609.

Townsend, B.L. (1998) 'Social friendships and networks among African American children and youth', in L.H. Meyer, H-S. Park, M. Grenot-Scheyer, I.S. Schwartz and B. Harry (eds) *Making Friends: The Influences of Culture and Development* (225–41), Baltimore, MD: Paul H. Brookes.

Unger, M.T. (2000) 'The myth of peer pressure', *Adolescence*, 35: 167–80.

Vygotsky, L.S. (1962) *Thought and Language*, Cambridge, MA: MIT Press.

—— (1978) *Mind in Society: The Development of Higher Psychological Processes*, ed. and trans. M. Cole, V. John-Steiner, S. Scribner and E. Souberman, Cambridge, MA: Harvard University Press.

Chapter 12

Large classes, small groups
A social systems approach

Shlomo Sharan

A large class: what is that?

Educators in Western countries generally consider classes of over thirty-five students to be large and to present difficult challenges to achieving instructional goals (Bennett 1996). An adequate definition of a large and difficult-to-teach class must take into consideration other factors in addition to the number of students present at any one time. Here, we focus on four critical variables affecting classroom teaching and learning. Later, we present a more complete list. The four factors to be discussed first are: (1) the physical size of the room, (2) the number of teachers functioning at one and the same time in that room, (3) the instructional method employed by teachers, and (4) the duration of a given class session. To be properly understood in educational terms, the concept of the large class must take into consideration all the features of classroom teaching that operate simultaneously.

Note that the focus of this discussion is on secondary schools. Class size in elementary schools has been treated at length by several authors (Bennett 1996; Slavin 1989; Zahorik 1999).

The spatial dimensions of the classroom

Some classes with more than twenty-five or thirty-five students are housed in relatively large rooms, often with more than one teacher or adult, as found in the British Open School, or in schools where classrooms have no walls and are marked off by movable room dividers. The entire school consists of a single and very large space built with the proper acoustical features. In all of the above kinds of classrooms, students have ample space to move around, work together in groups, prepare drawings, models and maps of fairly large size. Alternatively, classrooms in many countries may be relatively small in size yet still house a fairly large number of students. The variability in the space available in classrooms is highlighted by the following facts. In Singapore, for example, high school classrooms are usually 90 square metres for forty (or up to forty-five) students. In Finland classrooms are typically 64 to 70 square metres, but rarely are there more than twenty or twenty-five students per class. In Israel, classrooms are only 52 square metres for forty students or more.

Obviously, the classes in Israel have relatively high density and classes in Finland a very low level of density compared to other countries. Teachers in Israel claim that they cannot employ alternative methods of teaching in such cramped quarters that hamper freedom of movement. It seems reasonable to argue that classroom density (i.e. room size divided by number of students) certainly exerts an effect on teaching and learning. Nevertheless, in this author's experience, this straightforward measure of density, in and of itself, is far less significant as a factor that determines the pedagogical process in any given classroom than the teacher's pedagogical orientation and repertoire.

Number of teachers in the same class

The second in our initial list of four factors affecting classroom teaching in large classes is the number of teachers available to lead the class. Clearly, a large class with two or three teachers functioning together as a team constitutes a totally different instructional situation than a similarly large class with only one teacher. If accomplished with a reasonable degree of skill and co-ordination, a large class led by a team of teachers can be a very effective instructional setting, much more so than the large class with one teacher. However, secondary schools almost invariably assign only one teacher to a class and team teaching, in the sense of two or three teachers assigned to the same class for the same session, is virtually unheard of. The practice of team teaching is limited to a minority of elementary schools.

One of the potential contributions of team teaching to the practice of instruction in large classes is the opportunity to engage students in the analysis of, and pursuit of solutions to, trans-disciplinary, real-life problems instead of the study of single-discipline topics, as is generally practised today (Doll 1993; Sharan *et al.* 1999). Team teaching of trans-disciplinary subject matter requires a restructuring of the curriculum to provide teachers with the academic perspective needed as a basis for instructional team work. It also requires a distinctly innovative allocation of time to team members to plan and co-ordinate their instructional work.

The conclusion is clear: large classes can be taught effectively. To do so requires several fundamental structural changes in the organization of teaching and learning. The changes mentioned thus far are: using teams of teachers in the same class, and conceiving the curriculum in trans-disciplinary rather than uni-disciplinary terms. Some educators will point out that these are complicated changes, and it would be easier to implement more simple solutions. To this claim we must refer readers to the many writings of Seymour Sarason who frequently quoted the saying of H.L. Mencken: 'For every complex problem there is always one simple solution, and it is wrong!' Teaching large classes is a complex problem and requires complex solutions. Simple solutions will not solve complex problems. No one can build today's airplane in a carpentry shop!

Alternative instructional methods

One feature of classroom teaching that appears to be the most malleable in the equation of classroom change to meet the challenge of the large classroom is the use by teachers of new and varied instructional methods that have been shown to exert positive effects on student learning, motivation and on social interaction with peers in the classroom (Sharan 1990; Slavin 1995). Moreover, the use of interactive forms of classroom learning, as distinct from the lecture-and-recitation approach, is related in many essential ways to real change in classroom structure, such as reducing the number of students in the class, team teaching, longer class sessions and so on. However, the fact cannot be ignored that retraining teachers to implement new instructional methods often poses formidable impediments of various kinds (Sharan 1990). Teachers in Finland, Israel, Singapore, or most countries, for that matter, do not employ co-operative learning in small groups because, for one reason, they generally lack the pedagogical skills needed to implement these methods effectively.

More important than skill, however, is the fact that these methods have not yet been officially accepted by secondary school systems. Consequently, the organizational environment conducive to employing alternative instructional methods thus far has not been developed. Teachers encounter official school or system-wide policies, particularly the policy of standardized testing, that contradict or even preclude the adoption of alternative instructional methods that clearly can assist teachers of large classes. In short, school systems create large classrooms that pose serious challenges to effective teaching. Yet simultaneously, they enforce organizational policies that prevent teachers from coping effectively with the situation in which they find themselves. The vast majority of high school classrooms are still conducted in the traditional manner (Cawelti 1994).

Duration of the class session

Another fundamental structural feature that affects classroom teaching in general, and teaching large classes in particular, is the duration of the lesson. Recently published programmes for the redesign of high schools introduce dramatic changes in the duration of class sessions. The main goal is to provide teachers and students with extended periods of time to pursue in-depth study projects individually or in co-operative groups

(Sharan *et al.* 1999; Sizer 1993). Increasing the duration of the class session can also make it possible to reduce the number of subjects that students study in school at any one time. Schools should create the conditions that allow students to concentrate their energy and not feel torn between many topics competing for their attention and time. The extension of time for the classroom lesson increases the chances that teachers will adopt alternative methods of instruction. This is precisely what is needed to cope more successfully with the challenge of the large class.

Classes today meet for relatively short periods in the upper grades of elementary schools and in secondary schools. The duration of a class meeting ranges from thirty-five minutes in some countries, to forty-five minutes in many countries, and to ninety minutes in numerous instances where classes meet for double sessions. The short thirty- to forty-five-minute class literally prevents teachers from making any change in teaching method from the standard lecture-recitation approach.

Given that the duration of a class session is an hour or less, students are usually scheduled to attend about six classes each day, including music/art and/or physical education. This organizational arrangement of schools seems to assuage two of teachers' widespread assumptions about large classes, namely that (1) students have short attention spans and consequently cannot concentrate on learning for extended periods of time, and (2) disruptive behaviour problems are on the verge of erupting at any moment. The relatively short length of the class session, coupled with rigorous control of students' behaviour through the lecture-and-recitation method of teaching, are seen as necessary to maintain order.

For the majority of teachers, their typical mode of instruction is intended to transmit information verbally to the students about a given subject over a given unit of time (usually between thirty and fifty minutes) dictated by the school's schedule of classes (Cawelti 1994). That is the situation deemed by many educators to be the bane of teachers who otherwise might be prepared to introduce marked changes in their mode of instruction (Zahorik 1999).

This form of organizing classes can hardly be justified on the basis of sound psychological and pedagogical considerations. Few teachers attain the insight that the lecture-recitation method used in classes with a large number of students as an audience creates the conditions that engender students' short attention spans. That kind of classroom inevitably must generate a lack of attention by perhaps as many as 60 per cent or more of the students. Students' disruptive behaviour follows from the boredom fuelled by the need for prolonged listening to the teacher and lack of personal involvement in the learning task. Extended lack of attention will lead to disruptive behaviour by some students and draw the teacher's attention away from the task of teaching. Ultimately, the concentration of other students in the class will be disrupted, giving the teacher the frustrating sense of being ineffective. Teachers then reach the conclusion that the large class is very difficult to teach. However, when teachers transform their classrooms to promote interactive, co-operative learning in small groups, they are often amazed at how long students can remain focused on their studies without disruptive behaviour. In Carroll's Copernican plan for restructuring the duration of classroom time, students and teachers reported that they enjoyed the four-hour-long lessons that Carroll's plan afforded them (Carroll 1994; Sharan et al. 1999).

Of course, some teachers have the capacity for strikingly dramatic presentations. Along with a generous use of technological teaching aids, such presentations can manage to attract the attention of the majority of the students in the room, even in large classes. However, highly successful actor-teachers comprise only a small fraction of the millions of teachers who appear every day in classrooms around the world.

Class size and school organization

School organization throughout the world is guided by the structural features of classrooms mentioned thus far: the number of participants, the number of teachers present, the breadth of subject matter taught/studied, and the duration of the class session. These features can be expressed in the following formula: one class (whatever its size), one teacher, one subject, one session (Sarason 1982, 1996; Sharan et al. 1999). This one (class)-by-one (teacher)-by-one (subject)-by-one (session) form of organization embodies many of the classical features of bureaucracy formulated a hundred years ago by Max Weber. Most important among them are the division of labour, fostering specialization and the demarcation of distinct territories of operation for personnel in order to promote efficiency and avoid conflict. These principles continue to dominate public education almost everywhere. The many negative pedagogical implications of these principles have been studied and analysed from a variety of perspectives by several astute observers of public schooling (Goodlad 1984, 1990; Sarason 1971, 1982, 1983, 1990, 1996; Sizer 1993). Add to this formula (of $1 \times 1 \times 1 \times 1$) the fact that, more often than not, the one class with one teacher who teaches one subject during one session is conducted by one method of instruction, namely the lecture or frontal method (including the usual question-and-answer interchange between teachers and students, and the frequent use of student work sheets). At any given time more public school classes in the world are organized and taught in this fashion than in any other way (Cawelti 1994). All of these five features (teacher, class, subject, duration, method or $1 \times 1 \times 1 \times 1 \times 1$) are included when educators talk about the difficulty of teaching large classes in secondary schools, whether or not they realize it.

Sarason (1971, 1982, 1996) identified the features of schooling mentioned above and others as the behavioural regularities that characterize daily life in schools. These patterns are so ingrained and taken for granted that it is the rare person who would ever question the educational validity of these arrangements, least of all the school principal. The one-teacher-one-class principle certainly dominates unchallenged the thinking of those people who determine policy regarding the allocation of resources to schools. School systems have long resisted many attempts by experimenters and innovators to have two or more teachers working together in the same classroom, even when the situation appears to beg for such a solution to a patently negative teacher–student ratio. Classes with more than forty-five or fifty students that have two or more teachers or adults assisting the students, and whose temporal duration is ninety minutes or more, hardly ever figure in discussions of what is known as the large class.

Research on class size: what it has not done

The conclusion from a sizeable body of research on the effects of class size on student achievement is that size does not matter (Cohen *et al.* 1983; Hanushek 1996; Slavin 1989). However, most studies evaluated the impact of an entire configuration of conditions on student achievement, and not the effects of class size alone in isolation from the context of organizational and pedagogical features. Of course it is methodologically legitimate to claim that, if and when the following variables are held constant, and only class size is allowed to vary (or, as will be discussed below, class size in conjunction with one or two other systematically controlled variables), a given study is in fact assessing the impact of class size *per se*. Many of the following critical variables (some of which were mentioned above) are frequently ignored in studies of class size: (1) the number of teachers in the classroom, (2) the nature of the instructional method employed, (3) the variety of informational resources available to students, (4) the size of the room, (5) the number of subjects being studied/taught, (6) the duration of the class session, (7) the students' ethnicity, (8) students' prior level of achievement, and (9) students' socio-economic status.

The variables mentioned in this list affect student learning in classrooms directly or indirectly even when investigators assert that they are doing research on the effects of class size. As discussed above, that term hides more than it reveals. When all or most of the above variables are held constant and the number of students is the only variable (or it is one of two or three variables being assessed systematically) only then is it legitimate to assert that a particular study *is* in fact assessing the effects of class size on achievement. Otherwise, it is really all the other features combined with class size, and not class size alone, that is exerting the effects being measured. This aspect of the situation suggests itself particularly when investigators find that class size does not affect achievement, when they are not hard pressed to explain the results of the research. Investigators are somewhat at a loss to explain the meaning of their findings when class size does affect achievement because that outcome is generally not expected. When the latter result is obtained in research it is difficult if not impossible to know what variable or set of variables produced that outcome because of the many hidden (i.e. uncontrolled) variables operating in the classroom.

In reality, what these studies are saying is this: a large class of forty or forty-five students usually has only one teacher. Most often the teacher lectures to the students about a given subject for a substantial portion of the thirty- or forty-five-minute class session. Students in a class of twenty-five will generally remember on a test the same amount of material that will be remembered by students in a class of forty-five who were also taught with the lecture method by one teacher for the same amount of time. Comparison of the test scores of students from the smaller and larger classrooms leads to the conclusion that class size does not matter.

However, let us imagine that several of the fundamental organizational features would be varied simultaneously. For example: (1) the class would last for ninety minutes or more, even for up to 200 minutes; (2) students would study by investigating a topic, individually or in small groups where they work together and exchange ideas (Sharan and Sharan 1992); (3) students would have direct access to a rich diversity of source material; and (4) teaching assistants would be available who could be consulted during the process of investigation. Would these conditions yield the same student outcomes compared to classes of the same size if there were twenty-five or forty-five students in the class (Sharan et al. 1999)? Few experienced educators accept the notion that the sheer number of bodies in a given space affects pedagogical outcomes while ignoring the nature of the instructional process (Zahorik 1999). Yet, to date, class size has not served as a variable in experiments that also employ teaching method as a co-independent variable, as in the 2×2 design shown in Table 12.1.

Evidence from existing research strongly suggests that there would be a difference in student learning outcomes as a function of simultaneous variation in *both* size and instructional method. For the experiment whose general structure is suggested in Table 12.1, some possible hypotheses would be: (1) there will be no difference in student achievement (however defined or measured) between the small and large classes taught with the

Table 12.1 Suggested design for a classroom experiment with teaching method and class size as independent variables

Method	Lecture and recitation		Co-operative learning	
Number of students	20	45	20	45

lecture-recitation method; (2) there will be no difference between the two sets of smaller (twenty students) classes taught with either the lecture-recitation or with the co-operative learning methods; (3) the large classes of forty-five students taught with the co-operative learning method will achieve higher scores than those achieved by either the smaller or the larger classes taught with the lecture-recitation method; and (4) there might be a difference between the smaller and larger classes taught with the co-operative learning method, but the direction of the difference, whether favouring the small or large class, cannot be predicted at this time.

It is strongly recommended that research about class size undertake a series of studies in which size interacts with other major independent and intervening variables. Such variation is necessary to assess the manifold effects of class size on students. Moreover, the entire nature of the achievement data collected by investigators would be different if data were collected not only about what students remember on a test, but also about the depth of understanding they disclose regarding the subject matter at hand. More important, studies of class size are usually not conducted as experiments at all, but as correlational studies, since most investigators do not interest themselves in variables such as instructional method in addition to the formal changes in class size. The prevailing guideline for many decisions in educational policy-making seems to be saying: Keep doing the same thing over and over again with smaller or larger groups of people, and you will see that it does not make any difference. Perhaps it is assumed that changes in teachers' professional behaviour are improbable or completely beyond the realm of possibility, so the only real thing that can be changed is the number of students in the room, and we all know that that does not really change anything.

Class size as an inhibitor of innovation

One aspect of class size that has not been evaluated or emphasized adequately is the extent to which the number of students in the large classroom with one teacher affects the likelihood that such teachers will adopt alternative methods of instruction, such as individualized instruction, co-operative learning with small groups of students, or the pursuit of study projects outside of the classroom in settings such as industry, hospitals and clinics, art and music centres, the judiciary system and so on. Does the presence in the class of more than thirty-five students inhibit teachers' willingness to learn new methods, or to apply them even after they have learned new methods? How can instruction in large classes be improved if teachers are not able to adopt new and more effective methods of teaching?

A group of researchers concerned with precisely this question found that reduction of class size may lead to the gradual emergence of individualized instruction (Zahorik 1999). However, these investigators did not indicate if the teachers in their study participated in special inservice courses aimed at providing them with the concepts and pedagogical skills needed to change their methods of instruction along with reducing the number of students in their classrooms. It seems that the change in classroom size was not perceived by principals or supervisors to require a change in instructional technology. In fact, what the researchers reported was that the changes in teaching method consisted primarily of an increase in direct instruction aimed at individuals or at small groups of students; that is, forms of tutoring. Teachers in this study did not seem to know about alternative methods of instruction (Zahorik 1999). What may be concluded at this time from the latter and from other studies is that student outcomes can be an indirect function of class size as an inhibitor of instructional innovation.

One of the negative consequences of prevailing official policy regarding class size in the majority of school systems in the world is that even those teachers who are prepared to implement innovations in instructional methods are effectively dissuaded from doing so. The structural features of the classroom are most often mandated by official decision-making bodies located outside of the school. These features typically are based on the $1 \times 1 \times 1 \times 1 \times 1$ concept of classroom organization and instruction. As we have seen, that kind of organization results in maximum separation of people and classes from one another and is generally inhospitable to change. System-wide testing procedures that lack a direct and essential relationship to particular classrooms is another feature mandated by school systems. That feature frequently precludes teachers' adoption of new instructional methods. Under such conditions, teaching to the test almost automatically becomes the norm. It is the rare teacher who can afford to withstand the pressures of official policy on the grounds of his or her pedagogical convictions (Griffin 1995).

A systems approach to classroom organization and instruction

A social systems approach to school organization seeks ways of connecting people, departments and subjects rather than separating them, as is generally practised in light of bureaucratic theory. Systems theory emphasizes the free flow of information between parts of the system, which often entails direct contact between those parts or people. Organizations as systems rely heavily on the ongoing flow of feedback regarding its operations and the use of this feedback for problem-solving and decision-making. Significant problems facing schools most often have more than one solution, so that the road to that solution is best identified by teams of participants rather than by a solo leader. Teams are far more effective than individuals for suggesting alternative solutions to complex problems, and all schools bar none are confronted by myriad complex policy problems all the time. Foremost among these problems is the challenge of making day-to-day instruction meaningful for hundreds of students grouped into large classes. The conduct of a school with hundreds or thousands of students and dozens of teachers whose time should be invested constructively in the pursuit of knowledge or positive social activities *ipso facto* arouses countless questions and problems. These problems require persistent attention from many of the people involved and a wide range of alternative solutions. The functioning of teams for feedback and problem-solving in a variety of domains (e.g. class scheduling, teaching teams, multi-disciplinary curricular studies, special projects) can inject a high degree of flexibility into the school's operation so that the diverse needs of teachers and students can be met in a satisfying and edifying way.

In contrast, many schools solve these problems by conforming to a mandated or inherited policy that the school applies as uniformly as possible to the majority of events and people. Such schools – that probably constitute a majority of high schools in the world – impose a quasi-military uniformity on a staff of approximately a hundred teachers (or more) and one or two thousand students in order to retain reasonable predictability in a situation that some people fear could potentially deteriorate into maximum disorganization unless a system of centralized control is strictly maintained. Indeed, there are more than a few 'inner-city' schools where violence, drug abuse, gang warfare and other antisocial phenomena have reduced the school to something more akin to a penal institution than to an academy in pursuit of learning. However, to date these schools are still a minority.

Another feature of a systems approach, in addition to the functioning of different teams of teachers for problem-solving and curricular implementation, is the need to view all the various subject matter departments and classes as connected and related to one another, rather than as self-contained units. Classes as well as individuals must be included in the continuous flow of information within the system. Today, most secondary schools make little or no attempt to relate or integrate the many subjects that the same students study at any given time (Griffin 1995; Petrie 1992). Yet subject matter integration, team teaching and co-operative learning in small groups are the central avenues for dealing creatively with large classes without necessarily reducing the number of students in a given classroom (Sharan *et al.* 1999).

A system is not a collection

To transform a school from a collection of teachers, classrooms, disciplines and students into an organization that functions as a social system, it is recommended that the principal and his or her administrative team view the entire school as an interrelated set of four units or subsystems: (1) the teaching staff, (2) the student body, (3) the intellectual contents to be studied and educational experiences to be made available (including the curriculum), and (4) instruction (i.e. how point 3 is to be accomplished) (Sharan *et al.* 1999). The primary challenge confronting the school's leadership and staff is: How can these units or subsystems be interrelated to achieve maximum benefit for everyone, teachers and students? Any combination of these subsystems, or parts of them, that can yield educational benefits for the staff and the students are to be pursued. The combinations – such as different disciplines taught together in an integrated fashion, or teachers working together as a teaching team – should not be determined in advance by traditional categories (e.g. ninth grade biology, tenth grade physics, eighth grade history, eleventh grade English). Nor need the study of disciplinary or trans-disciplinary domains be determined by an unalterable schedule of class sessions whose duration is immutable, such as thirty, forty-five or sixty minutes. Similarly, students and teachers should not be viewed as collections of individuals, each working in isolation from peers. Finally, plans to introduce significant changes in any of these subsystems must take the other subsystems into consideration and co-ordinate their functioning. Efforts at educational reform can fail because, among other reasons, they focus on some specific feature of the school as if that feature is not intimately related to other organizational features of the school. Instead, the principles of relatedness, communication between elements (people), integrated domains of teaching and studying, flexible scheduling of classes, co-operative team work among teachers and students, can and should be applied to all levels of the school's functioning (Canady and Rettig 1995; Carroll 1990; Jenkins 1996; Newman and Wehlage 1995; Sarason 1996; Senge 1990; Sharan *et al.* 1999; Sizer 1993).

Weick (1969) defined an organization as a group of groups. The school can certainly be viewed as an organization precisely in these terms, and much to the benefit of all concerned. The size of classes can be changed in many ways for short or long periods of time. Classes can be combined and led by a team of teachers or given a relatively short lecture (twenty minutes) well prepared in advance by a single teacher, only to be subdivided into relatively small groups for discussion or other activities associated with the topic, led by several adults. Classes can be divided into ten or more groups of four students per group, each group pursuing the same or different aspects of the topic under study, or even different topics if so desired (Sharan 1994). The school as a whole can be subdivided into houses (Sizer 1993) that number 200 or 250 students, and a team of teachers assigned to each house which is then subdivided in a variety of ways depending upon the prevailing circumstances (e.g. student interest, the availability of teachers' aides, flexible scheduling allowing groups of students to spend several hours, or days, concentrating on a given project). Decisions regarding the manner in which the various houses within the school will function in terms of scheduling, instructional methods, curriculum and so on must be made at house level by the relevant staff, and not at the level of the entire school. Of course that does not prevent the school's leadership from reaching agreement with the teachers in all the houses regarding the nature of some core curriculum or common set of goals. Moreover, the houses can implement multi-aged grouping or they can maintain traditional class levels, as deemed appropriate for the students involved. The school will be administered by a steering committee consisting of representatives from all the houses.

In this kind of relatively flexible organizational environment, the distressing phenomenon of the large class can become a non-issue, even though, if one simply counts the number of bodies in a particular room at a given time, that class might still qualify as a large class, but without the side effect of creating a pedagogical hurdle. Large can be beautiful when supported by the wide variety of alternative methods of organization and instruction discussed above.

Can schools move from adherence to the century-old model of uniform bureaucratic organization to the dynamic organization envisioned in light of systems theory? Many commercial and industrial organizations have made this transformation in the past few decades, but schools lag far behind. Informed observers of the educational scene over the course of the past three decades or more remain sceptical about the prospects for implementing genuine educational reform (Sarason 1990). Nor have many secondary schools demonstrated much responsiveness to new ideas that entail essential, and not just cosmetic, changes, even when these changes hold out much promise for enormous improvement in the process of schooling (Fullan 1993; Hopkins *et al.* 1994; Zahorik 1999). Parents and school personnel at all levels are clearly opposed to large classrooms, as research has shown unequivocally (Bennett 1996). Perhaps this fact will ultimately provide a powerful political force that can affect the school system both from without and within and ultimately influence the educational administrators to relinquish the notion of organizational uniformity in schools, and thereby release the reins on change.

References

Bennett, N. (1996) 'Class size in primary schools: perceptions of headmasters, chairs of governors, teachers and parents', *British Educational Research Journal*, 22: 33–55.

Canady, R. and Rettig, M. (1995) *Block Scheduling: A Catalyst for Change in High Schools*, Princeton, NJ: Eye on Education.

Carroll, J. (1990) 'The Copernican plan: restructuring the American high school', *Phi Delta Kappan*, 71: 358–65.

—— (1994) 'The Copernican plan evaluated: the evolution of a revolution', *Phi Delta Kappan*, 76: 105–13.

Cawelti, G. (1994) *High School Restructuring: A National Study*, Arlington, VA: Educational Research Service.

Cohen, L., Filby, N., McCutchen, G. and Kyle, D. (1983) *Class Size and Instruction*, New York: Longman.

Doll, W. (1993) *A Post-Modern Perspective on Curriculum*, New York: Teachers College Press.

Fullan, M. (1993) *Change Forces*, London: Cassell.

Goodlad, J. (1984) *A Place Called School*, New York: McGraw Hill.

—— (1990) *Teachers for Our Nation's Schools*, San Francisco, CA: Jossey-Bass.

Griffin, G. (1995) 'Influences of shared decision making on school and classroom activity: conversations with five teachers', *The Elementary School Journal*, 96: 29–45.

Hanushek, B. (1996) 'A more complete picture of school resource policies', *Review of Educational Research*, 66: 397–409.

Hopkins, D., Ainscow, M. and West, M. (1994) *School Improvement in an Era of Change*, London: Cassell.

Jenkins, J. (1996) *Transforming High Schools: A Constructivist Agenda*, Lancaster, PA: Technomic.

Newman, F. and Wehlage, G. (1995) *Successful School Restructuring*, Madison, WI: University of Wisconsin-Madison, Center on Organization and Restructuring of Schools.

Petrie, H. (1992) Interdisciplinary education: are we faced with insurmountable opportunities? *Review of Research in Education*, 18: 299–333.

Sarason, S. (1971) *The Culture of the School and the Problem of Change*, Boston, MA: Allyn & Bacon.

—— (1982) *The Culture of the School and the Problem of Change* (2nd edn), Boston, MA: Allyn & Bacon.

—— (1983) *Schooling in America: Scapegoat and Salvation*, New York: The Free Press.

—— (1990) *The Predictable Failure of Educational Reform*, San Francisco, CA: Jossey-Bass.

—— (1996) *Revisiting 'The Culture of the School and the Problem of Change'*, New York: Teachers College Press.

Senge, P. (1990) *The Fifth Discipline: The Art and Practice of the Learning Organization*, New York: Doubleday.

Sharan, S. (ed.) (1990) *Cooperative Learning: Theory and Research*, New York: Praeger.

—— (ed.) (1994) *Handbook of Cooperative Learning Methods*, Westport, CT: Greenwood Press.

Sharan, S., Shachar, H. and Levine, T. (1999) *The Innovative School: Organization and Instruction*, Westport, CT: Bergin & Garvey.

Sharan, Y. and Sharan, S. (1992) *Expanding Cooperative Learning Through Group Investigation*, New York: Teachers College Press.

Sizer, T. (1993) *Horace's School: Redesigning the American High School*, Boston, MA: Houghton-Mifflin.

Slavin, R. (1989) 'Class size and student achievement: small effects of small classes', *Educational Psychologist*, 24: 99–110.

—— (1995) *Cooperative Learning: Theory, Research and Practice* (2nd edn), Boston, MA: Allyn & Bacon.

Weick, K. (1969) *The Social Psychology of Organizing*, Reading, MA: Addison-Wesley.

Zahorik, J. (1999) 'Reducing class size leads to individualized instruction', *Educational Leadership*, 57: 50–3.

Chapter 13

Guiding intellectual and personal growth across educational contexts

Adrian F. Ashman and Robyn M. Gillies

In the early 1980s, Ashman and Conway developed a classroom-based teaching-learning model called Process-Based Instruction. At that time, many of the cognitive interventions being advocated by researchers to improve classroom teaching outcomes were more relevant to work undertaken in the controlled climate of the psychological laboratory than the dynamic environment of the classroom. This is not to say that there were not excellent ideas developed through theoretical research which were relevant to teaching practice, but often their translation from the laboratory to the practical realities of the classroom left much to be desired.

In their exposition of Process-Based Instruction, Ashman and Conway (1993) asserted that many teachers are understandably wary of innovation for the sake of change alone and the introduction of any new method must take into account the way in which classrooms operate and be based firmly in instructional theory and good teaching practice.

In this concluding chapter, we review peer mediation in the context of the Ashman and Conway (1993) approach. We also extend the discussion to the manner in which peer mediation accommodates a four-component model that deals with the various influences on successful learning and problem-solving.

Bringing innovation into the classroom

Ashman and Conway's (1993) approach might be seen to constitute a minimum standard necessary for the acceptance of any new approach into a teacher's repertoire of classroom strategies. While they recognized that new programmes and methods may be designed specifically for one-to-one or small group instruction, teachers most often work at the level of whole class instruction. In arguing for the adoption of their approach, they elaborated four criteria that new teaching technologies must satisfy to maximize teacher acceptance and implementation.

Any new initiative should:

- operate as part of the regular classroom activities and involve the teacher directly rather than require a laboratory-type context or content-free intervention;
- include instruction about how to learn and problem-solve within the framework of the curriculum content being presented by the teacher;
- actively involve students in the teaching-learning process and enable them to recognize the value of their participation rather than provide only activities that are teacher designed, presented and controlled;
- directly address the generalization of learning and problem-solving skills and strategies so that students clearly see the relevance of how, and what, they are learning.

These four criteria encapsulate the expressed concerns of teachers about the relevance and value of making changes to classroom procedures and practices. They apply to the range of behavioural, social and cognitive interventions and, hence, apply to the variety of peer-mediated approaches developed over the past two to three decades. How do they fare under scrutiny?

First, most applications of peer-mediated learning are classroom-based. Indeed, the extensive body of research reported in this volume is evidence of teaching procedures and practices that involve all students in classroom activities. In the overwhelming majority of cases reported in the professional literature, the introduction of a specific programme or model will have been initiated by a research team. Its ultimate implementation, however, has become the responsibility of the teacher to the extent that he or she will have to generate curriculum objectives, appropriate teaching materials and assessment.

In Gillies and Ashman (1996, 1998), we relied on teachers involved in the projects to integrate co-operative learning into existing work units that were part of the curriculum. They were provided with the guidelines for evaluation of learning outcomes, but they ultimately had the responsibility of constructing the orientation of the unit and authentic assessment. The only addition to the participating teachers' usual practice was the training of students to work co-operatively. Perhaps of more significance are the many other local peer-mediation activities that have been solely teacher initiated although they have never been reported in the professional literature.

Second, most peer-mediated programmes emphasize, as essential elements, the training of students in how to solve problems and how to interact with others to achieve the group goal. Moreover, there is a body of research that documents the importance of the essential elements involved in constructing successful co-operative learning groups (Slavin 1996), the importance of training students to solve problems (King 1994, 1999), and how to structure interactions among group members as they work on assigned tasks (Gillies and Ashman 1996, 1998; Meloth and Deering 1999; Webb and Farivar 1999). If these elements are not evident, children will not reap the benefits of working together with others.

Third, peer-mediated learning clearly involves the process of students helping students, but what of the outcomes? The overwhelming majority of reports documenting the effects of peer-mediated learning testify to academic and social benefits. In saying this, we are mindful of an imperative in academic publishing to report positive outcomes only (see Heath 1999) and of the few reports of outcomes in the longer term; that is, beyond the life of the research project. We are also aware of McMaster and Fuchs' (2002) review of co-operative learning studies with students with special needs that reported mixed results, in part, because of the limitations posed by the design of many studies. However, these authors observed that if co-operative learning strategies incorporated individual accountability and group rewards they were more likely to improve the achievement of the students involved in the project. Given the equivocal results obtained on measures of academic achievement, one wonders whether students experiencing learning problems are less motivated and so have lower academic self-esteem in comparison to their same-age, non-disabled peers. This is not so according to Meltzer et al. (2001) who, in a study of self-perceptions in 308 adolescents with learning disabilities, found that they viewed themselves as motivated, hard-working and academically competent, thus reflecting positive academic self-concepts.

Fourth, peer-mediated learning approaches have relevance in almost every aspect of life. There are reports of the application of these approaches across curriculum areas and student groups in school and community settings. Dyson and Grineski (2001) described how co-operative learning structures may be used in physical education classes to enhance social interaction and learning. Dudley et al. (1997) reported that co-operative learning experiences may be used to enhance the academic and social experiences of freshman college athletes, and Van Stralen (2002) and Evanciew and Rojewski (1999) reported a study of peer-mediated learning that facilitated skill acquisition and adjustment in the workplace. Importantly, peer-mediated approaches provide for the modelling of appropriate learning behaviours, including how problems can be addressed and solved. Thus, the interdependence of group members and the way in which goals are achieved provide a clear message to students about the value of co-operation inside and outside of school.

Factors affecting successful peer-mediated learning

Leaving aside the fifty or so hours when we are asleep, the balance of the week provides opportunities for learning and, more often than not, is spent in the company of others. Some of these people will be work colleagues, others may be family or friends. Indeed, for nearly everyone, learning with and from others is arguably the most common and efficient way of gathering information about the world in which we live and our interactions with it.

Much of the literature presented in this book is associated with learning in a structured setting (i.e. the school classroom) in which the way knowledge is transferred from one person to others has been prescribed. However, our authors acknowledge that learning is not limited to the context of the classroom or the location of research. In Chapter 11, we drew attention to learning outside of the classroom in situations in which few of the participants, if any, have as their agenda a learning experience involving the systematic transmission of knowledge or the ways of society. In those situations, learning just happens almost without awareness or warning.

The accumulation of these many learning and problem-solving events in formal and informal settings across the course of our lives has given each of us a unique education history. Even for monozygotic twins, the overlap of learning experiences is not 100 per cent. At a very early age, their learning circumstance – largely located in the family and the neighbourhood – are distinctive. Family characteristics and the attitudes and beliefs of parents will have a differential effect on the way in which each child develops language, grows cognitively and emotionally, and responds to new experiences. In addition, while there remain remarkable similarities that characterize twins as they grow up, the interactions with adults, siblings and other children create a matchless constellation of social and intellectual inputs and outputs that mark each twin as a unique individual.

For most children, as the teaching-learning ecology expands to include the school, community and the wider world through television, the Internet and the World Wide Web, others become increasingly significant contributors to the individual's education. As the social networks expand, access to informal learning environments grows, and visits to libraries, museums, art galleries, shopping centres, parks, and recreation and leisure facilities further enhance the learning and socialization processes (e.g. about interactions, boundaries, the nature of relationships, right and wrong, and the rudiments of identity, position and status within groups).

While the intellectual, emotional, spiritual, physical and interpersonal outcomes of any teaching and learning event will be different for each participant, the success of any teaching-learning episode is a function of four components, namely the interaction between the learner and the other three – the setting in which learning occurs, the nature of what is to be learned (curriculum) and the facilitator involved in the event (most often a teacher or instructor). Moreover, the process of learning in any situation (formal or informal) may not occur in the same way, proceed at the same rate, or achieve the same outcome from one time to another. Hence, the interplay of these four components governs the success (or otherwise) of a learning or problem-solving experience. These components operate in every learning context and are relevant in every peer-mediated learning context.

The learner

For decades, the individual has been the focus of research into learning and problem-solving. It was taken for granted, for example, that the student was the responsible party when learning did not occur. This may have been theorized to have been as a consequence of flawed personal characteristics that included modest genetic endowment, physical capability, health status plus the involvement of any number of attributes and traits that limited learning outcomes. In dealing with successful learning and problem-solving, Ashman and Conway (1997) argued that a balance was needed across three interactive components: knowledge, affect (here referred to as inclination towards learning) and problem-solving strategies.

Knowledge

This refers to the building blocks of learning and problem-solving that are accumulated across one's lifetime. There are two forms. The first relates to specific detail (declarative knowledge) and the second to information about how to perform tasks (procedural or process knowledge). The knowledge we possess also includes all-purpose plans that have been developed for general forms of activity (e.g. how to get to work, shop for groceries, solve complex personal, social and intellectual problems). Our knowledge base, therefore, is the complex storehouse of information to which the individual has ready access.

Inclination towards learning

This second component refers to learners' belief systems about themselves and the experiences that affect their involvement in future learning and problem-solving. Inclination towards learning relates to the learner's state of readiness to receive and process information, the relevance or importance of the task to the individual, and motivation that is influenced by past experiences, personality characteristics, resourcefulness and creativity. Yet another influence is the emotional response a person may have towards a certain experience.

Problem-solving strategies

This third component relates to one's capabilities to adapt to novel situations and activities. Adaptation is a sophisticated endeavour that draws on the planning and decision-making skills developed over the course of one's life. This involves making decisions about the relevance of information to a particular problem, setting and amending priorities, evaluating the effectiveness of the learning and problem-solving process, and making corrections if needed.

Interactions between the three components

Without an appropriate knowledge base, sufficient motivation, or the ability to organize and manage knowledge and process acquisition, success in any learning or problem-solving event may be limited. In some cases, it is hard to compensate for a deficit in one area or another. For example, inadequate general knowledge will usually act against a player in the game Trivial Pursuit. While the person's motivation and general problem-solving capability may be high, it is unlikely that this can compensate for a general knowledge deficit. For those who do not like parlour games, a lack of application, enthusiasm and competitive spirit can also limit success. Conversely, advanced competencies and/or positive dispositions can aid performance and compensate for shortcomings. For example, an individual with limited organizational skills but high motivation might persist with a task long after others have given up and eventually solve the problem.

The setting

The conditions under which learning occurs influence the outcome of teaching and learning. Some writers have collected these conditions under the heading 'quality of life', and have drawn attention to its effect on educational outcomes (e.g. Babad 2001; Mitchem and Young 2001; Wheldall et al. 1999). Issues relating to the setting in which learning occurs may be considered under three headings.

Resources and space

The resources needed for successful teaching and learning will vary greatly depending upon the event. A backpacker exploring the world may need little in the way of resources beyond his or her physical and mental capabilities. Similar limited resources may be required by a sportsperson learning a new tactic or strategy. In other situations, a person may need manuals and computer equipment and the tension that might come from the buzz of excitement in an office. Others may need access to quiet spaces and expansive resources.

Data have been gathered over the years to show that children respond differently to the arrangement of space in which they work. Wheldall (1991), for example, found that students' productivity rose around 15 per cent when they were placed in rows and fell about 15 per cent when they returned to sitting around tables. Some children's performance rose by over 30 per cent in the row configuration and some even complained about having to work again in groups. Similar results were reported by Pointon and Kershner (2000), and Marx et al. (1999) identified action zones within different classroom configurations. For example, there was an action zone in the row-and-column arrangement in which children asked more questions per lesson, and a similar zone when they sat in a semicircular seating arrangement.

Climate

There is universal agreement among teachers that climatic conditions affect students' learning. In Australia, for example, students become unsettled and erratic when there has been constant strong wind over a number of days; and high ambient temperatures during the school year, where classrooms are generally not air-conditioned, lead to considerable student (and teacher) lethargy. Ambient noise can also affect attention although this appears to be a matter of personal choice. Some young (and older) students can study while a radio, CD or television is playing in the background while others find it impossible to maintain concentration with any level of noise whatsoever. Working in classrooms that are located adjacent to busy roads or railway tracks can adversely affect the performance of students and teachers alike.

Curriculum

In this context, curriculum refers to a general concept that includes the teaching-learning processes and procedures in addition to the sequence in which the skill-related material is presented, used and adapted. The sequencing of instruction, in particular, has been a major focus of educational research for decades. Analysis of the development of reading, mathematics and language skills and the establishment of a hierarchy within a curriculum area remains one of the positive contributions of curriculum research undertaken in the final quarter of the twentieth century. Here, curriculum also refers to learning away from the school and classroom, the information that is transmitted among peers, from one to another.

The facilitator

Arguably, the instructor is the most important component in the teaching–learning equation. The instructing entity might be a textbook, audio-visual or computer-based learning product, a parent, peer or classroom teacher. In formal teaching–learning settings, the instructor not only mediates the learning or problem-solving process but must also facilitate a high level of motivation through encouragement and reward if success is to be achieved. Intrinsic motivation may be involved when students are working with computer equipment, or they may be encouraged by a teacher's confidence and familiarity with the content being presented. In class, however, many students respond to instruction passively, waiting for teacher-initiated, monitored and reinforced learning rather than responding to encouragement to adopt an active role in the learning process.

The teacher's disposition and experiences (as learner and teacher) are important. Crucial issues include the manner in which instruction is provided (e.g. emphasizing group work, a chalk-and-talk didactic teaching approach, discovery learning methods, peer-mediated negotiation about what is to be learned and how), how feedback is given (e.g. the language used) and how personal attributes, qualities and attitudes contribute to successful learning (e.g. demeanour, competence in controlling classroom behaviour, enthusiasm for the job, and respect for the rights and views of others).

In a sense, it is the teacher's responsibility to ensure that all four components in the model facilitate students' progress. This means: considering the student's learning history, existing needs, and capabilities; providing a setting that is conducive to the student's learning profile; and presenting the curriculum in a way that dovetails with student and environmental characteristics. Placing the responsibility on the teacher for the learners' performance is a major obligation, one that teachers may find difficult to accept in its entirety. They may argue that the educational experience of a child is such that it will mitigate against any educational intervention, regardless of the enthusiasm and skill of the teacher. It is in this context that we move now to consider peer mediation and its potential for facilitating an appropriate interplay between the four components of the model.

Co-operation among students

The teaching practices used in any learning situation generally depend most upon the teacher's experience and the mix of student abilities. For example, in a class of low-achieving children a teacher may choose to be more directive, decide not to assign a textbook because it is too difficult, and introduce content in the morning when the students are more responsive. In other circumstances, where there is a mandatory curriculum, the teacher may decide to use concrete, hands-on materials or even an approach that employs discovery as the underlying principle.

Regardless of the approach or strategy used by the teacher, there will always be a number of students in every class who learn very quickly and there will be some who do not. The important question to consider is whether there are correct combinations of teaching, learning and context factors that can maximize learning for each child. Peer mediation has been offered as an effective way of achieving this objective.

Throughout this volume, the contributors have provided many examples of students working together successfully on projects and other learning experiences. It is clear that the notion of a student assisting others on difficult tasks is part of school life even though it may not be a dominant part. Young and older people also work together collaboratively to assist each other outside of formal instructional environments where a considerable amount of learning takes place. Team work within partnerships, sporting groups, community welfare agencies, and among families and friendship networks are important (if not essential) elements of living within, and being supported by, society.

We have seen many examples of how peers can support others inside and outside of the classroom to such an extent that the nature of the helping relationships is quite comparable. Moreover, competition is not necessarily anathema in co-operative ventures. A player can strive to be the fastest runner in a football team while still being the most supportive player. A student can strive to finish his or her assigned piece of work first and then look for ways in which others may be helped. Thus elements of co-operation and competition can exist within school-based peer-support programmes in the same way as they exist outside of the classroom. What is important for success in the classroom, however, is the way in which co-operation is established and supported. This involves developing students' skills in contributing ideas, providing appropriate feedback to others, organizing time and resources, and working on tasks in which the involvement of all is a necessary condition for successful completion, although not all peer-mediated learning approaches demand the shared commitment of students. Furthermore, this is not an essential element of co-operation that occurs outside of the classroom and informally.

At this point, we again consider peer-mediated learning within the context of the four components outlined above (learner, setting, curriculum, instructor).

Student characteristics and learning styles

Our own work and that of others (e.g. Brinton *et al.* 2000; Putnam *et al.* 1996) has demonstrated that co-operative learning and other peer-mediated learning approaches have not been universally successful. Some students do not work well in small groups because of limited social and interaction skills while others prefer to learn on their own. The question is: How can peer-mediated learning approaches assist the learner to maximize his or her contribution in any learning and problem-solving situation?

If we consider first the knowledge base that students possess, peer-mediated approaches bring together the resources of a number of participants thereby relieving the individual of responsibility for all the knowledge required for the specified activity or problem. In so doing, each participant benefits from every other, learning not only relevant declarative knowledge that will assist in task completion, but also procedural knowledge that includes metacognitive aspects related to learning and solving problems (King 1994). In peer-mediation situations, the learners talk about how and, often, why things are done in certain ways. Students are often more inclined to ask questions of their peers than to show their presumed ignorance to the teacher. Webb and Farivar (1994) even suggested that peers are often more aware of what other students do not understand, can point out relevant aspects of the problem, and can give explanations in language that is readily understood.

Students' motivation can be encouraged in peer-mediation settings although an improvement in this area is not necessarily guaranteed. Some students prefer to work alone and some will not interact effectively with others in a small work group because of limited social skills. Nevertheless, many peer-mediation approaches in the classroom provide a secure working environment that often reflects the positive attributes of successful informal learning activities, especially by providing time to consider the problem from a number of perspectives. Peer-mediated learning is success-driven, and hence has the potential to support students with special difficulties whose past learning experiences at school may not have been positive. When they experience success there is an increased likelihood of their willingness to engage in similar or new learning activities.

One important positive attribute of peer-mediated learning is the opportunity provided to those involved to consider alternative ways of solving problems. There is commonly a richness to the exchange of ideas among participants that brings to light alternative views about the planning process, priority-setting and decision-making in a context that supports the expression of alternative views. In a real sense, peer-mediated learning approaches provide the building blocks for independent learning and problem-solving in a context where repetition of process and diverse problem-solving is the norm (King et al. 1998; Webb and Farivar 1999).

Co-operation in context

There are few instances in the literature of advocates proposing peer mediation as the sole teaching and learning method. Most often, it is viewed as an important addition to didactic teaching and private study. Certainly, within the education and psychology literature, it is recognized that learners do not acquire their knowledge in the same way or at the same speed, and have preferences in how they approach a learning or problem-solving task.

While Wheldall's (1991) study drew attention to the way in which seating arrangements affect student productivity, there was no indication given in his article to suggest that the activities undertaken in small groups conformed to the principles of co-operative learning or class-wide peer tutoring in which the task requirements and interactions between participants are arranged to promote productive activity. Indeed, our own observations of interactions in classrooms where traditional teaching methods are employed would confirm Wheldall's findings. When tasks are poorly defined, when there is no requirement for interdependence and when students are largely working independently, much time is spent on activities and interactions that are unrelated to task completion.

Informal discussions with classroom teachers confirm their misgivings about small group learning. Most express the view that such an arrangement leads to an increase in chatter with very little being achieved by students unless the teacher monitors the group process closely. For these teachers, close monitoring means deterioration in order, a greater need for the regulation of student behaviour (discipline) and higher stress levels in what might otherwise be a supportive and productive class group.

These interactions confirm the importance of preparing students to work in small groups and developing activities following the principles of the more successful peer-mediation approaches, such as co-operative learning and class-wide peer tutoring (Delquadri *et al.* 1986; Johnson and Johnson 1981). It is our view that peer mediation is only one of several approaches to learning that enable teachers in a wide range of educational contexts to provide support to the diversity of learners with whom they work. Using peer mediation exclusively, or any other method including didactic instruction, is unlikely to accommodate the learning needs of all.

Co-operation and the curriculum

Once again, various contributors to this volume have highlighted the application of peer-mediated learning approaches across a range of curriculum areas. Many have drawn attention here and elsewhere to enhanced academic and interpersonal outcomes. It is our belief that peer mediation in its various forms facilitates the acquisition of curriculum content in an intellectually and interpersonally fertile environment that emphasizes not only the content that is to be learned or accommodated, but also the way in which learning and problem-solving may occur.

While there are concerns associated with the inclusion of some students with special learning needs in co-operative learning settings, the information presented in Chapter 6 suggests optimism if students with and without learning difficulties are prepared adequately for the experience. Certainly, there are numerous reports that describe successful learning outcomes for students with a disability working on the same curriculum objectives and within the same classroom context as their non-disabled peers.

Of importance to the success of peer-mediation approaches is the structure of the learning activity. Ashman and Conway (1997) drew attention to the structure of the knowledge and strategies that are required for successful learning, and the specification of outcomes and assessment. Most peer-mediation approaches provide clear indications to the learners about what is to be achieved and how. (See the extensive review in Chapter 3 of the importance of structuring peer-learning experiences to facilitate student interactions and guide their understandings.)

Peers and teachers

Perhaps the greatest benefit of peer mediation derives from the type and level of interaction that occurs in a context in which the responsibility for learning does not rest solely with the teacher but is shared among teacher and students. Consequently, students are participating members of the teaching–learning process and have a joint responsibility to provide and receive support.

In effect, peer-mediation approaches place a responsibility upon each participant to interpret the demands of the task, establish what is needed to complete the task, and evaluate the extent of their own (and others') knowledge base in terms of existing curriculum content and strategies needed to achieve success. Student language and elaboration (i.e. putting the content and the problem-solving process into students' own words) are the bases of integrating the new content and the new learning strategies. The learning process then becomes more relevant to the students and more likely to be retained and generalized.

Conclusion

Peer-mediated learning methods are not new, having been employed in a number of societies down through the centuries (see e.g. Bonner 1950; Wagner 1990). The contemporary notions of peer collaboration and co-operation described in this volume derive their conceptual foundation largely from the interactional perspective described by Vygotsky (1978).

Through peer mediation, all students gain relevant information, new patterns of thought and problem-solving strategies from the interactions they have with peers. Through these collaborative exchanges, new strategies and metacognitive concepts that are implicit in their communications are internalized, and this, in turn, leads to academic and social benefits that otherwise may not be available through traditional instructional methods.

In this volume, contributors have explored many notions relating to peer-mediated learning. Some have devoted considerable attention to theories relating to groups and group dynamics, others have reported new and innovative research to show the effectiveness of collaboration among peers. Since the inception of contemporary peer-mediation approaches, researchers and practitioners alike have stressed their practical value and, in this chapter, we have shown that peer mediation satisfies several criteria that classroom teachers argue are essential for success.

Certainly, the last word has not been written on peer-mediated learning. Researchers will continue to explore new ways in which learners can assist each other, and education practitioners will continue to provide opportunities for students to work with and support each other.

References

Ashman, A.F. and Conway, R.N.F. (1993) *Using Cognitive Methods in the Classroom*, London: Routledge.

—— (1997) *An Introduction to Cognitive Education: Theory and Applications*, London: Routledge.

Babad, E. (2001) 'On the conception and measurement of popularity: more facts and some straight conclusions', *Social Psychology of Education*, 5(1): 3–29.

Bonner, S.F. (1950) *The Education of a Roman*, Liverpool: Liverpool University Press.

Brinton, B., Fujiki, M., Montague, E.C. and Hanton, J.L. (2000) 'Children with language impairment in cooperative work groups: a pilot study', *Language, Speech, and Hearing Services in Schools*, 31: 252–64.

Delquadri, J.C., Greenwood, C.R., Whorton, D., Carta, J.J. and Hall, R.V. (1986) 'Classwide peer tutoring', *Exceptional Children*, 52: 535–42.

Dudley, B., Johnson, D. and Johnson, R. (1997) 'Using cooperative learning to enhance the academic and social experiences of freshmen student athletes', *Journal of Social Psychology*, 137: 449–59.

Dyson, B. and Grineski, S. (2001) 'Using cooperative learning structures in physical education', *Journal of Physical Education, Recreation and Dance*, 72(2): 28–31.

Evanciew, C. and Rojewski, J. (1999) 'Skill and knowledge acquisition in the workplace: a case study of mentor–apprentice relationships in youth apprenticeship programs', *Journal of Industrial Teacher Education*, 36(2): 24–54.

Gillies, R.M and Ashman, A.F. (1996) 'Teaching collaborative skills to primary school children in classroom-based work groups', *Learning and Instruction*, 6: 187–200.

—— (1998) 'Behavior and interactions of children in cooperative groups in lower and middle elementary grades', *Journal of Educational Psychology*, 90: 746–57.

Heath, S. (1999) 'Discipline and discipline in education research: elusive goals?', in E.C. Langmann and L. Shulman (eds) *Issues in Education*, San Francisco, CA: Jossey-Bass.

Johnson, D.W. and Johnson, R. (1981) 'Effects of cooperative and individualistic learning experiences on interethnic interaction', *Journal of Educational Psychology*, 73: 444–49.

King, A. (1994) 'Guided knowledge construction in the classroom: effects of teaching children how to question and how to explain', *American Educational Research Journal*, 31: 338–68.

—— (1999) 'Discourse patterns for mediating peer learning', in A. O'Donnell and A. King (eds) *Cognitive Perspectives on Peer Learning* (87–116), Mahwah, NJ: Lawrence Erlbaum.

King, A., Staffieri, A. and Adelgais, A. (1998) 'Mutual peer tutoring: effects of structuring tutorial interaction to scaffold peer learning', *Journal of Educational Psychology*, 90: 134–52.

McMaster, K. and Fuchs, D. (2002) 'Effects of cooperative learning on the academic achievement of students with learning disabilities: an update of Tateyama-Sniezek's review', *Learning Disabilities Research and Practice*, 17: 107–17.

Marx, A., Fuhrer, U. and Hartig, T. (1999) 'Effects of classroom seating arrangements on children's question-asking', *Learning Environments Research*, 2: 249–63.

Meloth, M. and Deering, P. (1999) 'The role of the teacher in promoting cognitive processing during collaborative learning', in A. O'Donnell and A. King (eds) *Cognitive Perspectives on Peer Learning* (235–56), Mahwah, NJ: Lawrence Erlbaum.

Meltzer, L., Katzir-Cohen, T. and Miller, L. (2001) 'The impact of effort and strategy use on academic performance: student and teacher perceptions', *Learning Disability Quarterly*, 24: 85–98.

Mitchem, K.J. and Young, K.R. (2001) 'Adapting self-management programs for classwide use: acceptability, feasibility, and effectiveness', *Remedial and Special Education*, 22(2): 75–88.

Pointon, P. and Kershner, R. (2000) 'Making decisions about organising the primary classroom environment as a context for learning: the views of three experienced teachers and their pupils', *Teaching and Teacher Education*, 16: 117–27.

Putnam, J., Markovchick, K., Johnson, D.W. and Johnson, R.T. (1996) 'Cooperative learning and peer acceptance of students with learning disabilities', *Journal of Social Psychology*, 136: 741–52.

Slavin, R. (1996) *Education for All*, Exton, PA: Swets & Zeitlinger.

Van Stralen, S. (2002) 'Making sense of one's experience in the workplace', *New Directions for Adult and Continuing Education*, 94: 13–21.

Vygotsky, L.S. (1978) *Mind in Society: The Development of Higher Psychological Processes*, ed. and trans. M. Cole, V. John-Steiner, S. Scribner and E. Souberman, Cambridge, MA: Harvard University Press.

Wagner, L. (1990) 'Social and historical perspectives on peer teaching in education', in H. Foot, M. Morgan and R. Shute (eds) *Children Helping Children* (65–92), Chichester: John Wiley & Sons.

Webb, N. and Farivar, S. (1994) 'Promoting helping behavior in cooperative small groups in middle school mathematics', *American Educational Research Journal*, 31: 369–95.

—— (1999) 'Developing productive group interaction in middle school mathematics', in A. O'Donnell and A. King (eds) *Cognitive Perspectives on Peer Learning* (117–50), Mahwah, NJ: Lawrence Erlbaum.

Wheldall, K. (1991) 'Managing troublesome school behaviour in regular schools: a positive teaching perspective', *International Journal of Disability, Development and Education*, 38: 99–116.

Wheldall, K., Beaman, R. and Mok, M. (1999) 'Does the Individualized Classroom Environment Questionnaire (ICEQ) measure classroom climate?', *Educational and Psychological Measurement*, 59: 847–54.

Index

Page references for figures and tables are in *italics*